Reason for the Hope

The Futures
of
Roman Catholic Theologates

Reason for the Hope
The Futures
of
Roman Catholic Theologates

by

Katarina Schuth, O.S.F.

Historical Introductions by

Joseph M. White and
John W. O'Malley, S.J.

 Michael Glazier, Inc.
Wilmington, Delaware

About the Author

Sr. Katarina Schuth, a member of the Sisters of St. Francis of Rochester, Minnesota since 1960, is currently director of planning and registrar at Weston School of Theology in Cambridge, Massachusetts. Since 1984 she also has directed the research project on Roman Catholic Theologates sponsored by the Lilly Endowment Inc. Her doctorate in cultural geography is from Syracuse University, and she has earned both a masters and licentiate in theology from Weston School of Theology. Her bachelor's degree in history is from the College of St. Teresa. Sr. Schuth serves on numerous boards of trustees and does extensive consulting in areas of goverance, planning and management for Catholic institutions.

First published in 1989 by Michael Glazier, Inc., 1935 West Fourth Street, Wilmington, Delaware 19805.

Library of Congress Cataloging-in-Publication Data

Schuth, Katarina.
  Reason for the hope.
  Bibliography; p.
  Includes index.
  1. Theology—Study and teaching—Catholic Church.
2. Catholic Church—Education—United States. I. Title.
BX905.S38   1989   207'.112   89-1917
ISBN   0-89453-772-5

Cover Design by Maureen Daney
Printed in the United States of America by Edwards Brothers

*For My Father
In gratitude for his faith,
integrity, and love*

Contents

Acknowledgements

As I deliberated about a title for this book, it occurred to me again and again that I can readily identify many "reasons for the hope" that I have about the futures of Roman Catholic theologates. The reasons often reside in the persons who are associated with these institutions, from faculty and boards, to administrations and students. So many of these individuals assisted me in every phase of this research, and to all who participated so openly and willingly I am most grateful, especially to the more than four-hundred who responded to an hour-long interview. The hopes and challenges that they shared with me constitute the basis of the book.

Among those associated with this project are several whose contributions are so important that without them this book would not exist. David Nygren, C.M., is first among them. In the early phases of the research he assisted me in developing and testing questionnaires and doing interviews. His insights and knowledge were highly significant in the design and direction of the research, especially the sections on formation. Only a faithful friend would offer such sustained support, and to him I say thank you.

The abiding interest and concern of John O'Malley, S.J., whose wisdom comes from both experience and learning, endured through several years of this project. Not only did he offer insights and ideas, but he also wrote a section for the book on the history of religious formation, and his extensive editing work on early drafts was of tremendous value. I am grateful to him for his distinctive scholarly contributions, for his constant encouragement, and even for his occasional prodding.

Many others deserve specific mention. Joseph M. White, who has thoroughly researched the history of diocesan seminaries in the United States, graciously took time from his own work to write a chapter on that topic. In the final stages of writing, Elizabeth Burr's dedication, along with her considerable skill as an editor, made it possible for me to complete the book. Without her facility at this specialized task, the book would be less precise and clear. I am grateful to her for the substantial contribution she has made. Special recognition must be given to Adrian Fuerst, O.S.B., for his dedicated and faithful work in collecting data on seminaries through the Center for Applied Research in the Apostolate. With his twenty-year data base, which he so willingly explains and shares, research today is immensely enriched.

Others had special roles: research assistants Mary Sweeney, S.C., Theresa Carlow, S.N.D., Geneva Gorgo, O.S.F., Charlotte Prather, and Roger Bergman, and the local and national advisory committees, who are named in the book. The National Catholic Educational Association Seminary Department, under the leadership of Msgr. William Baumgaertner, gave early critical support and endorsement of the project, which was continued by his successor, Rev. Charles Kavanagh. Rev. Robert Sherry, Executive Director of the Bishops' Committee on Priestly Formation, provided important insight and knowledge about concerns and issues on a national level. To each of them I express my genuine appreciation.

My Franciscan community of Rochester, Minnesota graciously missioned me to undertake this special task, and my family in Minnesota has also sustained me by their interest and concern. I acknowledge with gratitude my sisters and my family for their solicitude and their prayers.

My colleagues at Weston School of Theology were always ready to discuss the many topics related to theological education that are covered in the book, and their reflections offer depth in areas with which I was less familiar. The two presidents of Weston under whom I served, John Padberg, S.J., and Edward O'Flaherty, S.J., have consistently endorsed and supported my participation in this research project. For all that this excellent working environment has provided, I am thankful.

As I come to the end of the acknowledgements, I am brought back to the beginning of the project. Thomas Savage, S.J., introduced me to the staff at the Lilly Endowment, Inc., which has generously funded this project. Mr. Fred Hofheinz, Senior Program Officer at the Endowment, has not only provided valuable connections with those who are most knowledgeable about theological education, but he has also given consistent encouragement and support. To him and to the Lilly Endowment, I extend my appreciation.

These are but a few of the many who deserve to be named as "reasons for the hope" that I have for the present and for the future.

Preface

The Roman Catholic Church has made more changes in its think-ing about the education of its priests during the past two decades than it did over the previous four centuries. The seminary system in place before the Second Vatican Council had its roots in the Council of Trent. Bishop John Carroll followed those sixteenth-century guidelines when he established the first American seminary in Balti-more in 1791 and, from that time until the end of Vatican II in 1965, priestly education in the United States remained virtually unchanged. The years since then have been marked by upheaval, experimen-tation, and uncertainty. It is against this background that Sister Katarina Schuth, O.S.F., makes an immeasurable contribution to anyone who seeks either to make sense of the recent past or to make informed plans for the intermediate future.

Sister Schuth approaches this work from a special perspective. She is not exclusively an educator, historian, or theologian—though her competence surely extends to these and other disciplines. By training and temperament, however, she is a cultural geographer, and it is from that perspective that she is here mapping the terrain of the contemporary world of theological education in the United States. To be sure, she reminds us of the past and offers clues to the future, but most fundamentally she presents us with a penetrating and powerfully accurate snapshot of the present.

When Sister Schuth began this work in 1984, she was a newcomer to the world she proposed to chart, having just recently arrived at the Weston School of Theology after serving as a teacher and administrator at the College of St. Teresa in Winona, Minnesota.

Those of us who have been around this enterprise for a longer period stand somewhat in awe of the encyclopedic knowledge of the American seminary that she has amassed in such a relatively brief time. In the manner of every good explorer, she started her work with extensive forays into the field. Over a period of four years she and her colleague and collaborator, Father David Nygren, C.M., traversed the nation interviewing more than four hundred trustees, administrators, faculty, and students at most of its Catholic seminaries. During the same period, she presented reports on her research-in-progress at virtually every gathering of seminary leaders held anywhere in North America. Her travels will continue after the publication of this book as she, Father Nygren, and other colleagues discuss its content and its ramifications with theological educators in the United States and Europe. She has become a major figure in American theological education in her own right.

For most of the decade of the 1980s, the Lilly Endowment has supported various research efforts aimed at leading American Catholics to a better understanding of the seminary enterprise. These studies have helped to illuminate the contemporary scene and have provided useful information for those who must plan for the future. The Schuth study is the latest in that series. I know it will be avidly read and carefully studied by seminary rectors, presidents, and deans. It should also be read by bishops, religious superiors, seminary trustees, and indeed by every person who has a stake in the future of the Catholic Church in the United States. I think that latter category includes us all.

Fred L. Hofheinz
Lilly Endowment, Inc.

Introduction:
Background, Methodology,
and Scope of the Study

Background

"Simply reverence the Lord Christ in your hearts, and always have your answer ready for people who ask you the reason for the hope that you all have" (1 Peter 3:15, *The Jerusalem Bible*). Four years ago when I began this research on the futures of Roman Catholic theologates, it was unclear to me if my findings would yield reason for hope or reason for discouragement. After visiting half of the theologates in the United States, and interviewing more than four hundred administrators, faculty, and students at these institutions, it has become clear to me that the title of this study must reflect hope—hope that was unmistakably present among the men and women who work and study in theologates.

As I listened to accounts of improvements in personal and spiritual formation, in carefully designed academic programs, and in competently integrated pastoral field education, it became apparent to me that unfounded criticism of all seminaries, from high school through college and theology, has negatively influenced the public's view of these institutions, and has had a demoralizing effect on many people in the Church. The enrollment of a smaller number of priesthood candidates has been unjustifiably interpreted as the failure of the seminaries. Low numbers have been confused with low quality. The wide publicity given to these negative perceptions was in part responsible for the careful scrutiny of seminaries by Church officials in the 1980s. After intensive review of every seminary, their reports led to the conclusion by Cardinal William Baum that seminaries are "serving the Church well in preparing candidates for priesthood."[1] But their generally positive assessment has not stopped the right-wing attacks and uninformed negative criticisms that are so disruptive to the life of the Church and so disheartening to all persons associated with the education of future "laborers in the vineyard." A vital purpose of this extensive research and thorough analysis of data is, therefore, to illuminate the understanding of those who are anxious about the condition of theologates. The work accomplished over the past twenty years offers every reason for the hope we all have in our hearts that the Church will be well served by those who are now preparing for ministry.

The hope was illustrated most convincingly by rectors/presidents of theologates when they responded to a questionnaire about changes and trends over the past twenty years.[2] They identified many reasons for a positive outlook in answer to questions about changes in institutional arrangements, enrollment, programs, and various other facets of their schools. In all they listed 332 changes. Of these, forty-nine were institutional changes related to expanding the mission of the school or augmenting boards of trustees. Changes of one form or another in admissions policies were mentioned 166 times; as a result of these changes, women religious, lay students, ordained priests, permanent deacons, diocesan candidates from more dioceses, and men religious from more provinces were enrolled. Program changes numbered 117, with thirty-four schools adding the Master of Divinity (M.Div.) degree, twenty-five adding the Master of Arts (M.A.), twenty-one adding a continuing education program, and thirty-seven adding a variety of other new programs. Of all the changes identified, only three or four in each category could be construed as negative, that is, representing a loss to or diminishment of the institution.

Next the respondents were asked to identify up to three of the

---

[1]From Cardinal William Baum's letter of 14 September 1986 to the cardinals, archbishops, and bishops in the United States, in which he assessed the findings from the visitations to seminaries.

[2]This questionnaire was sent in preparation for a triennial meeting of all ordinaries—cardinals, archbishops, bishops, and religious superiors—who have theologates under their jurisdiction, and all rectors/presidents of theologates. The meeting was held in June 1987 at Seton Hall University, Immaculate Conception Seminary.

most important changes in their institution, and they cited 145 changes. Organizational/structural changes numbered thirty-eight, and related to sponsorship, governance, mission, closing of programs, affiliations, and changes in location or facilities. Personnel changes numbered forty-nine, and generally pertained to adding administrators or faculty in new positions; broadening the composition of personnel to include women religious, laywomen, and laymen; and adding different categories of students. Program changes numbered fifty-eight, and concerned the addition of degrees, programs, and special orientations, as well as improvements made in the curriculum, in spiritual formation, and in pastoral formation. Several also noted accreditation of their institution as one of the three most important changes. Only one or two changes in each of the three broad categories were negative.

Respondents were then asked to weight the significance of possible reasons for making these changes, using a scale that ranged from 7 signifying "very important" to 0 signifying "of no importance." They also evaluated the impact of the changes, using a scale ranging from +3 ("very positive") to -3 ("very negative"). The reasons for organizational/structural changes were most heavily weighted toward making better use of financial resources (4.8), followed by responding to the needs of the Church (4.6) and responding to the theological changes of Vatican II (4.5). The greatest impact of these changes was on the quality of theological education (+2.1) and the quality of priesthood formation (+2.0). Changes in the composition of administrations, faculties, and student bodies were made primarily because of the theological changes of Vatican II (5.5), and secondarily out of a desire to meet the needs of the Church (5.2). The impact of these changes was considered most positive in its effect on the quality of the priesthood formation program (+2.3), overall the highest figure for any category. The second most positive impact was on the quality of theological education (+2.1). Reasons for adding or improving programs were the theological changes of Vatican II (5.7) and the needs of the local Church (5.6). The impact of program changes was viewed as most positive in its effect first on the quality of the priesthood formation program (+2.1) and second on the quality of theological education (+1.9).

In summary, fifty-three out of a possible total of fifty-four rectors/ presidents identified more than three hundred changes in theologates over the past twenty years, and with very few exceptions, these changes were positive. Moreover, the impact of these changes on both the quality of the priesthood formation program and the quality of theological education as a whole was assessed as highly positive. These are reasons for hope.

The decidedly positive evaluation by the respondents of developments since 1967 is confirmed by other significant indications of reason for hope yielded by the interviews conducted for this study. Reason for hope also comes from bishops and religious superiors who appreciate the value of the formation provided for their candidates, from administrators who are successfully fostering professional advancement at their schools, from faculty who are experiencing satisfaction with their teaching and research, and from students who are fulfilling their goal of acquiring excellent preparation for ministry. This book is about these positive findings.

Realistically, the book is also about the many concerns and challenges, the intractable problems that persist, the new difficulties that arise from day to day in these institutions. The less optimistic observations come from the same groups of people who find reason for hope—from bishops and religious superiors who are discouraged by the small number of firstrate candidates applying for ordination, from administrators who are concerned about enrollment and finances, from faculty who fear loss of academic freedom and feel overburdened by the multiple expectations attached to their positions, and by students who are uncertain of their role and identity as ministers in an unpredictable future. This study is also about these negative findings.

The study originated in 1984 with a grant from the Lilly Endowment, and was designed as a parallel study to *The Futures of Protestant Seminaries*, completed by John C. Fletcher in 1983. Within the Roman Catholic Church, the aftermath of the Second Vatican Council brought renewed interest in theological education. Fundamental changes in the content and structure of priestly formation programs were accompanied by equally radical changes in enrollment patterns and student life. In light of this altered context, the goal of the study was to collect and present to decisionmakers and leaders in theologates pertinent data about these changes and their effects, so that they could begin to plan for the futures of their institutions.

Methodology

Several sources of data were significant for this research. The primary data were collected during interviews. Advised by a national advisory committee and a Boston-based committee,[3] we selected half of the theologates in the United States for site visits. A random selection was made with the purposes of covering a broad geographical area, including theologates of different sizes, and incorporating at least some theologates representing each of the three models (see below). All twenty-four theologates that were selected agreed to participate. The interviews were conducted by me or by David Nygren, C.M., or by both of us. I conducted interviews at twenty-one theologates, seven of them with Fr. Nygren; he visited three others alone. A standard set of questions was sent to each respondent several weeks in advance of the site visit, indicating the broad topics that would be covered. Each interview was about an hour long, and all but a few were done individually. It was agreed that, unless a person wished to be quoted, the responses would be anonymous, assuring confidentiality for the person and the school. Cooperation was remarkable, and the interviews could be characterized as candid and open, with a sense of trust obviously present. Only two persons out of the more than four hundred who were asked declined to be interviewed.

At each theologate fifteen to twenty people were interviewed, typically comprising about five administrators, ten faculty members, and five students. All rectors/presidents, all except one academic dean, all formation directors, and all field education directors at the twenty-four theologates were among the respondents. Depending on the size of the school, we interviewed one or two other administrators, drawing from development directors, business officers,

---

[3]The national advisory committee met five times, and the Boston-based committee every two months, between 1984 and 1987. They reviewed work-in-progress and critiqued every aspect of the research; they also contributed to the contents of questionnaires used during interviews and sent to selected constituents. The members of the national committee were Msgr. William Baumgaertner; Most Rev. Daniel Buechlein; Msgr. Edward Cuiba; Rev. John Grindel, C.M.; Mr. Fred Hofheinz; Rev. Charles Kavanagh; Sr. Theresa Monroe, R.S.C.J.; Rev. David Nygren, C.M.; Rev. John Padberg, S.J.; Most Rev. John Roach; Rev. Robert Sherry; and Sr. Jean Marie Sullivan, R.S.M. The Boston committee members were Rev. Richard Clifford, S.J.; Rev. John Farrell; Sr. Suzanne Kearney, C.S.J.; Rev. David Nygren, C.M.; and Rev. John O'Malley, S.J.

librarians, and others. In several settings it was also possible to interview ordinaries and other members of boards of trustees, totaling about fifty. The approximately two hundred faculty members were selected at each site according to teaching discipline, so that all the major areas of theological study were covered. Within each discipline a random sample of faculty was chosen. Four or five students were interviewed at each site, one or two student leaders and others selected by the dean or rector/president. Informal discussions took place with dozens of other students as well. In reporting the results of the interviews, specific numbers have not generally been used, since everyone in every category was not in a position to respond to all the questions. The categories of persons who did respond are identified, and then the approximate measure is designated as "a few" meaning under 10 percent, "some" meaning 10 to 40 percent, "about half" meaning over 40 but under 60 percent, "many" meaning between 60 and 90 percent, and "almost all" meaning over 90 percent.

To supplement the field research, I did a comprehensive review of catalogs, brochures, and handbooks issued by the theologates, as well as of the statistical data (primarily from the CARA seminary directories), and a thorough survey and analysis of the previous literature. Questionnaire responses were another important source of information. The survey of rectors/presidents concerning changes and trends at their institutions between 1967 and 1987 is referred to above. Vocation directors were also sent a questionnaire in which they were asked to provide information about their own backgrounds, education, and preparation for vocation work; their methods of screening candidates for priesthood; the criteria they use in selecting theologates for their students; and recommendations they had concerning their interactions with theologates.[4]

Social-science research of this kind, which includes interviews and surveys and statistics, has both its limitations and its capabilities. One of its limitations is that the information is never "all there" in static form at any one time, waiting to be located and measured. Since institutions are dynamic and vital, they are always being

---

[4]In June 1986, 229 vocation directors, representing approximately 66 percent of the total number, responded to the questionnaire. A summary of the findings of this survey is found in appendix B.

transformed, always being modified, always in flux. Because they represent an infinitely complex reality, the findings about them are not merely true or untrue, and statements about them cannot be simply accepted or rejected. Rather, the research reveals trends, directions, accomplishments, and failures. The findings are to be evaluated according to their usefulness in furthering the development of the institutions from which they derive. Seen from this perspective, the capabilities of social-science research are enormous. This study provides an opportunity for each theologate to review its own status and circumstances in relation to the other theologates. Perceptions can be appraised, ideas generated, and horizons expanded in light of the data. At its best, this research penetrates to the heart of an institution and discovers what is being created and what is being conserved, what is being valued and what is being discarded. It discovers the purpose, the identity, the spirit of each place, and transmits part of that life to all the others. That is the greatest contribution of this research.

Scope of the Study

The study covers all facets of theologates, and information was collected from all of the institutions that are members of the National Catholic Educational Association (NCEA) Seminary Department. These theologates are named in various ways—as seminaries, as schools of theology, or as divinity schools. The generic term used consistently in this book to identify institutions that enroll students who are studying theology in preparation for priesthood is "theologates." It distinguishes these institutions from seminaries that operate at the high school and college levels. Fifty-four theologates were operating in 1987-88 (see appendix C). Four of them are excluded from this study unless otherwise noted, however, because their structures and programs are not comparable to those of the other fifty.[5]

---

[5]Two of the four excluded theologates prepare men for other rites: St. Gregory the Theologian Seminary in Newton Centre, Massachusetts, (Eparchy of Newton), or Melkite Greek Catholic Seminary; and Byzantine Catholic Seminary of Saints Cyril and Methodius in Pittsburgh, Pennsylvania (Byzantine Archdiocese). The other two institutions are both Cisterian (OCSO) and provide monastic preparation for priesthood candidates: Monastery of the Holy Spirit in Conyers, Georgia; and St. Joseph's School of Theology and Institute of

The fifty theologates that are central to this research are of several types, as defined in *The Program of Priestly Formation* (*PPF*). The document states that "one of the results of the call for greater breadth, flexibility, and creativity in the formation and education of priests in the pluralistic context in our country has been the development of new models of seminary structures to effect greater renewal..."[6] The *PPF* then identifies three models: the traditional or freestanding model, the supplemental model, and the collaborative model, the latter being further divided into the union model, the federation model, and the mixed model.

Freestanding theologates, of which there are thirty, provide "the entire program of spiritual, intellectual, and pastoral formation/ education."[7] Within this category, they can be differentiated on the basis of who conducts them (sixteen are run by dioceses, and fourteen by religious orders) and who attends them (nine are for seminarians only, and twenty-one enroll both seminarians and other students). Ten theologates are identified as supplemental, that is, ones that provide "one or more parts of the program from [their] own resources while other parts (such as the academic) are provided by another institution (such as a university)."[8] This category includes all the houses of formation, which do not have academic programs. Since our study examines only theologates that also administer the academic programs for priesthood candidates, houses of formation are not included here in order to avoid counting students twice, once at their residence and once at the academic institution they attend. In our description of personal and spiritual formation programs, however, those programs that are located in houses of study are reviewed.

The collaborative model is described in the *PPF* as one that "recognizes the sharing of resources in a different way for the formation and education of priests."[9] A variation of this type is the

Monastic Studies in Spencer, Massachusetts. I gratefully acknowledge the response of these institutions to requests for information.

[6] *The Program of Priestly Formation*, 3rd ed. (Washington, D.C.: United States Catholic Conference, 1982), 7.

[7] Ibid.

[8] Ibid.

[9] Ibid.

union model, according to which "several specific groups (such as religious orders and/or dioceses) unite their resources in one institution under a single administrative and academic structure."[10] Two theologates identify themselves as "unions." Another variation of the collaborative type is the federation model, following which "seminaries of religious orders or of dioceses or of other, non-Catholic Churches, or 'union' seminaries ... make their resources available to each other to be shared according to several patterns of agreement. Each entity remains distinct and separate, but through the shared resources, they combine to form a cluster, a consortium, a coalition."[11] The five theologates that fit this definition vary among themselves, but the federation category corresponds to their configurations better than any other. The third type of collaborative arrangement is the mixed model, in which "some administrative and academic offerings belong specifically to the federation while others remain as the responsibility of the individual member institutions."[12] Three theologates conform to the mixed model. These fifty theologates (thirty freestanding, ten supplemental, and ten collaborative) are the basis for the findings reported in this study.

Early in the course of my research, I decided that whatever facets of theologates were represented in interviews and other sources of data would be incorporated insofar as reasonable. The scope of the study is, therefore, broad. Two early chapters supply the historical context. The first is a condensed version of "How the Diocesan Seminary Developed," by Joseph M. White , and the second is an essay entitled "The Houses of Study of Religious Orders and Congregations: A Historical Sketch," by John W. O'Malley, S.J. The remaining chapters describe the present status and suggest the future directions of theologates: Part two explores the purpose and management of theologates—their evolving missions, the emerging role of boards, and their growing command of finances. Part three considers personnel and students: changing administrative patterns, expanding faculty composition and education, and types of students—seminarians, women religious, laywomen and laymen, brothers, and

[10]Ibid.

[11]Ibid.

[12]Ibid.

priests. Part four examines programs: personal and spiritual formation for ministry, academic programs and curriculum development, and pastoral formation and field education. Part five reviews all of these areas in light of the needs of the Church and the changing Catholic population. It concludes by identifying future challenges and highlighting future opportunities.

Part I

Historical Background

A. How the Seminary Developed

by Joseph M. White

1. ORIGINS

The Catholic seminary originated at the Council of Trent's twenty-third session, which recessed on 15 July 1563, having framed its eighteenth chapter requiring every cathedral to support a college to train poor boys for the diocesan priesthood. The decree did not create a new institution, the clerical seminary as known in the twentieth century; instead it assigned responsibility to the bishop to train diocesan priests within an existing institution, the cathedral, with its urban location, its proximity to the episcopal curia and household, its rich liturgical life at which students were regularly to assist, and its chapter of canons, two of whom were to oversee the program. The decree gave only general directions to the effect that boys not younger than twelve were to study "grammar, singing, ecclesiastical computation, and other useful arts," progressing to "sacred scripture, ecclesiastical books, the homilies of saints, the manner of administering the sacraments, especially those things that seem adapted to the hearing of confessions, and the rites and ceremonies." This program was intended for poor youth, the well-to-do boys having other paths to the priesthood. The decree, then, did not make the seminary the required road to the diocesan priesthood, but it was a significant step toward developing a tradition of training diocesan priests. It made the bishop the central figure in the formation of priests and permitted him to determine the ideas appropriate for their training over the next 350 years.

The seminary decree did not address several issues. It did not pertain to the formation of priests of religious orders, which already had their own traditions of formation. Nor did it elaborate an ideal model of the diocesan priest as a guide to clerical formation, though other areas of Trent's legislation provided the basis for a model by insisting on the priest's good morals and behavior. Trent also issued a decree on the priesthood that defined the doctrine of the sacrament of orders, stating that "a character is imprinted which can neither be effaced nor taken away." It thus insisted on the distinctiveness of the priesthood as separate from the laity. The fuller implications of the sacrament of orders on methods of clerical formation would be worked out subsequently.

The founding of seminaries proceeded slowly after the council. It would be well into the eighteenth century before most European dioceses had one. Their uneven size, quality, and length of studies reflected the varying resources, population, and episcopal interest in clerical formation in dioceses across Catholic Europe. Several seventeenth-century French figures played a crucial role in informing the church's attitude on the subject of creating an influential method for the training of diocesan priests. The so-called French School of Pierre de Bérulle, Jean Jacques Olier, and St. Vincent de Paul elaborated a spirituality specifically for diocesan priests, which became the basis of their training. Bérulle, the seminal figure, sought the interiorization of religion in the believer's identification through mental prayer with the attitudes and actions of Christ's life, regarded not simply as past events but as "states" always available for contemplation. Priests and seminarians were to associate themselves with the role of the risen Christ as eternal priest and victim. As priests they were representations of Christ the victim-priest, imparting grace through the ministry of sacraments. The seminarian's interior identification with Christ was accompanied by an attitude of self-abnegation, or even self-annihilation, so that Christ would live in him.

The seminary training that was inaugurated in France by Jean Jacques Olier, founder of the Society of St. Sulpice (Sulpicians), and St. Vincent de Paul, founder of the Congregation of the Mission (Vincentians), began with retreats for candidates for ordination based on Berullian spirituality. The candidates for orders would have taken their theological training at universities. In 1642 Olier established his famous seminary at the church of St. Sulpice, the largest parish in Paris, of which he was pastor. Here candidates for orders were given spiritual preparation of undetermined length according to the wishes of their bishop; they lived a community life, pursued their studies at the university if not already completed, taught catechism to the parish children, and assisted in the parish church's liturgical life. Olier's Sulpicians and St. Vincent de Paul's Priests of the Mission were gradually invited by bishops throughout France to train diocesan clergy at local seminaries in cathedral towns where the format varied.

Some seminaries sponsored no more than retreat programs for candidates educated elsewhere, often at a local university. Where prior formal training was not possible, the retreats were lengthened to include a short course in theology and practical training for such ministerial tasks as hearing confessions, administering sacraments, and directing spiritual formation, which lasted from a few months to two or even three years, depending on the desires and resources of the local bishop. The preseminary training of the students would very likely have been at the colleges for boys conducted by religious orders throughout France. By the eighteenth century, nearly every French diocese had its local seminary, conducted either by Vincentians or Sulpicians or by a smaller company of priests.

The French model of the seminary had as its starting point the end of theological training, that is, preparation for ordination according to the new spirituality of the French School, as opposed to the Tridentine seminary decree's idea of starting with boys. Emphasizing spiritual training, it did not assign much importance to theological study as preparation for ministry. The spiritual dispositions and the development of what the French called *esprit ecclésiastique,* or what a modern observer might call "clerical spirit" or "clerical culture," were considered essential to preparing for the priesthood. The priest was to exemplify the loftiness of the priesthood, as defined by the Council of Trent, by manifesting a personal spirituality and a code of clerical behavior that set him apart from the unordained.

2. EARLY SEMINARIES IN AMERICA

As the methods of seminary education were taking shape in seventeenth-century France, English Catholics founded Maryland in 1634, where priests of the Society of Jesus were responsible for their pastoral care. The English Jesuits were trained and educated in Europe, so that there was no need or expectation of conducting diocesan seminary training in English-speaking North America. After the suppression of the Jesuits by Pope Clement XIV in 1773, the same priests (though no longer Jesuits) continued their work among Catholics in Maryland and in southeastern Pennsylvania. One of these priests, John Carroll, seeing the isolation of American Catholics from Europe after the American Revolution and the need for a succession of priests, made plans and raised funds during the 1780s for a Catholic college. The purpose of the college would be to educate Catholic laymen, recruiting candidates for seminary studies from among them and gradually developing a native American clergy. His efforts resulted in the establishment of Georgetown Academy (later University) in 1789 which opened officially in 1791. Meanwhile, in 1789 the Holy See provided for the spiritual care of American Catholics by creating the diocese of Baltimore, and appointed John Carroll as its bishop. In 1790, Bishop Carroll accepted the offer of the superior general of the Society of St. Sulpice to open a seminary in the new diocese. The Sulpicians wanted to continue their work of seminary training in Paris, but were beset by the upheaval of the French Revolution.

The arrival of four Sulpician priests with five seminarians in 1791 to open St. Mary's Seminary in Baltimore was the starting point of Catholic seminary education in the United States, and the beginning of a series of events leading to the formation of several clerical institutions in the Baltimore diocese. The Sulpicians had very few seminarians to train in the seminary's initial years, its enrollment dropping to one in 1799. From 1799 to 1852 they conducted a lay college, affiliated with the seminary, that provided institutional sup-port to maintain the small seminary program. Since Georgetown also functioned as a lay college under the restored Society of Jesus, the Sulpicians planned a minor, or preparatory, seminary to train boys in the humanities and piety as preparation for theological studies at St. Mary's Seminary. In 1808 they opened Mount Saint

Mary's College at Emmitsburg, Maryland, for this purpose. The small enrollment there of young aspirants to the priesthood soon led to the admission of boys who did not intend to become priests, in order to bring in more revenue to sustain the college. The Sulpicians ceded control of St. Mary's Seminary to a corporation of diocesan priests, who introduced theological instruction for seminarians teaching college boys in order to support themselves. The college at Emmitsburg continued as a "mixed" seminary, that is, one in which seminary training was combined with a lay college conducted by priests and seminarians. The Sulpicians closed their lay college in 1852, and developed St. Mary's as a freestanding seminary where seminarians and clerical faculty devoted themselves exclusively to the task of clerical formation in an environment separated from other activities. The Sulpicians also succeeded in opening the country's first freestanding minor seminary, St. Charles College, in 1848 near Baltimore.

By the middle of the nineteenth century, therefore, the Baltimore diocese was the location for two major or theological seminaries, St. Mary's Seminary at Baltimore and Mount Saint Mary's College at Emmitsburg, and a minor seminary, St. Charles College. The archbishop of Baltimore was not directly responsible for administering or financing these seminaries, which were patronized by bishops of dioceses from across the country. Thus the Baltimore experience did not reflect a literal compliance with the model of training set forth in the Tridentine seminary decree.

The diocese of Baltimore did not long remain the only diocese in the United States. In 1808 Baltimore was raised to the rank of an archdiocese, and new dioceses at principal cities were periodically established over the following decades. Some bishops sent their seminarians to Baltimore and Emmitsburg for training, but most were eager to start their own diocesan seminaries. The grants of money that European mission-aid societies gave the bishops of newly formed dioceses enabled them to construct a small cathedral to carry on episcopal functions, with an adjacent residence. The subsequent scenario varied from diocese to diocese, but often the next concern was to establish a school. The early building of cathedral, residence, and school, either on the same site or on separate sites, enabled the bishop to provide living arrangements for seminarians recruited from Europe. The immigrant seminarians usually came late in their training to their adopted diocese, where they resided in the bishop's residence and received the final stages of their instruction, usually in practical matters such as the administration of sacraments and the English language if they were not English speakers. They might also teach in the local Catholic school part-time during the short period before their ordination. There were seldom local youth aspiring to the priesthood who would need longer training.

The domestic seminary, or the small seminary united to a local Catholic academy, combined the practical wisdom of preparing immigrant seminarians under the bishop's eye with minimal outlay, thus avoiding the expense of sending them to a distant seminary. This arrangement complied literally with Trent's ideal of episcopal supervision for clerical formation in each diocese. The pattern of episcopal sponsorship was so prevalent that by 1843 there were twenty-two seminaries in the country with a combined enrollment of 277, or an average of thirteen students per seminary. Most of these local seminaries collapsed during the 1840s and 1850s for one or more reasons: the dearth of local youth attracted to the priesthood, the uneven supply of immigrant seminarians, the lack of clerical personnel to conduct the seminaries, and the absence of regular funding to sustain their operation.

3. SEMINARY EXPANSION IN THE MID-1800s

From the late 1840s through the 1870s, as some forty new dioceses were formed, only a few attempted to start a local seminary. By 1850, however, four dioceses had been promoted to the rank of archdiocese, with neighboring dioceses grouped around them to form ecclesiastical provinces, and efforts were made to form a regional seminary in each province. Thus the Cincinnati archdiocese opened Mount Saint Mary's Seminary of the West at Cincinnati in 1851, and the New York archdiocese opened St. Joseph Seminary at Troy, New York, in 1864. The financial and administrative challenges were such that the archdioceses of St. Louis and New Orleans failed in their attempts to sustain seminaries. On the other hand, two large Catholic dioceses that became archdioceses in the 1870s founded successful seminaries: Milwaukee, drawing on the financial support of German Catholics in the Middle West, opened St. Francis Seminary in 1856, which became a regional center for clerical formation especially of Germans. And Philadelphia, which had sponsored its local St. Charles Seminary since the 1830s, relocated its seminarians to a spacious and costly building in the suburb of Overbrook in 1871. During the same period Chicago failed in an ambitious attempt to sustain a seminary.

The seminaries of Cincinnati, Milwaukee, New York, and Philadelphia represented a significant stage in the evolution of the American Catholic seminary as an institutional form. These seminaries had antecedents in either episcopal residences or "mixed" structures or both. They were refounded in modern buildings, usually after a fund-raising effort, and located on spacious grounds that separated the resident seminary community from its surroundings. Except for New York's, these seminaries had minor seminary programs to prepare candidates for the major seminary. St. Mary's Seminary after 1852 shared some of these characteristics, though it retained its location in downtown Baltimore. The freestanding seminaries thus moved away from the Tridentine ideal of clerical formation taking place within the context of a cathedral and its allied activities. Each seminary that offered an entire course of theology achieved an enrollment of between fifty and one hundred students during the 1860s and 1870s. There were no competing activities such as teaching for the seminarians at these institutions. The freestanding seminaries were what social historians of nineteenth-century life label "total institutions," whose internal life is ordered for one specific purpose, in this case the training of priests.

The freestanding seminary was not the only institutional model for American diocesan seminaries; communities of priests also sponsored diocesan seminaries. The Vincentians, who came to Missouri in 1818 to open a seminary for the local diocese and later staffed several local diocesan seminaries, also conducted diocesan programs at their colleges for laymen: St. Vincent's College in Cape Girardeau, Missouri (1858); and Niagara College in Niagara Falls, New York (1857). Likewise, Benedictine monks from German-speaking Europe came to the United States to serve German communities. The monks established monasteries where monastic life was observed, schools for laymen were operated, the land was farmed, ordained monks engaged in parish ministry, and seminary training was conducted for diocesan and monastic seminarians. This was the case at St. Vincent's

Archabbey and Seminary (1846), St. John's Abbey and Seminary in Collegeville, Minnesota (1857), and St. Meinrad Abbey and Seminary (1854). Italian Franciscans were invited to western New York State in 1863, where they started a similar lay college and seminary, which became St. Bonaventure College. These seminaries trained candidates from a range of dioceses, and reflect the fact that the responsibility for conducting diocesan seminaries was sometimes assumed by interests other than bishops. As instances of diocesan seminary training in a "mixed" context, they joined Mount Saint Mary's College and Seminary at Emmitsburg, and the sole mixed seminary and college to succeed under the sponsorship of a diocese, Immaculate Conception Seminary with Seton Hall College, at South Orange, New Jersey.

The dependence of the American Catholic church on Europe led to various proposals for establishing seminaries in Europe near sources of funding and students. Eventually an American College was established in the shadow of the Catholic University of Louvain, Belgium, in 1857. Here many Europeans, especially Germans, were trained for the American missions during the first half century of the college's history. Pope Pius IX ordered the opening of an American College in Rome in 1859 exclusively for American seminarians.

Priests of religious orders were trained within the context of the educational and ministerial activities of monasteries, friaries, and religious houses around the country. Vincentians and Benedictines trained their own candidates as well as diocesan seminarians. The Jesuits were foremost in ending diffuse local training of their members and unifying their seminary program in a single, national, freestanding seminary, the College of the Sacred Heart, founded in 1869 at Woodstock, Maryland, near Baltimore. Woodstock College, as it was subsequently named, remained the Jesuits' national seminary until the early twentieth century.

The vision of ministry in the developing American Catholic church influenced the nature and length of seminary programs. The urgent need for priests to minister the sacraments to the rapidly growing Catholic immigrant population required quick training. Dogmatic and moral theology "tracts," or short articles on theological topics bound together in "manuals," were the basis of instruction, with other subjects being either secondary or not offered. There was no church legislation governing the length of programs. As the rector of

Cincinnati's seminary remarked in 1861, "We have known cases of persons having been ordained after their first year's theology; and some have graduated in ecclesiastical science, after an extensive course of six months." The rise of the well-organized freestanding seminaries ensured longer courses in theology. For instance, at Baltimore's St. Mary's Seminary, the future Cardinal James Gibbons pursued a course of studies in the 1850s comprising one year of philosophy and two of theology. The better seminaries by the 1870s offered no more than four years of philosophy and theology.

4. SEMINARY REFORM AND NEW INSTITUTIONS IN THE LATE 1800s

The volume of seminary activity, substantial though it appears by the 1870s, had not produced enough priests for the growing Catholic population. Only a small proportion of priests ministering in the United States were born, trained, and ordained there during the nineteenth century. The American church depended on continuous recruiting of priests from western Europe. It was not until 1849, sixty years after the founding of the diocese of Baltimore, that the number of priests in the United States reached one thousand. Accompanying the massive Catholic immigration that began in the middle of the century, the number of clergy doubled to two thousand by 1857 and then tripled to six thousand by 1880.

The growing body of clergy inspired mixed appraisals. Deriving from several countries, they had various national characteristics, levels of education, and standards of behavior. Some came to America because they had failed at ministerial careers in Europe. All came to a country where the church enjoyed missionary status, meaning that canon law was only partially in force. There were no canonical parishes, only missions to and from which the local bishop could and did transfer priests at will. American dioceses, unlike those in Europe, had no cathedral chapters of senior clergy to serve as checks on a bishop's authority. This lack of priests' rights as under canon law caused a movement among priests to defend their rights. Bishops, on the other hand, maintained that they had to be able to transfer priests at will, if individuals from this mixed body of clergy proved to be lax or unsuitable for the position to which they had been assigned. The issue of clerical rights and behavior related naturally to the issue of seminary training, which came to be regarded as too brief and inadequate. To resolve these and other pressing issues in the American Catholic community, the American bishops convened for their Third Plenary Council of Baltimore in 1884.

The council took steps to ensure the protection of priests' rights by creating a diocesan board of consultors consisting of the senior pastors of the diocese. The local bishop had to obtain the approval of the consultors in specified areas. Grievance procedures for priests were also clarified. These measures dealt with the current body of clergy, but the bishops looked to the future development of an American clergy trained along standard lines. The council's seminary decrees aimed to improve the content and extend the length of seminary training by requiring a six-year course for minor and major seminaries. The major-seminary decree listed and described the courses of the curriculum, giving unprecedented attention to formerly neglected subjects such as biblical studies, homiletics, and church history. The minor-seminary decree concerned the preparation of students for the major seminary through instruction in the humanities, classical languages, and the rudiments of clerical spirituality and culture. These decrees were based on drafts submitted by Roman authorities, but the bishops eliminated Roman suggestions about summer villas to house seminarians during vacations. The decrees were unprecedented in the history of the American bishops' conciliar legislation for their attention to issues of clerical formation. Diocesan seminary educators now had the guidance of a curricular program for a prescribed number of years, though it would be decades before all seminaries complied fully with the six-year requirement for the major seminary.

During the council the bishops also heard one of their younger colleagues, Bishop John Lancaster Spalding of Peoria, Illinois, deliver an eloquent speech on "University Education Considered in Its Bearing on the Higher Education of Priests," in which he set forth the need for a Catholic university. His idea was not a school for advanced theological and professional study, but a place for priests to develop a mental culture permitting them to deal with a range of ideas; Catholic spokesmen could then participate in the "controversies of the age." The bishops agreed to establish the Catholic University of America, which opened with a pontifical charter from Pope Leo XIII in 1889 in Washington, D.C.

The attention given to clerical learning at Third Baltimore was continued in discussions of new ideas about the seminary by such leading bishops as Archbishop John Ireland of St. Paul, Minnesota, and Bishop Bernard McQuaid of Rochester, New York, who advocated a liberally educated, theologically well-trained clergy capable of being articulate spokesmen for Catholicism in a pluralistic society where ideas were openly discussed. A new generation of American-born Sulpicians also attempted to alter seminary traditions in response to the rising educational needs of the time. These seminary reformers rejected the older view that the priest should have just enough formal learning to administer sacraments. They were aware of the great advancement of theological learning and secular knowledge in the nineteenth century, and saw the need for priests to come to terms with it. Their views received systematic treatment in both *Clerical Studies* (1896) by John B. Hogan, a Sulpician who explained the purpose of each discipline in the modern seminary curriculum prescribed at Third Baltimore, and *Our American Seminaries* (1895) by John Talbot Smith, a diocesan priest whose ideal American diocesan priest was to be an educated gentleman fitted for public life, physically sound, acquainted and in sympathy with his environment, and imbued with the true missionary spirit. This clerical model was a reaction against an older ideal of the narrowly schooled priest whose mind was exclusively on the supernatural, whose asceticism and unexercised body rendered him sickly and useless, whose European background caused him to disdain American values, and who lacked the necessary flexibility for the varied demands of ministry in America.

The 1880s and 1890s were decades of institution building in the interest of improved training for priests. In addition to the Catholic University of America, dioceses opened St. John's Seminary at Boston in 1884, St. Bernard Seminary at Rochester in 1893, St. Paul Seminary at St. Paul in 1894, Kenrick Seminary at St. Louis in 1894, and St. Patrick's Seminary near San Francisco in 1898. New York's St. Joseph Seminary was refounded at Yonkers in 1896, and Baltimore's St. Mary's Seminary was greatly enlarged. Unlike the improvised diocesan seminaries earlier in the century, the new seminaries were normally housed in modern structures, thanks to careful planning and fund raising. Their dioceses were able to raise sufficient funds to build them and then sustain their operation, since most of the students needed to have their expenses provided. A full generation had elapsed since the massive immigration of Irish and Germans in the 1850s; for the first time, the Catholic community now had a large pool of potential seminarians born and raised in American Catholic culture. Accordingly, the freestanding seminaries achieved enrollments of between one hundred and two hundred by 1910. Although these seminaries represented the assertion of an American style in institutional life and clerical training, ethnic consciousness still remained important in the Catholic community. National diocesan seminaries were opened for Germans at the Pontifical Josephinum in Columbus, Ohio, in 1892, and for Poles at Sts. Cyril and Methodius Seminary in Detroit, Michigan, in 1885.

The opening of Catholic University at Washington, D.C., stimulated interest among several religious orders in improving their seminary programs. Some smaller orders opened houses of study near the university so that their members could attend the university's theology programs. The Dominicans opened their own Dominican House of Studies in 1905 as a freestanding seminary across the street from the university; here the order's distinctive theological program and pontifical degrees could be pursued without recourse to the university. Several other orders likewise founded separate freestanding seminaries near the university, but affiliated only minimally with it. This network of freestanding seminaries and houses of study in the neighborhood of Catholic University in northeast Washington was the closest manifestation of a larger cooperation among Catholic seminary interests in the area of theological education. The growing number of religious order seminarians kept pace with the increase in diocesan seminarians. By 1900 there were some 76 seminaries, minor and major, diocesan and religious, enrolling 3,395 seminarians.

5. ROMAN INFLUENCE ON AMERICAN SEMINARIES

The renewal and expansion of seminaries in the United States paralleled initiatives taken by the Holy See that impinged on the quality of intellectual life in the Church. First and foremost among these was the encyclical *Aeterni Patris*, issued by Pope Leo XIII in 1879, which proposed the scholastic method of St. Thomas Aquinas for Catholic philosophical and theological studies. Concurrently in Europe the advancement of biblical studies, archaeology, and the historical study of Christian antiquities taking place outside the Catholic community had an inevitable impact on Catholic intellectual activity. Catholic theologians and scholars saw a clear need to reexamine Catholic theology and to reconcile it with the new scholarship. The European Catholics undertaking this task soon found their work under suspicion, however. Pope St. Pius X came down sharply against these important developments in 1907 by condemning a series of theological and philosophical propositions that he labeled "Modernism." This action was followed in 1910 by the decree issued *motu proprio* (i.e., on the pope's own initiative) and entitled *Sacrorum Antistitum*, which required seminary instructors to take an annual oath against Modernism. The decree also forbade seminarians to read periodicals, and contains remarkable words about the importance of controlling the enthusiasm for learning. It was directly opposed in spirit to the idea that seminarians and seminary faculty should keep abreast of contemporary theological issues, which American seminary reformers strongly advocated. Though serious scholarship had scarcely taken root at Catholic institutions in the United States, the crusade against Modernism effectively prevented it from developing for a generation.

Pope St. Pius X also initiated a compilation of universal church law known as the Code of Canon Law, which was completed and took effect in 1917. The code provided the first general legislation pertaining to the seminary since the Council of Trent, defining its nature and purpose, enumerating its officials including the new office of spiritual director, and listing the subjects to be studied in the major seminary. It stipulated that all candidates for holy orders take their training in seminaries. By requiring that the study of philosophy and theology proceed according to the scholasticism of St. Thomas Aquinas, it precluded the rise of historical and critical methods of study. It greatly enlarged the powers of the Holy See's Sacred Congregation of Seminaries and Universities, which in the following years issued regulations, dispensed permissions, and received triennial reports on matters pertaining to seminaries.

The Holy See had wrought a profound change in thus relocating responsibility for the diocesan seminary. From the Council of Trent to the dawn of the twentieth century, the local bishop had been the pivotal figure in forming diocesan clergy; now the bishop served as an agent of Roman authorities in executing decrees that he had had no part in making. Increasing numbers of American bishops appointed since the turn of the century had been trained in Rome, where they assimilated the new trend of Roman centralization. When they became bishops, they had no knowledge of and no interest in developing an American tradition of seminary education such as had concerned nineteenth-century bishops like Ireland and McQuaid. The new trend also affected the religious orders, which had to conform to standards of uniformity set by the code. The Sacred Congregation of Religious regulated their affairs with unprecedented closeness. In turn, the religious orders that were headquartered in Rome enforced uniform standards on their own members' activities, including seminary training.

The new Roman vision of the priesthood that came to inform seminary training was articulated by Popes St. Pius X, Pius XI, and Pius XII, who issued encyclicals and apostolic exhortations and letters on the priesthood with unprecedented regularity. Their statements indicate how much the concepts of the priesthood arising from the seventeenth-century French reformers had penetrated the church generally. These popes reinforced the church's adherence to this Baroque tradition by emphasizing the loftiness of the priest to the point of conferring near magical powers on him, and by binding clerics to a spirituality different from that prescribed for the unordained. Pope Pius XI, who reigned from 1922 to 1939, also issued statements on the importance of clerics' mastering the church's official teaching. His particular interest in the areas of clerical spirituality and learning was evident when he ordered an official visitation of all the seminaries in the Catholic world, beginning in 1937, to determine how well the new Roman standards had been implemented.

The training offered in seminaries continued the same methods of spiritual formation that had been pursued since the seventeenth century. Moreover, the separation of seminary communities from lay culture was more complete within the self-contained world of the freestanding seminary and under the more rigorous standards decreed by church authority. The methods of formal learning in most diocesan seminaries and in many seminaries of religious orders shared similarities.

Dogmatic and moral theology dominated the major seminary curriculum, and the so-called manuals written in Latin dominated the study of these subjects. Although church authority did not prescribe the choice of textbook, a consensus formed around the works of the French Sulpician Adolph Tanquerey, whose dogmatic manuals written in clear and simple Latin achieved an extraordinary influence in American seminaries during the first half of the twentieth century. The manuals generally presented church teachings in brief theological propositions, followed by objections normally advanced by opponents of Catholicism; the objections were then answered with a rebuttal that included quotations from Scripture, the church fathers, official teachings, and Catholic authors. The contents of moral theology manuals were closely related to topics that might arise in the confessional. Normally no collateral reading, written work, or independent research was assigned in dogma and moral theology courses. It was mastery of official teaching as presented in the manuals that was expected.

Other subjects were secondary. Biblical studies improved as instructors at many seminaries gained formal graduate training, but these studies did not displace dogma and moral theology courses. Church history emphasized the institutional progress of the church without teaching the development of church doctrine and practice, which was also neglected in the dogma and moral manuals. Canon law gave an introduction to the church's operation as prescribed by the code. Roman officials often commended or even commanded the introduction of such subjects as sacred music, catechetics, and social problems, which greatly enlarged the curriculum with minor courses. They issued regular exhortations that Latin was to be thoroughly taught, and that theological instruction was to be carried out in Latin. There was no assertion that this system of introductory courses produced scholars, but it provided what was considered a useful general survey of what a priest should know.

6. PROFESSIONAL DEVELOPMENT AND TWENTIETH-CENTURY REFORMS

The professional development of the seminary faculty advanced gradually, with instructors earning degrees from pontifical institutes as required by the code. In this area Pope Pius XI was responsible for a far-reaching reform when he issued the apostolic constitution *Deus Scientiarum Dominus* (1931), which set standards for graduate

degrees in pontifical universities by prescribing formal programs of
graduate study lasting a period of years accompanied with a dissertation. This reform ended the easy Roman doctorate conferred by
examination based on a defense of theological propositions, and
brought pontifical universities in Rome closer to modern university
practices. It also acted as an entering wedge for the education of
future seminary instructors in historical and critical methods of
theological research. Awareness of developments within seminary-
related academic disciplines was manifested after the late 1930s in
the founding of professional organizations of biblical scholars, canon
lawyers, and theologians. Their memberships consisted largely of
seminary educators. The organizations had annual meetings, sponsored publications, and provided a forum for the exchange of views,
thereby encouraging the idea that theological knowledge was in the
process of evolving.

The Catholic minor and major seminary network provided not
only theological programs according to church practices, but also
high school and undergraduate liberal arts programs. Seminary
educators gradually saw the need to bring their liberal arts programs
up to the standards of modern American education. High school
programs were increasingly conformed to state requirements. Some
older seminaries possessed state charters from the nineteenth century
that permitted the conferral of degrees, but had refused to use them
to grant bachelor's degrees because of the strong tradition of the
vanity of degrees. From the 1920s onward, the practice of conferring
bachelor's degrees for liberal arts studies gained ground based on
state charters or state certification. By the 1950s, seminary educators
began to think about seeking accreditation from regional accrediting
bodies, which would make seminary bachelor's degrees equivalent to
those granted by colleges and universities in the United States. The
accrediting process advanced slowly, since many seminaries fell below
accepted standards of American higher education in such areas as
administrative procedures, library holdings, course offerings, and
faculty qualifications.

The organizational structure of the seminary network prevented
rapid adjustment in these areas. The lines of authority in the church
were vertical: from the seminary officials to the bishop to the Roman
authorities, in the case of diocesan seminaries; in the case of religious
orders, from the seminary officials to the local religious superior to

the international superior to the Roman authorities. There was no provision for horizontal interaction among seminary educators thinking and acting collectively to improve seminary education. Roman authority, with its concern for universal standards of its own, usually took no cognizance of the need for seminary educators to interact or to relate seminaries to local educational standards. Seminary reformers were therefore greatly encouraged in their efforts by the words of Pope Pius XII, in the apostolic exhortation *Menti Nostrae* (1950), to the effect that seminary courses in the liberal arts should not be inferior to those offered at equivalent secular institutions.

Seminary educators by the 1950s began to develop among themselves a sense of common concerns, initially through educational conferences sponsored by religious orders that were engaged in educational activities, including the administration of their own seminaries or of seminary education for dioceses. At such conferences the need for reform was discussed, and common educational policies within a religious order's institutions were formulated. The national forum for seminary educators had been the seminary department of the National Catholic Educational Association, where for many years papers had been presented at annual conventions on seminary topics. In 1958 the association appointed a full-time executive for the seminary department, Rev. J. Cyril Dukehart, a persistent advocate of measures to reduce the Catholic seminary's isolation from the rest of the educational world, which often regarded it as inferior. Dukehart targeted three major areas for seminary reform: first, the accreditation of seminaries so that unordained former seminary students and clerical alumni would have academic records and degrees that would be recognized in the educational world; second, the formation of an American Association of Catholic Theological Seminaries as a means of improving seminary standards and establishing a professional degree for seminaries; and third, addressing the acute problem of the more than one hundred minor and major seminaries with an enrollment of fewer than fifty students.

Many seminary educators shared Dukehart's vision of the needs of Catholic seminaries. Regional meetings of seminary educators were held at which these progressive ideas were discussed. The Middle West was especially important because of the relationship that seminary educators there formed with the North Central Association of Colleges and Universities to advance accreditation, especially for degrees in theological studies.

Seminary educators took the initiative of formulating their views on educational reform against the background of the burgeoning growth of the Catholic seminary network. In 1959 the seminary department of the National Catholic Educational Association reported that there were 381 seminaries, major and minor, diocesan and religious, in the United States: This meant that 34 percent of the total number had been founded since World War II, 28 percent of them since 1950. It represented a 53-percent increase in the number of seminaries since 1945, and a 40-percent increase since 1950. By 1961 the total number of all seminarians, diocesan and religious, was 42,349, distributed in 402 seminaries and houses of religious formation. These institutions ranged in size from great freestanding seminaries of large dioceses and large religious orders, many of them established after 1900, to programs of small religious orders training a handful of seminarians. The increasing number of seminarians attested to the attractiveness of the priesthood to youth born and raised in American Catholic culture. Many seminary educators believed that this growth would continue indefinitely, and that the need for the improvement of seminaries was therefore urgent.

By 1962, the year of the opening of the Second Vatican Council, the main lines of an agenda for seminary reform in the United States had been determined. The following decade saw the implementation of most reforms that were designed to end the isolation of the seminary and to enlarge its educational purposes. These changes were accompanied with the theological renewal engendered by the Second Vatican Council, which would alter the content of seminary learning, and by the rapid cultural changes taking place within the American Catholic community, which would change the attitude of young men toward entering the seminary.

B. The Houses of Study
of Religious Orders and Congregations:
A Historical Sketch

by John W. O'Malley, S.J.

Whereas the origins of the seminary for the training of diocesan priests can be pinpointed to the decree of the twenty-third session of the Council of Trent (1563), the origins of the correlative institutions for members of religious orders and congregations are much more diffuse. They are also, by and large, older than the Tridentine tradition of seminary. It would be difficult to summarize these origins and the subsequent histories even if we possessed the monographic studies that are the necessary preconditions for such an endeavor. In actual fact, however, the training of their members is an aspect of the history of religious orders that has been singularly neglected, especially for the modern period and for the United States. The only notable exception to this generalization is a doctoral dissertation on the Jesuits' Woodstock College, submitted to the Catholic University of America in 1964.

For the earlier histories of these institutions, some few studies exist that examine aspects of the spiritual and academic training of members, but they are scattered in highly specialized journals and leave many questions unanswered, even for the largest and most influential orders. This means that the oldest traditions of systematic attempts to educate young persons for the ministry remain almost a closed book to us, and therefore that only comments of the most general nature can be adduced here, in contrast to the foregoing history of seminary education, which has been better researched. Nonetheless, even from the little we know it is clear that, historically and canonically speaking, we are dealing with traditions that are significantly different from the seminary tradition properly so called. The two should not be identified as essentially the same, as is the current trend. The traditions of the orders and congregations derived their distinctiveness in part from the historical periods in which they came into being. On a deeper level, however, their distinctiveness derived from the life-style embraced by the order or congregation, which itself was largely determined by the specific ministries in which the members engaged—or did not engage—and by the general understanding of ministry that these choices implied. Thus from the very beginning, diversities in ministry account for diversities in training between the diocesan and regular clergy, and within the regular clergy itself.

1. ORIGINS

From the twelfth century onwards, a number of monasteries following the Rule of St. Benedict increasingly encouraged, or at least tolerated, study as having a place in the life of the monk. From the abundance and high quality of the literature produced as a result of this development, we must infer that in many monasteries the standard of education of the monks was high relative to the period. Particularly in the twelfth century, monks like St. Anselm, St. Bernard, and others were among the most respected intellectual figures of their time. The monasteries and, later, the monastic congregations continued to foster learning among their members, as is clear from the Congregation of S. Giustina in Italy in the fifteenth century, the Congregation of St. Maur in France in the seventeenth, and many other examples.

While detailed information about the academic training of the "average monk" in almost any of these monasteries is not easily accessible, certain general features are obvious. By the twelfth century many monks were priests, yet they lived in monasteries that were for the most part exempt from episcopal jurisdiction. Although they were ordained, the care of souls was sometimes forbidden them, as we see in canon 16 of Lateran Council I (1123). They in fact often exercised such care, but they did not seem to think of their priesthood in terms of ministry. Hence, the aim of their studies was contemplative rather than practical or pastoral, in the usual sense of these words. There was thus a coordination between the style of theology that was learned or created and the style of life that was led—a coordination between intellectual and spiritual training that was so perfect that the distinction is almost without meaning in monastic culture. This integrated training took place entirely in the monastery, that is, in a "freestanding" institution. This "total institution" stood apart from "the world" and was located in the countryside. The training was, moreover, much less formalized and structured, though not for that reason less effective, than other systems that first came into being in the thirteenth century. The training and relationship to ministry of canons regular would fall somewhere between the monastic and these other systems.

By the early years of the thirteenth century, several great universities like Paris and Bologna had already achieved a mature organization and had created graduated and fully articulated curricula in programs that led to publicly recognized degrees. Thus a wholly new style of education was born about the year 1200, which produced "professionals" in learning. The new style began slowly to displace the informal, highly personalized traditions that had long held sway. This revolution affected those relatively few members of both the secular and monastic clergy who attended the universities, even when they did so for just a short time and without obtaining degrees. It had an impact on the new mendicant orders, however, in ways that were much more profound and systemic. The mendicants and the universities were, in a sense, creatures of the same generation.

In this regard the Dominicans are particularly important. They came into being under the leadership of their founder in response to a precise pastoral need, namely, the need for preachers who could by the soundness of their doctrine and the example of their poverty convince the Albigensian heretics of their errors. From its very inception, therefore, learning was central to Dominican ministry, and both ministry and learning were related to a spiritual training that would begin in the novitiate and continue throughout the friar's entire life. St. Dominic deliberately founded major houses near universities, so that a close relationship was established right away between those institutions and the ministerial training of the friars.

The pattern established by the Dominicans almost immediately became paradigmatic for the Franciscans, and then for the other mendicant orders like the Augustinians, Carmelites, and Servites. This is not to say that every member of these orders who engaged in ministry attended a university, but rather that explicit programs of education were formulated within these orders that were inspired by the same principles that undergirded the university programs. As early as 1290, for instance, the Augustinians could speak of a *Ratio Studiorum*, or "plan of studies," formulated under the influence of Giles of Rome at the general chapter at Ratisbon.

The Franciscans manifested, especially through the life of St. Francis, another important aspect of the mendicants' self-understanding that bore on their training. St. Francis was, in the strictest sense of the term, a charismatic leader—a charismatic leader whom the love of God impelled to undertake the ministry of preaching. He began this ministry even before he was tonsured by Pope Innocent III, and he never was ordained a priest. Thus Franciscan ministry derived not from ecclesiastical office or priestly ordination, but from pastoral needs and personal inspiration. The lay origins of the Franciscans and the gradual "clericalization" of the order is a complex historical problem, but we must at the same time be aware that all the mendicant orders of the thirteenth century manifested close and special relationships to the laity in their lay brothers and in their so-called second and third orders.

As would again be true for all the mendicants, Franciscan ministry was officially exempt from direct episcopal supervision and was carried out under the "apostolic" structures within the order. Not contained therefore within diocesan boundaries, it extended everywhere, even to the infidel—as St. Francis showed so graphically by his own preaching before El-Kamil, the sultan of Egypt.

The Society of Jesus, founded in 1540, was the self-conscious heir to many of the ideas about ministry and training for ministry first implemented by the mendicants, and it in turn set a pattern followed by many subsequent orders and congregations. Moreover, St. Ignatius and his five original companions were all graduates of the University of Paris, and that first generation soon became convinced of the ministerial potential of the new humanistic education both for Jesuits themselves and for those whom they served. For the first time in the history of the Church, teaching in schools came to be considered and exercised as a formal ministry.

In the earliest years of the order, young members were sent to universities to study, but soon the Jesuits established schools for their members in imitation of and sometimes in tandem with the universities, and so always in centers of population. It is significant that five of the ten parts of the lengthy Jesuit *Constitutions*, composed mostly by St. Ignatius, deal with the admission and training of members. It is also noteworthy that, although St. Ignatius certainly assumed that the "fully formed" members of the order would be priests, there is no mention of priesthood or ordination in the whole of the *Constitutions* with respect to the training of Jesuits. The *Ratio Studiorum* of 1599, although of broader scope as well, codified the

Jesuit ideal of the academic aspects of training for ministry.

"Ministry" is in fact the word and idea that recurs again and again in the early Jesuit documents (*ministerium, ministeria*), especially various forms of "ministry of the Word." In some of these documents, even sacramental confession is sometimes subsumed under that designation as a kind of "personalized sermon." The various ministries of the Word—preaching, teaching, lecturing, spiritual direction, directing retreats, publishing books, ministering to heretics and the infidel as well as to the faithful, et al.—required a fully developed spiritual and intellectual training.

In even more explicit and emphatic fashion than the mendicants, the Jesuits, who were also exempt from episcopal jurisdiction, envisioned the scope of their ministries as extending not only beyond diocesan boundaries but far beyond Christendom itself, as indicated by their special vow to obey the pope "concerning missions." Implied here, besides, was a broad understanding of ministry as almost any form of pastoral care that could be devised to meet the spiritual needs of persons marginalized or alienated, persons with no religious faith or with a different religious faith, persons as well who sought a deeper and more closely guided spiritual experience. To be free for such work, Jesuits were forbidden by their own legislation to accept parishes, properly so called. Most orders and congregations shared at least in some degree this same broad designation of the locus and forms of pastoral service.

By the middle of the seventeenth century, therefore, training programs for the so-called active orders had been fully articulated and correlated with their ministries. Granted that there was considerable diversity among the orders and even within any given order, some common elements existed: an intense spiritual program begun in the novitiate, whose foundations were assumed in later phases of training; an equally intense academic program conducted in special *Studia* located in cities, which imitated or stood in some close relationship to universities; a close relationship in community with nonordained members, and with other men and women through second and third orders and through closely attached confraternities or sodalities; a sense of calling to certain ministries that met needs not being attended to by what we might by this time call the "parochial structures"; the persuasion that the shape and finality of both the spiritual and academic programs be determined by these special ministries; and self-determination regarding these programs, without reference to diocesan or papal regulation.

2. UNITED STATES

The earliest missionaries to the territories that would later be the United States were members of religious orders, but the history of the founding of their novitiates and houses of study does not really begin until the late-eighteenth and early-nineteenth centuries. In Europe this very period was a particularly difficult one for most orders. The suppression of the Society of Jesus in 1773 was followed by the more general religious upheavals of the French Revolution and its long aftermath, whose effects were felt in all countries on the Continent and throughout the Catholic world. The Dominicans, for instance, were unable to hold a general chapter of the order for over half a century, from 1777 until 1832.

This turmoil surely affected the training the orders gave their members and in many, perhaps most, cases interrupted the continuity of their traditions of formation. The transplanting of those traditions to the newly founded United States of America would put that continuity to further tests. Nonetheless, the traditional programs of a solid spiritual training begun in a novitiate established for that purpose and an integrated intellectual training conducted in houses of study where the humanities, philosophy, and theology would be taught continued to be the ideal in the New World.

Since novitiates were easier to staff, they seem to have been established earlier and had more continuous histories. For academic training, the orders tended to send their young members to Europe or, more often, to settle for a haphazard patchwork of courses and private reading that was a far cry from what the various "plans of study" enjoined. As late as 1866, a Jesuit who was then superior of the large midwestern province complained that he had never had a single year for study since he had entered the order, and that whatever philosophy or theology he knew he had had to teach himself from textbooks while he was at the same time engaged in practically full-time ministry.

Nonetheless, efforts were being made to regularize the situation, as the following few instances will show. As early as 1834, the Dominicans founded their first *Studium Generale* in the United

States at Somerset, Ohio. About 1860 they established a similar institution on the West Coast at Monterey, California, which was soon transferred to Benicia, where it remained until 1932. By 1820 the Vincentians had begun a log rectory-seminary at Perryville, Missouri, whose student body included not only Vincentians and diocesan seminarians (until 1842), but also lay students earning a college degree (until 1866). The institution transferred to St. Louis in 1862 and thence to Germantown, Pennsylvania, where St. Vincent's Seminary opened in 1868. The Benedictines founded St. Vincent's Archabbey in 1846, St. Meinrad's Abbey in 1854, and St. John's Abbey in 1857, where not only diocesan candidates for the priesthood but also Benedictines were trained.

The Redemptorists opened their first house of studies in 1849 in New York City, whence it moved two years later to Cumberland, Maryland, only to be moved in 1862 to Annapolis and again in 1866 to Ilchester, where it remained until moved in 1907 to a farm at Esopus, New York. The Conventual Franciscans established a house for philosophical and theological studies at Trenton New Jersey, in 1876, but closed it for lack of students in 1885 and sent the friars to Europe for their postnovitiate training. Reestablished in 1889, the house at Trenton went through several later transfers and reorganizations until settled in 1912 at St.-Anthony-on-Hudson in a "free-standing" situation outside Albany, New York. The origins of the Franciscan School of Theology now at Berkeley, California, can be traced back to rudimentary beginnings in 1854.

In 1823 the Jesuits established a novitiate at Florissant, Missouri, outside St. Louis, and a few months later began to teach philosophy and theology there to a half-dozen candidates. The rural location seems to have been chosen simply because the countryside was less expensive than the city. By 1837 five scholastics were being taught philosophy and theology at St. Louis University. For over half a century, from 1806 until the Civil War, Jesuit scholastics from the East Coast were trained in philosophy and theology at Georgetown University in Washington, D.C. On 30 March 1833, Georgetown received from the Sacred Congregation for the Propagation of the Faith the power to grant ecclesiastical degrees in philosophy and theology.

By common admission, however, the academic training of Jesuits throughout the country remained woefully inadequate, and recognition of this situation eventually led to the founding in 1860 of a common scholasticate at Boston College for all the provinces in the United States. But since the scholastics could be supported more cheaply on a farm, they were transferred in 1869 to Woodstock, Maryland. Although the General of the Society urged in 1910 that the scholasticate be moved to the campus of Fordham University, it remained at Woodstock until 1968. By contrast, the Jesuits from the Midwest had withdrawn their scholastics from Woodstock as early as 1899 and relocated them at St. Louis University. In 1931 these scholastics were, again for financial reasons, transferred from St. Louis to the countryside, this time to St. Mary's, Kansas.

Until more information is assembled and analyzed, we may assume that the above patterns were somewhat typical for religious orders through much of the nineteenth century. There seem to have been many foundations that lasted only a few years, and "plans of study" legislated by the orders were observed in only a most approximate fashion. The period between the Civil War and the early decades of the twentieth century, however, brought improvement and stabilization. For instance, Jesuits of considerable competence, who had been expelled from Italy for political reasons between 1860 and 1870, began to teach at Woodstock. An academic tradition was thus established that, for all its shortcomings, would eventually lead to the founding of *Theological Studies* in 1939. In 1905 the Dominicans transferred their *Studium Generale* from Ohio to Washington, D.C., in order to be near the newly founded Catholic University of America, and that *Studium* was later empowered to grant ecclesiastical degrees.

Smaller and newer orders occasionally entered into a more than nominal relationship with institutions of higher learning. In 1916 the Oblates of Mary Immaculate established a house at Catholic University, as did the Oblates of St. Francis de Sales in 1924. In the latter case, the candidates completed all their academic preparation for priesthood at the university. The Oblates of St. Joseph pursued their theological studies either at Catholic University or at the Gregorian University in Rome. The Congregation of the Holy Cross established Holy Cross College in 1901 and Holy Cross Foreign Mission Seminary in 1924, near Catholic University; it also carried out formation through houses abroad that were attached to other institutions, like the Gregorian University in Rome, the Catholic

University of Chile, and the Grande Seminaire at LeMans, France.

It was the freestanding pattern that predominated, however, a pattern that persisted during the great multiplication of such houses of study between World War I and the end of the Second Vatican Council. By that time the Jesuits, for example, had five freestanding theologates, three freestanding philosophates (plus two others located on university campuses), and ten freestanding juniorates, to each of which a novitiate was attached. These institutions almost invariably had, it is true, some affiliation with a nearby Jesuit university, which meant that their students were often enrolled in degree programs recognized by the university and, therefore, by civil authority. This important development presaged changes soon to come.

Nonetheless, the houses of study remained "total institutions," fully staffed with their own professors and having students who rarely, if ever, set foot on the campuses at which they were matriculated. Besides civil degrees, the students usually also received ecclesiastical degrees in philosophy and theology. At institutions like these, run by nearly all the religious orders and congregations of men, no students were admitted to classes except members of the organization in question who were preparing for ordination.

Even at this late date, some provinces and houses of study of a few congregations were founded in certain parts of the country precisely in view of the cultural and linguistic problems encountered by certain ethnic groups. Houses to prepare ministers for a French-speaking population, for instance, were established in the Northeast by the Missionaries of Our Lady of La Salette and the Oblates of Mary Immaculate. Also in the Northeast, Stigmatines directed their ministry especially to speakers of Italian, an emphasis that was reflected in the training their members received.

After World War II many religious orders and congregations began to pursue a vigorous program of sending ordained and sometimes nonordained members to Catholic and non-Catholic universities for advanced degrees, often doctorates. This was an extremely important development, which fell outside the patterns prescribed by the "plans of study" of the orders. The program was occasioned by the heavy commitment of some orders to missionary work, to the publication of books and journals, and to higher education, that is, to ministries requiring training beyond the standards adequate for more conventional pastoral duties. But it also had repercussions on the internal life of the orders. Members with experience of education outside the order brought new and sometimes critical perspectives to bear on the traditional "plans of study" and on certain assumptions then operative in the Church about the training of clerics.

3. FROM VATICAN II TO THE PRESENT

It is against this general background, and especially against the impact of the Second Vatican Council, that the dramatic series of relocations and reorganizations of houses of study that took place in both larger and smaller orders during the postconciliar years must be viewed. Between 1966 and 1970, an extremely large number of theologates related themselves in a variety of formal and informal ways to other religious bodies and institutions of learning. At that time in the United States there were about 3,200 members of religious orders studying in theologates, compared with about 4,760 diocesan seminarians at the same stage of preparation for ordination. Thus about 40 percent of the students in theologates were members of religious orders or congregations.

The Catholic Theological Union at Chicago originated in 1967 from the joint sponsorship of provinces of the Franciscans, Servites, and Passionists. Augustinians, Norbertines, Capuchins, Viatorians, and many others joined later. All these orders or congregations eventually closed their own schools to form the new corporation, located near the University of Chicago and associated with the Chicago Cluster of Theological Schools. A somewhat similar arrangement came into force with the Washington Theological Union, which was incorporated in 1969 as the Washington Theological Coalition. Corporate members soon came to include provinces of the Franciscans, Carmelites, Trinitarians, and others. Pope Paul VI had provided canonical grounds for such unions on 6 August 1966, with his *Ecclesiae Sanctae* (II, n. 37; AAS 58:781).

The Franciscan, Dominican, and Jesuit theologates associated themselves at Berkeley with the Graduate Theological Union and the University of California in the late 1960s. Although this meant cooperation with the union on many levels, including the granting of some joint degrees, all three schools retained clear institutional autonomy. Even looser affiliations were entered into, as with the Cluster of Independent Theological Schools in Washington, D.C., which included DeSales School of Theology, Dominican House of Studies, and Oblate College. An arrangement similarly based on complete institutional autonomy was created in 1968 with the Boston Theological Institute, comprising the divinity schools of several universities, some freestanding Protestant and Orthodox schools, St. John's Seminary (diocesan), and the Jesuits' Weston School of Theology, the only school in the institute run by a religious order.

In many cases these new arrangements entailed moving an institution to a city from a freestanding situation in the country. The motivations behind such relocations and reorganizations were certainly complex, but until now the phenomenon has not been systematically studied. There is little doubt, however, that many religious orders interpreted Vatican II as encouraging or mandating a rather radical reform of their programs of training so that they would be equipped to address the "new era" of which the council spoke. In particular, the training of priests at institutions relatively isolated from the cultural milieu in which they would later exercise their ministries was seen as a deficiency to be remedied. More effective use of resources through collaboration was also surely a powerful motive, especially since with passing years the number of candidates for any given order had declined.

Some scholasticates or clericates, like the Franciscans' St. Anthony-on-Hudson, did not relocate or seek affiliations with other schools. In 1968 the Congregation of the Holy Cross transferred its theological students from Catholic University to Moreau Seminary on the campus of Notre Dame University, retaining its legal autonomy. The Oblate School of Theology, founded in 1903 at San Antonio, Texas, exclusively for the education of Oblates, exemplifies yet another pattern. It remained at the same location but evolved into a freestanding graduate school, which now educates priesthood candidates from six different orders and sixteen dioceses, and also provides programs for men and women who are not candidates for ordination.

Despite the considerable diversity among these postconciliar patterns, certain features are common to most or many of them. Schools that relocated generally did so in order to achieve proximity to a university, and then sought some degree of formal relationship with it. These scholasticates, and some that did not relocate, tended to have closer relationships with nearby Protestant schools of divinity, often joined with them in ecumenical endeavors, and allowed or encouraged a certain amount of cross-registration for courses. Most of these institutions matriculated students who were not seeking ordination, including women. All of the formal clusters or unions, and most of the individual schools, soon became affiliated with the Association of Theological Schools and subsequently accredited by it. The first such affiliations took place in 1968. The Oblate School of Theology is an example of a school that was further accredited, in this case, by the Commission on Colleges of the Southern Association of Colleges and Schools.

The factors just outlined account for the introduction of the Master of Divinity degree for clerical students, and also for the introduction of other degrees like the Master of Arts and the Master of Theological Studies. Even schools that had authority to grant ecclesiastical degrees now began to make provision for other programs. Under the impact of such changes, older curricula prescribed in this or that *Ratio Studiorum* of the orders were modified.

But the most fundamental impetus for changes in curriculum came from the documents of Vatican II that in one way or another related to formation for priesthood. The most obvious of these was, of course, the decree specifically addressing that subject, *Optatam Totius.* In the years right after the council, however, religious orders and congregations seem to have been more deeply influenced by the various decrees relating to ecumenism and evangelization, and particularly by *Gaudium et Spes,* the pastoral constitution on "The Church in the Modern World." The special concern of the orders for these decrees, over *Optatam Totius,* is noteworthy and quite consonant with their general traditions of ministry and ministerial training. The orders also took special account of the review of their more properly spiritual and ascetical traditions urged by *Perfectae Caritatis,* the decree on religious life.

After the council, religious orders and congregations held general chapters during which their programs of formation and study were scrutinized in light of the whole range of conciliar documents, and a number of changes were legislated. Various administrative decrees from the curias of the orders then began to reduce the new legislation to practice. A further specification took place in some orders when adaptation was made to the needs of a given country or culture. In 1969, for instance, a Regional Order of Studies for the American

Assistancy was established for the Jesuits in the United States.

In brief, changes were introduced by the orders in the immediate postconciliar period that significantly modified the way their candidates for priesthood were prepared for ministry in comparison with settings and structures that had been securely in place only a few years earlier. For the most part, moreover, the changes seem to have been more notable than those experienced at diocesan seminaries, which in the larger dioceses continued, for instance, to adhere to the freestanding model.

To a large extent the changes introduced between about 1966 and 1970 were a result of self-determination on the part of the orders and congregations, and were not imposed or proposed in any specific fashion by ecclesiastical agencies outside them. Such self-determination accorded with the way religious orders had traditionally dealt with the training of their members, for which as exempt ecclesiastical bodies they were responsible only to themselves, aside from a few very general norms principally concerning novitiates. Beginning in the late nineteenth century, however, an ever-increasing series of decisions originating with other ecclesiastical authorities began to be taken that eventually greatly affected the curriculum and the functioning of scholasticates and, in recent years, even their self-understanding.

Only a few of these decisions can be mentioned here. Leo XIII's *Aeterni Patris* concerning Thomistic philosophy (1879) was in essence only an exhortation, but it was the basis for the obligation to teach philosophy and theology according to the doctrine of Thomas that was laid down for religious orders in the Code of Canon Law of 1917. Pius X's prescriptions and proscriptions for seminary professors in the wake of the Modernist crisis also applied to teachers in the houses of the religious orders.

In at least one respect the code was more traditional. While it imposed certain measures on all programs leading to ordination, it did make a clear distinction between seminaries, for which it legislated in considerable detail, and the *Studiorum Domus* of the orders, for which its provisions were few and mainly generic. Nonetheless, the code clearly stated that the competence concerning studies rested with the Sacred Congregation for Religious, thereby giving added warrant to interventions by the congregation.

Pius XI's apostolic constitution *Deus Scientiarum Dominus* (1931) dealt directly with pontifical faculties, many of which were staffed by members of religious orders and so, along with its *Ordinationes,* it had perhaps a more immediate impact on training within orders like the Dominicans and Jesuits than it did on smaller orders or diocesan seminaries. Each order was required to bring its *Ratio Studiorum* into accord with the norms of the constitution insofar as the *Ratio* related to ecclesiastical degrees. The general intent of the constitution was to raise academic standards at all institutions that trained candidates for the priesthood, and in that regard it was altogether appropriate for the day. It was also, however, one of the first documents from outside religious orders that broadly affected the academic training of members within them by specifically determining curriculum.

Documents like these, as well as the series of statements on the priesthood issued by the popes from Pius X to Pius XII, formed much of the background to *Optatam Totius.* Brief as that document is, it is considerably longer than the few lines the Council of Trent devoted to seminaries. Most significant from our perspective, though, are three other features of the document. First of all, along with *Presbyterorum Ordinis* on the nature of the priesthood, it clearly states a doctrine of "the unity of the Catholic priesthood." Second, seemingly as a corollary to the foregoing, it affirms that the same "priestly formation is required for all priests—secular, religious and of every rite." Third, it assumes that the diocesan priesthood with its basically parochial ministries is the analogue according to which the appropriateness of all priestly training is to be measured.

This last feature, which also strongly undergirds *Presbyterorum Ordinis,* means that priesthood is conceived as a ministry that is: (1) exercised in a stable community of faith and practice, (2) exercised most normatively in a parish, and (3) exercised by priests who are in "hierarchical union with the order of bishops." True, the document allows for "due qualification" to be made for members of religious orders, who at the time of the council comprised over 35 percent of the priests in the Church. But the assumption seems to be that such qualification will be minor, even though in fact the traditions of priestly ministry within most of the orders have conformed to none of these three conceptions.

Optatam Totius and *Presbyterorum Ordinis* provided the principles out of which was constructed the *Ratio Fundamentalis* concerning priestly formation, issued in January 1970 by the Sacred Congregation for Catholic Education, in which all the foregoing assumptions and conceptions were clearly operative. It was thus in this document that the implications of *Optatam Totius* and *Presbyterorum Ordinis* began to be specified and applied even to the orders. Furthermore, in the *Ratio* the term "seminary" was used in the general sense of "institution organized for the formation of priests." This usage is symptomatic of the erosion of the older distinction between *seminarium,* the diocesan institution, and the *Studiorum Domus* of the orders, a distinction that has also disappeared from the new Code of Canon Law of 1983.

When the first edition of the *Program of Priestly Formation* was published by the National Conference of Catholic Bishops in 1971 in accordance with the provisions of the *Ratio Fundamentalis* of the previous year, it contained a special section entitled "The Religious Priest's Formation." The preface to the document included the following statement: "The Conference of Major Religious Superiors of Men... agreed to accept the *Program* as the recommended program for religious priests' formation, if there were added to the *Program* a short section prepared by them on religious life (Part Four). The National Conference approved the *Program* as the one program for all seminarians, diocesan and religious, and the addition of Part Four" (pp. xii-xiii). Thus within the short period between the publication of the *Ratio* and the publication of the first edition of the *PPF*, "seminaries" of the orders and congregations found their training for the first time in history seeming to require episcopal approval.

What was noteworthy about "Part Four," moreover, was that it dealt almost exclusively with the ascetical traditions of religious life in general and with the three vows of poverty, chastity, and obedience. Entirely missing was any description of ministry that would suggest models, goals, settings, or persons ministered unto different from those of the parish clergy. By its separate treatment of novitiates, however, Part Four did implicitly call attention to a training in the spiritual life that began upon entrance and was tested and matured over some years, often through extensive ministerial experience, before the student began the formal study of theology leading to ordination. This means, inter alia, that at the time of theological study the student would be some five or more years older than the diocesan seminarian, but the rest of the *PPF* makes no allowance for this difference.

The second edition (1976) of the *PPF* contained the same Part Four unchanged. But the third edition (1981) dropped this section on religious priests because, according to the "Statement from the Conference of Major Superiors of Men" (p. 3): "Religious and diocesan priests share an increasingly pluriform priesthood; their needs for priestly formation as such do not differ.... Thus the Conference of Major Superiors of Men adopts the program of priestly formation as the one program for all United States religious seminarians." It is not altogether clear, however, that this statement in fact perfectly reflects the reasons why the CMSM urged or conceded the dropping of Part Four. The statement should not in any case be taken as reflecting a fully matured theological position on the underlying issues. In the light of developments like these, it is not surprising that the visitations enjoined by the Papal Seminary Study, which got under way in the United States in 1984, included the institutions run by religious orders for their own members, unprecedented though such visitations were. Even more striking and unprecedented was the fact that the chairman of every team visiting these institutions was a bishop, not a religious ordinary.

Since the council, then, the following important changes have taken place in the United States regarding the formation of religious priests: By and large unlike their diocesan counterparts, the schools of religious orders have relocated in urban areas and abandoned their freestanding status by establishing important relationships with similar institutions and sometimes with prestigious universities; these actions, plus the decline in vocations, have led to the amalgamation of institutions and even to the closing of many, which have in turn led in many orders and congregations to a significant curtailment of the numbers sent on for advanced degrees in theology, since responsibility for staffing is no longer so pointedly operative; at many theologates religious women and lay students have been admitted into various degree programs; the whole program of formation has undergone important changes, beginning with the novitiate; while retaining some degree of independence, the design of the theological curriculum and ministerial preparation has become increasingly determined by standards set by outside agencies like the Association of Theological Schools and especially by the National Conference of

Catholic Bishops; perhaps most important of all, a new self-under-standing seems evident both from repeated affirmations concerning a single priestly ideal in the Church and from the assertion that in formation for ministry and priesthood there is no appreciable dif-ference between diocesan candidates and those of religious orders. Regarding that last point, it must be noted that such a conclusion, so crucial for the self-understanding religious orders have of their mission and ministry, seems to have been simply conceded by them, never challenged or systematically argued.

In summary, the history of the houses of study of religious orders of men in the United States falls into three phases, with considerable chronological overlap between the first two: (1) the late-eighteenth into the mid-nineteenth century, when many members were born and/or trained in Europe or received rather haphazard training here; (2) the late nineteenth century until Vatican II, when theolo-gates proliferated and programs became ever more regularized by virtue, for the most part, of the internal mechanisms of the orders themselves; and (3) the postconciliar period, when the whole series of developments took place that are outlined in the preceding para-graph.

Part II

Mission and Management

A. Missions of Theologates

OVERVIEW STATEMENTS

Several different structural models are represented among the theologates where education for priesthood is provided; they include freestanding, supplemental, and collaborative, as well as certain combinations of these.

During the past ten to fifteen years, the missions of more than two-thirds of all seminaries and schools of theology have changed from being exclusively for ordination candidates enrolled in a single program to serving a diverse student body enrolled in a variety of programs.

Theologates are at the symbolic center of the Church's effort to come to terms with the implications of Vatican II and of a still rapidly changing culture. This reality lends urgency to discussion about what the mission and role of seminaries will be in the future.

Distinctly different views on what is the best environment in which to prepare men for priesthood are represented by various schools, based largely on the ecclesiology and the theology of priesthood of those who govern, administer, and teach at each institution.

The "market," or "consumer," mentality is a strong driving force in determining the missions of theologates; to ensure enrollment, schools must try to provide programs that are responsive to the needs and goals of the bishops and religious superiors who support them, not

always the same programs that faculty and administration believe are the best preparation for ministry.

Responsible stewardship poses the crucial question about how many theologates should remain open. Though some argue for reducing the number of theologates, regional differences and needs, as well as diverse modes of education, constitute valid arguments against closing most of the schools.

1. THE STATUS OF THE MISSIONS OF THEOLOGATES

Present reality: The missions of theologates vary from the preparation of ordination candidates only to the preparation of a variety of students for a variety of ministries. In the latter case, programs are sometimes integrated, with seminarians and other students taking some of the same classes; otherwise the programs are entirely separate. These distinct contexts for studying theology arise out of different understandings about the kind of preparation for ministry that best serves the needs of the Church. Many schools have recently reevaluated their position on this question, and have redefined or reaffirmed their missions. At least half of the schools where we conducted interviews for this study had reviewed their statements of purpose over the past two or three years. Among the reasons for these deliberations are the following:

   a. some are maintaining and solidifying their present mission of only preparing men for ordained ministry;
   b. others are expanding their mission by preparing lay students for ministry in response to the needs of the Church in their particular region;
   c. some are maintaining a mixed model out of the conviction that the most effective preparation for priesthood takes place in a school with a diverse student body;
   d. finally, others are reviewing their mission because of impending accreditation and the requirement imposed by visiting accreditors that each school be aware of its mission and of the programmatic implications of that mission.

In some cases the process of reevaluation has led to new life and enthusiasm for the work being carried on at a given institution. In other cases it has caused consternation, since the status quo had not been questioned previously. Serious disagreement has sometimes arisen among the various bodies that, in their totality, constitute the school—governing and advisory boards, religious communities, faculty, students, and others—about what its mission should be.

On the whole, research shows a striking number of changes in mission over the past twenty years, especially regarding the student body. In 1966-67 some 8,325 seminarians were enrolled in about 110 theologates; by 1988-89 some 3,606 seminarians were studying theology at 52 schools, along with at least 3,500 full-time and part-time students who were not preparing for ordination (see table 1 on the following page). About three-fourths of all theologates have made significant changes in their mission since 1966-67, for the most part in relation to the student body and to program structure and content.

During the past two or three years, the question of mission has rapidly emerged as an issue of considerable concern and debate. The sources of concern are multiple, but the most significant is the difference in viewpoint between the Sacred Congregation for Catholic Education and many American seminary leaders about what is the appropriate mission for theologates. For example, Cardinal Baum's report of 14 September 1986 on the freestanding theologates emphasizes the specialized nature of priestly formation and the need to limit the number of lay students enrolled. This document also stresses the importance of having a faculty made up largely, almost exclusively, of priests. By contrast, rectors/presidents responding to a recent questionnaire[1] asserted that the changes that have had the most positive impact on the quality of programs for priestly formation and on the quality of theological education were the admission of lay students and the hiring of a more diverse faculty, that is, women religious and lay men and women. Thus quite opposite conclusions about the effects of these two changes were reached by Cardinal Baum on the one hand and most rectors/presidents on the other.

At the same time, though theologates with a mixed student body are numerically in the majority and are chosen by the vast majority

---

[1]In this questionnaire, completed in the spring of 1987, fifty-three out of the fifty-four rectors/presidents identified and evaluated important changes at their institutions over the past twenty years. See Introduction.

Profile of Enrollment in Theologates Based on CARA Statistics

	1967-68	1975-76	1985-86	1988-89
Diocesan Priesthood Students	4,761	3,109	2,672	2,616
Religious Order Priesthood Students	3,211	1,594	1,205	958
Unaffiliated	-	16	31	32
Total Priesthood Students	7,972	4,703	3,908	3,606
Other Full Time Students	—	479	2,289	2,295
Total Full Time Students	7,972	5,182	6,197	5,901
Other Part Time Students	—	914	613*	1,328
Total Headcount Enrollment	7,972**	6,096	6,810	7,229
Proportion of priesthood students	7,972 100.0%	4,703 90.8%	3,908 63.1%	3,606 61.1%
Proportion of other full time students	None listed —	479 10.2%	2,289 36.9%	2,295 38.9%

*Several schools did not report part-time students in 1985-86.

**For every 100 priesthood candidates in 1967-68, there were:

      59 priesthood candidates in 1975-76;

      49 priesthood candidates in 1985-86;

      45 priesthood candidates in 1988-89.

of religious superiors, American bishops more frequently choose schools for their priesthood candidates that enroll only seminarians. Only three (8.6 percent) of the thirty-seven schools with a mixed student body enroll as many as one hundred seminarians each, namely, the Catholic University of America, the Washington Theological Union, and the Catholic Theological Union. By contrast, eight (61.5 percent) of the thirteen schools with separate programs for priestly formation enroll more than one hundred seminarians each. In nine of these thirteen schools, the program is separate because it is the only program at the school; the remaining four schools sponsor other almost entirely separate programs for those not seeking ordination. Several leaders from among the thirteen schools have written a paper strongly defending the single-purpose program that enrolls only seminarians: "While interaction with women in such natural contexts as a parish plays a vital role in priestly formation, a mixed or coed seminarian community in the formative stages of preparation for priestly ministry seems to us unwise and unrealistic."[2] The authors make a case for what they call the "holistic" model of seminary formation, which they equate with a freestanding institution that enrolls seminarians in a program designed exclusively for them and includes spiritual formation, pastoral training, and academic education. They speak from the conviction that this type of institution is most effective in assisting seminarians to develop a strong sense of priestly identity.

During the interviews, respondents also differed about what the purpose of theologates should be. Those who are maintaining their institutions, in particular their M.Div. programs, solely for ordination candidates have several clear reasons for doing so. They believe that:

a. it is in the best interest of the seminarian to be educated in a setting where all formation is directed toward priesthood;

b. courses and formation programs need to have a specific emphasis that is not possible when nonordination candidates are enrolled, and too many new resources are needed to provide appropriate formation for different kinds of ministry;

---

[2]This position is articulated in *The Preparation of a Diocesan Priest* (1987), a pamphlet by Howard Bleichner, S.S., Daniel Buechlein, O.S.B., and Robert Leavitt, S.S.

c. the best environment for training future priests, especially given the discipline regarding celibacy, is one that is in comparative isolation from students who are not candidates for ordination.

Respondents from theologates that admit only ordination candidates commented frequently that it would be just too difficult to make all of the adjustments that would be needed if other students were admitted. Extensive resources would be required for expanded programs and student services. Moreover, they fear that too much tension would develop between seminarians and lay students. Stories were often repeated about the problems in schools that are trying to incorporate students who are not studying for priesthood. Though these incidents are sometimes exaggerated, they have become the stated reason for maintaining the status quo. A typical interrogative was, "Why create those problems for ourselves?"

On the other side of the debate, the leaders of theologates with a mixed student body are strongly convinced that a clear sense of priestly identity can be achieved and appropriated best when it is tested in the very process of formation by interaction with non-priesthood students. According to the statement of a representative leader of this persuasion: "The positive consequence of our kind of environment is that it forces the identity issues to the forefront, and it requires the seminarian to achieve a balance between the socially defined role of priesthood and the integration of his own beliefs in the context of the Church he will serve. Lay students, too, test their identity and role in an environment that is a somewhat realistic reflection of the ministerial contexts in which they will later serve. In other words, service to the Church is enhanced when there is clarity in terms of identities and roles and when these can be tested even as they are being shaped in the educational environment."

Those who have changed or are considering changing their mission to include other than ordination candidates share the following beliefs:

a. It is in the best interest of the seminarian to be educated in a setting that more closely approximates the secular milieu with respect to population. Most importantly, formation for celibacy in such a setting prepares men to interact with women as peers.

b. The Church today requires an education for its priests that equips them to address issues from a perspective that includes the laity. Often the ways in which lay students deliberate about issues in the Church more faithfully represent people who are not clerical or religious.

c. Responsible use of resources requires that education for lay ministers in the Church be provided at the facilities and with the faculties already assembled. Since some theologates are located in areas where other opportunities for theological education for the laity are not available, many believe that it is incumbent on their schools to provide this service.

Enrolled in the thirty-seven schools with a mixed student body are 1,114 (93.0 percent) religious order candidates, and 1,084 (40.5 percent) diocesan candidates for priesthood. Although three of these schools list no non-ordination candidates, their mission statements specifically indicate that their programs are open to all who qualify for admission. In fact, about ten schools enroll more lay students than are reported in the Center for Applied Research in the Apostolate (CARA) directories, and some administrators say the understatement is deliberate because of the negative perception that some bishops have about the presence of lay students in theologates.

Representatives of theologates that now include nonordination candidates acknowledge that the goal of integrating these students is far from being achieved. One president who has worked in an integrated setting for nearly ten years said: "We are trying to do something very difficult, that is, form a community that embraces men and women, lay and religious, who are preparing in common for ministry. Conversion of attitudes about its value is happening, but because of ecclesiastical structures, it takes a long time."

Two quite distinct models of education for priesthood thus emerge. One model enrolls only seminarians, and is subscribed to by institutions educating more than half of all diocesan candidates (59.5 percent) and a small minority of religious order candidates (7.0 percent). The other model enrolls a mixed student body, and includes schools that are educating virtually all candidates for religious orders (93.0 percent) and just under half (40.5 percent) of diocesan candidates. Religious orders have opted for a fairly uniform system, that is, the mixed student body. The consistency of this choice by the religious orders is itself noteworthy and deserves further analysis, for it seems to point to some deep, if not fully articulated, convictions about priesthood, ministry, and ecclesiology.

The diocesan system, on the other hand, is split almost in half, possibly reflecting the differing ecclesiologies of bishops who support the divergent models of seminary education.[3] In summary, of all priesthood candidates, 1,677 (42.8 percent) are enrolled in schools exclusively for seminarians or in totally separate M.Div. programs, and 2,240 (57.2 percent) are enrolled in schools with broader admissions policies.

There is no disagreement that theologates must adapt their missions to the larger needs of the Church rather than operating as isolated entities. There is disagreement, however, about what this task entails. For some it means that theologates should be on the cutting edge in preparing people not only for priesthood, but also for different kinds of professional lay ministry. This expansion, they say, will also enhance the preparation of priesthood candidates. Others, who value the tradition of education for priesthood candidates only, believe that seminaries should continue as in the past, with no lay students. In this position they feel supported by recent documentation from the Sacred Congregation for Catholic Education.

Many of those interviewed believe that central to the discussion about mission is concern about priestly identity and the appropriate formation of men who have rightful expectations of fraternal support. Those who believe in theologates for priesthood candidates only, argue that separation allows the seminarian to achieve a clearer sense of his identity as a priest. Others argue that separation leads to what they call clericalism. Those who advocate mixed settings believe that true priestly identity can best be achieved when it is tested during formation by interaction with students who are not studying for priesthood. This debate is likely to become more intense if the

---

[3]This difference is of significance, especially given the somewhat opposite premise of a statement in the 1981 *PPF* (p. 6): "Religious and diocesan priests share an increasingly pluriform but common priesthood; their needs for priestly formation as such do not differ." Research on priestly formation for religious, by John O'Malley, S.J., suggests that historically the mission and ministry of religious order priests has always been different from the parish ministry of diocesan priests. Consequently, their preparation has also been distinct. This fact explains in part the preference of religious orders for a different model of preparation for priesthood for their men today. See chapter 2.

role of lay ministers in the Church continues to expand, as seems highly probable.

Underlying all of the models in their various phases of development is the overriding desire to provide programs of priestly formation that prepare individuals whose actions will reflect the deepest beliefs of the Church about the gospel of Jesus Christ, and that create in them a desire to serve accordingly.

2. CHURCH NEEDS IN RELATION TO FORMULATION OF MISSION STATEMENTS

Present reality: Mission statements are generally formulated by faculty and administration, and then approved by governing boards. Accrediting agencies insist that boards, beyond merely approving the statements, be well informed about them. In several instances students and alumni have participated in discussions about mission. The goals needed to fulfill the mission often remain undeclared. Administrators commonly believe that the importance of the mission statement is not adequately acknowledged. They maintain that many Roman Catholic institutions do not sufficiently realize the crucial nature of their statements, either because the mission was always taken for granted or because the statements were not arrived at in a participatory fashion. Many faculty members regard them as poetic and vague, and so they are not inclined to reflect on them.

Three distinct approaches to the review of mission statements can be identified:

a. One approach is designed to retain the essential mission as it now exists.

b. Another approach seeks to keep the institution viable by making whatever adjustments in the mission are deemed necessary.

c. The third approach allows for more radical changes, arguing that it does so in response to changes in the Church and society that call for changes in seminary education.

Some combination of these approaches is generally found at every institution, with emphasis given to one over the others. In some cases the approach is framed in terms of a question like, Why is this the best way to carry on our mission? The second approach asks,

What do we have to do to survive? And the third, often with special regard for the region or constituency being served, What is most needed from this institution for the furthering of the mission of the Church?

Decisions about what the mission of a particular theologate will be are influenced by several factors. Since some schools exist primarily for the service of particular dioceses, they are guided most by the needs of the local church. Others have more general missions, since they are not based in any one diocese or region or religious community, and so must respond to the needs of broader constituencies. Many respondents expressed the belief that the mission is more or less determined by the governing or ownership group, with the institution being expected to work out the details. While the *PPF* was frequently mentioned as the major document informing the design of the priestly formation program as a whole, it was not necessarily the key element in writing the mission statement, since the mission often includes programs additional to those that prepare men for priesthood.

Another factor contributing to the nature of the mission statement is whether it is seen as visionary, that is, as the basis for future development, or as merely a reflection of the status quo. Respondents from at least seven or eight theologates said the statement was intended to be visionary in that the stated purpose of these institutions was broader than the reality of the moment. Generally this meant that the mission included the preparation of lay ministers even though few or no lay students were enrolled in those programs at the time. Most schools are attempting, however, to reformulate their present mission in clearer terms so as to reflect more adequately what the school is currently doing.

Issues for the future: At some institutions disagreements about the mission still need to be resolved. Many of those interviewed believe that the ecclesiologies of ordinaries vary substantially, and that the choice of a theologate for their priesthood candidates is made on the basis of the school's espoused, or even implicit, ecclesiology. Because of this method of selecting theologates, a number of administrators indicated that they are very cautious about how their mission is stated, since they do not wish to alienate ordinaries whose students come to them from a particular diocese or religious order. The support of these Church leaders is essential for the survival of a number of schools, a fact that is clearly recognized by virtually all who work in theologates. This perception is corroborated by the responses of vocation directors,[4] nearly 78 percent of whom indicated that the ordinaries are involved in the selection of a seminary for their students.

If a discrepancy exists between the espoused mission of a school and its actual mission, the consequences for students may be confusion between what is expected of them by their superiors and what is expected by the theologate. Students occasionally expressed dissatisfaction because they found the school in which they were enrolled to be different from what they thought their superiors wanted. But administrators and faculty questioned how necessary it was for a seminarian to be enrolled in a school whose ecclesiology closely paralleled that of the student's ordinary. Part of the experience of theological education, suggested many theologate personnel, is to assist the student in developing his own sense of identity within the Church. Theological education should not be ideological, but rather faithful to the broad tradition of the Church and open to discussion of many points of view. The ecclesiological issue is crucial, for it affects the whole future of ministry.

Many of those interviewed suggested that the discussion of mission must be framed in relation to the needs of the local church. Depending largely on the region of the country, the need for nonordained professional ministers varies significantly and, where the need is high, schools are more likely to be open to a diverse student body. In schools where preparation for a variety of ministries is an essential part of the mission, the position of the Church with respect to nonordained professional ministry is crucial. Will such ministry be supported, particularly by bishops, or discouraged? At this time the message is vague, and mixed signals are being given.

What positive steps might be taken to bring about better understanding of the various missions and purposes of theologates?

Faculty, administrators, students, and graduates need to be encouraged to be more reflective about mission statements. Many administrators believe that the best way to do this is to ask con-

---

[4]In 1986, vocation directors responded to a questionnaire about their interactions and relationships with theologates, as well as with their ordinaries, concerning the selection of a theologate for seminarians.

stituents to participate in drafting institutional statements. This process invites study of the documents of Vatican II and other seminary documents so that participants can gain awareness of local, national, and international ecclesial realities. Instead of "holding the line" or "caving in to modern pressures," each school can then evaluate its mission in light of its particular circumstances, including location, size, and alternatives for theological education in the area.

Leaders in theologates also recommended that a forum be established that would encourage dialogue about the implications of changing missions. Theologates are at the symbolic center of the Church's effort to come to terms with the implications of Vatican II and of a still rapidly changing culture. Thus they occupy the sometimes unenviable position of walking a tightrope between progressive and traditional forces. It is all too easy for theologates to become the scapegoat for what some consider is wrong with the Church. This problem places yet another burden on administrators and faculty, who often feel burdened enough already, and has serious implications for morale. Discussion of these common concerns among leaders could be a means of support and encouragement. Because of current tensions in the Church, however, the question is sometimes raised as to how willing and free leaders are to talk to each other about their schools' missions and possible futures, including continued existence as presently constituted.

Another fruitful form of dialogue might be instituted between various theologates and the ordinaries whose candidates are enrolled in them. Examining the expectations of seminary personnel and those of other Church leaders could help to focus formation questions appropriately, and to resolve potential disagreements or misunderstandings between the diocese or religious order and the theologate. To some extent this dialogue is already under way, especially in relation to individual students, but there is little discussion devoted to the overall needs of a diocese or community. This kind of exchange could aid theologates in determining which new program components to incorporate and which new directions to take. Several priests and bishops raised the question whether theologates ever ask dioceses about their mission statements or consider the special needs of a particular diocese. For example, as more Hispanic people move into dioceses where ministry has traditionally been geared to English-speaking people, theology requirements may need to change to accommodate the ministerial needs of a different population. In addition, the increasingly aged population may call for a special understanding of the nature of ministry in the average parish of the future. In promoting understanding and dialogue between theologate and diocese, the vocation director could play a crucial role, a role that the survey of vocation directors indicates would be a welcome one.

It has yet to be decided how one can measure which model is best suited to helping future priests come to a fuller sense of the role and meaning of priesthood. The divergence between the two main schools of thought on the mission of the seminary could grow; lines could be drawn so tightly that no dialogue would occur. Leaders at all types of theologates must discuss the consequences for the whole Church if they fail to come to terms with the underlying issues represented by diverse models of preparation for priesthood.

3. MISSION IN RELATION TO POTENTIAL FOR ENROLLMENT

Present reality: In the final analysis, a school is viable only if it has a sufficient number of students. Each school must enroll enough students so that a variety of courses can be taught, an adequate number of faculty can be hired, and the institution can remain financially viable. Whether enrollment patterns will lead to fewer theologates or to expanded missions is a vital question.

The dramatic change in the student population over the past twenty years is related both to the need for adequate enrollment and to a commitment to a different model of preparation for ministry. Theologates are "schools for the Church," with the primary mission of educating people for pastoral ministry. Theologate programs are not the same as nonministerial theology programs at universities; their academic standards are often as high, but the acquisition of pastoral skills that is integral to theologate programs is absent from the strictly academic programs of universities. Therefore, the distinct value of studying in a theologate is obvious for any future Church ministers.

In effect, competition for students who intend to study theology is increasing, regardless of the type of school. This point can be illustrated by several examples: Theologates that enroll only seminarians have in many cases expanded their mission beyond serving a single diocese or a local group of dioceses, and now recruit and welcome seminarians from any diocese in the country. Theologates that are operated by religious orders for their own candidates have opened their doors to include additional religious orders. Theologates that enroll students preparing for a variety of ministries are also recruiting more actively, but competition is increasing as the total pool of potential applicants decreases.

Issues for the future: In an effort to maintain adequate enrollment, many schools are reexamining recruiting methods and considering new programs. For example, one identifiable change occurring at a number of theologates is expansion of continuing education programs. In some cases this will mean better utilization of facilities and faculty, and it will provide the Church with a needed service. For those schools that are committed to having only priesthood candidates in their M.Div. programs, but at the same time consider more contact with women advisable, continuing education is a way of bringing women into the school while retaining the essential commitment to education for priesthood. But the pool of potential applicants for continuing education programs is also limited.

Other schools may extend full registration to a broader range of students. Some of these schools have also instituted M.A. programs for nonordination students. The kinds of interaction fostered by these full integrated programs, and their effects, are considerably different from those of the separate programs, but both types of programs are responsive to the need for increased enrollment. A few theologates, religious and diocesan, are unable to expand or change their mission because of governing policies or location or for other reasons. They may be forced to close or merge in the near future as a result of low enrollment.

Many of those interviewed believe that in the future a structure or plan for theological education will emerge that we have not yet imagined. The nature of the coming changes is uncertain, but some possibilities that were mentioned include more small houses of formation on university campuses and fewer freestanding seminaries, or more university theology departments offering an M.Div. degree designed for students not preparing for ordination. Some go so far as to suggest that ministerial education will be done largely on an apprenticeship basis. As is postulated later in this study, any decisive or broad change in the pattern of theological education must involve careful and extensive discussion, and comprehensive long-range planning. Regardless of how theological education is to be provided in the future, the determination of each theologate's mission is crucial to its strategic planning.

B. Governance

OVERVIEW STATEMENTS

Theologate boards serve in either a governing or an advisory capacity. The members of the 63 different boards currently number 820, of whom 533 (65 percent) are clerics and 287 (35 percent) represent other vocations.

Until recently, only a few theologates had effective boards of trustees that included persons other than clerics, but more diversity in board membership is beginning to appear for several reasons: to increase participation by lay people, to expand development efforts, and to strengthen boards in areas of competence that they do not currently enjoy.

In theologates, the prescriptions of canon law determine the juridical structures of boards, and so they have only the power that is delegated to them by the ordinary. The distinction between boards of incorporation and boards of trustees is peculiar to the legal status of Roman Catholic theologates.

The role of the ordinary is crucial in determining the functions of boards; if he is truly collegial, the effect can be extremely positive, but if the board merely ratifies decisions made by the ordinary, the effect on board members can be enervating.

Many rectors/presidents believe that it will be difficult to attract and retain competent lay board members unless boards are in fact governing and not merely advisory.

A common understanding about what should be the role of boards of trustees does not exist. Some function mainly for promotion and fund-raising purposes, while others are policy-making. Because of the brief history of diverse membership in the governance of Roman Catholic institutions, it will take some time to evolve new patterns.

Several institutions are experiencing difficulty in negotiating board responsibility in contradistinction to administrative responsibility, an issue of operations versus governance.

1. STRUCTURE AND ROLE OF BOARDS

Present reality: The extensive use of governing boards by Roman Catholic institutions is a phenomenon of the past twenty-five to thirty years, and at most theologates it is even more recent. During interviews, administrators often mentioned that "seminaries have always been considered the Church's schools, and have been the direct concern of bishops and religious superiors." Sharing governing authority is only now becoming common practice. Several factors were at work in bringing boards into existence. One such factor is the requirement of the Association of Theological Schools (ATS) and regional accrediting associations that every theologate have a functioning board.

Structure. Different types of boards function in theologates at present, some having a governance role and others being advisory. All of the forty-seven theologates based in the United States have a primary governing board.[1] In addition, twenty-one of them have a second board, and one has three boards; most of these are advisory. The primary governing boards for thirty-two theologates, including seven university boards, are identified as Boards of Trustees. Ten of the first-level boards are called Corporate Boards or The Corporation, four are Boards of Directors, and one is a Board of Governance. Those with more than one board identify the second-level board as a Board of Trustees in nine cases, eight of which have a first-level Corporate Board and one a Board of Directors. The other second-level boards are called Advisory Boards in four instances, the Board of Overseers in three, and in two single instances the Governing Board and the Board of Directors. Four theologates based at universities have identified Seminary Committees or Seminary Boards. The third board of one theologate is called a Board of Regents.

based at universities have identified Seminary Committees or Seminary Boards. The third board of one theologate is called a Board of Regents.

Role. Historically the responsibility for most theologates rested in

---

[1] The forty-seven include all except The North American College in Rome, The American College of Louvain, and Centro de Estudios de los Dominicos del Caribe, which have different governing structures.

the hands of ordinaries, and so the current movement toward new forms of shared governance can be a disturbing process. The proper role of boards is conceived of in widely divergent ways, and the convictions of ordinaries about shared authority usually determine the extent to which a board is empowered. Clear articulation of the board's role is crucial to its ability to function effectively. Conflicts arise when operating policies are not articulated, and when the question of who is in charge of what aspects of the theologate is left unanswered. Contradictory expectations around issues of governance and power can lead to disillusionment, if not resolved early in a board's history. Who convenes the Church? From whom does power come? How do we deal with issues of governance and power? Rectors/presidents emphasized that it is essential to discuss these questions if a board is to satisfactorily discharge its responsibilities. Board members must understand the ecclesiologies espoused by ordinaries, and they must hear them articulated. As one board member said: "The role that the board performs is directly related to the ecclesiology of the bishop or religious superior. The ability of boards to guide the direction of schools depends entirely on ecclesial officials. Many ordinaries are inclined to shift to others the responsibility for finances, but they want to retain control of every other aspect of the theologate. An independent board will not tolerate that position for long."

Once the fundamental question of where each area of authority resides is answered, the responsibilities of the board must be delineated. Typically boards select the rectors/presidents, or at least approve of the selection made by ordinaries; they clarify the mission of the theologate, ensure its financial health, attend to planning processes, oversee programs, interpret the theologate to its public, and lead it to a vision of service.[2] But in Roman Catholic theologates, and many other institutions, further clarification of responsibilities is essential. The role of governing boards is significantly different from that of advisory boards, in that the former often have a strong voice in the operation of the institution and are involved with policy

---

[2]A publication of the Association of Governing Boards, *The Good Steward: A Guide to Theological School Trusteeship,* is a useful resource about governance. In particular, Robert Wood Lynn's article on "The Responsibilities of Stewardship," (pp. 1-9) outlines the duties of a competent board.

making. The power of governing boards varies, depending on how their role was established and on the length of time they have been in existence. At least two prototypes can be distinguished: Some boards promote the theologate, perform an advocacy function, and do fund raising; others have regulatory or oversight functions, including selection and evaluation of major administrators—and sometimes faculty—and determination of the content of educational programs and policies. Although some boards combine these functions, a clear distinction can be drawn between boards that are decision-making and those that merely "rubber-stamp" decisions made elsewhere. Board members are selected in accordance with the functions they are expected to perform, and the outcomes that are achieved depend on how involved and committed members are to the goals of the theologate.

In theologates operated by religious communities, these same issues of governance and power are of equal concern, but they may be resolved in slightly different ways. Individual congregations and religious orders, or groups of them who are responsible for financing the institution, maintain control by carefully selecting board members, and more often by reserving governance exclusively for members of the sponsoring group or groups. Nonetheless, motivated by the desire to be in contact with the broader constituencies of the Church and to gain their financial support, seven theologates with all-clerical governing boards have established advisory boards.

The role of being advisory is more limited by definition, but it too has a variety of meanings and interpretations. Some boards are advisory to bishops, others to the administrations of theologates. Advisory boards may recommend policies, but their primary role is to provide counsel and feedback from a point of view that is not available with narrower representation. Lay people, in particular, fulfill this role on advisory boards and also on governing boards. It was reported by many rectors/presidents that in the past, when boards were predominately clerical in composition, their deliberations were not as concerned with the impact of theological education on the local church. "Lay people bring a dimension that was lacking," one respondent explained. "They can assess more objectively the effects of the way we train people for ministry. They have told us, for example, that we needed to improve our homiletics program, since they are the ones listening to homilies week after week."

Issues for the future: It is the intention of some theologate leaders to extend the governing functions and the responsibilities of boards; these leaders will be seeking assistance to ensure that such a policy leads to more effective boards. If the need for fund raising at theologates continues to increase, it is likely that boards will become more diverse in membership. Increasing lay participation in the Church in general may also lead to more board involvement with theologates. Issues of control will be unresolved until there is more experience of sharing power at this level. Canon law and Church documents like *Sapientia Christiana* will determine the parameters but, even so, considerable flexibility for development will remain. Moreover, the relation between canon law and civil law will have to be carefully explored and precisely understood.

2. MEMBERSHIP AND SIZE OF BOARDS

Present reality: Membership. Depending on the type of board, its membership varies considerably, with some boards being composed only of clerics and others of both lay people and clerics; some advisory boards comprise a majority of lay people. A total of 820 members serve on the 63 boards of theologates, excluding the 7 university boards. The other 40 first-level governing boards have 482 members, and the 22 second-level boards and one third-level board have 338 members. The boards are constituted as follows:

Title	First-level		Second-level		Total	
	Number	*Percent*	*Number*	*Percent*	*Number*	*Percent*
Cardinal/Bishop	60	12.0	38	11.0	98	12.0
Diocesan priest	97	19.0	60	18.0	157	19.0
Men religious	185	38.0	93	28.0	278	34.0
Women religious	15	3.0	15	4.0	30	4.0
Laymen	88	18.0	100	30.0	188	23.0
Laywomen	28	6.0	32	9.0	60	7.0
Other	9	2.0	-	-	9	1.0
TOTAL	482	100.0	338	100.0	820	100.0

Of the total board membership, 533 persons (65 percent) are ordained, and 287 (35 percent) represent other vocations. The first-level governing boards are composed of 342 ordained persons (71 percent) and 140 others (29 percent). The second-level boards are composed of 191 ordained (57 percent) and 147 others (43 percent). The nine members not included in other categories are two religious brothers, two Protestant ministers, one permanent deacon, and four students.

Size. The size of boards ranges from three to twenty-eight members. The distribution is as follows:

< 10 = 17 boards (11 first-level; 6 second-level)

10 - 14 = 17 boards (13 first-level; 3 second-level; one third-level)

15 - 19 = 17 boards (9 first-level; 8 second-level)

20 + = 12 boards (7 first-level; 5 second-level)

Many theologates have increased the size of their boards over the past five to ten years, for the following reasons: Boards can be an active force for fund raising and the maintenance of financial stability; they can assess programs from an external, objective perspective; and they can contribute to the school's ongoing advancement and planning. Their potential for cooperation in development efforts was sighted as the main reason for involving lay members, but rectors/presidents acknowledged that this rationale is seldom articulated. Some leaders also value the contribution of mixed boards to policies and programs. Thus it is common practice to establish a second, "advisory" board to assist with fund raising, and if it functions effectively to ask it to help the school reflect on its mission and operations.

The criteria for membership depend somewhat on the category to which the person belongs. Some rectors/presidents stated that the appointment of certain bishops to boards may be enrollment-driven, that is, the bishop is more likely to support the school by sending students to it if he has a stake in its operation. The criteria employed most often in selecting lay members of boards are the possession of a special expertise, especially financial or legal, or significant financial resources. Most boards are self-perpetuating, but new members must be approved by the bishop or the governing body of the religious order. Although this is not always the case, it was pointed out by rectors/presidents that lay board members tend to be conservative in their ecclesiological viewpoint and in their understanding of society and culture. Their conservatism can have an impact on theologate programs that may or may not be compatible with some of the values the school wishes to further, for example, an emphasis on social justice concerns.

Regarding membership, a comment representing the attitude of many rectors/presidents was made by one who has worked with two levels of boards: "A desirable criterion is that boards be reflective of the broader Church rather than that they be composed of wealthy people exclusively, or too many who are reformers. Boards ought to be balanced; and members must be able to work with bishops or religious superiors, reflect the Church at large, and support the theologate leadership in carrying out the mission of the school."

Issues for the future: Boards of trustees (governing boards) will continue to be expanded to include a broader representation of church members. The process will be gradual, and mixed boards will only gradually have the freedom and desire to extend their roles. The need for fund raising will occasion some changes, but very slowly if the dominant ecclesiology is strictly hierarchical. Determining how to incorporate the insights and use the expertise of lay members is considered one of the most important tasks of governing bodies in the next decade. Rectors/ presidents are looking for models of participation to guide them in modifying the structure and composition of boards.

A second issue concerns the education of board members. If boards are to function competently, they must have opportunities to learn about the theologates they serve, and they must be willing to commit themselves to educational opportunities. Occasional board seminars lasting two or three days are recommended as a means of helping boards to understand their roles and live out their commitment. Boards might also review their performance regularly, using tools such as the "Self-Study Criteria" and "User's Guide" from *The Good Steward*.[3]

3. AREAS OF BOARD RESPONSIBILITY

Present reality: For a board to be effective, it must have access to adequate information about the operations of the institution for which it is responsible. In a sense the board has ultimate responsi-

---

[3] Ibid., 136-160.

bility for the entire institution, but it must exercise its authority with discretion so that while maintaining control it does not interfere with administration. Board members can evaluate their knowledge of the theologate they serve by asking themselves a series of questions divided into four broad categories: mission and management, personnel and students, programs, and future goals and directions. Some typical questions that rectors/presidents cited as important, or that board members wanted to explore, are identified below.

Mission and Management: As boards become more aware of the different models of theological education that are operative in the 1980s, they must have answers to questions about the mission of the school for which they are responsible. They must also monitor their own performance as a board and be knowledgeable about the financial status of their institution. Regarding mission, pertinent questions are: What are the primary purposes of the theologate? Are these purposes relevant to the needs of the Church in general and to those of the particular constituencies of the theologate? What Church trends are affecting the direction of the school? Is the school responding to any need at all, or does it remain open only to survive? Is recruitment being extended into a region traditionally reserved for another theologate, thus eroding the potential enrollment of that institution and threatening its survival?

In evaluating itself, the board should ask whether its charge is clear. In other words, what authority does the board possess in relation to the ordinary, and are its purposes and objectives, its policies and procedures, carefully defined? Does the board limit its role to setting policy, or does it meddle inappropriately in operations? Who are the best board members, and how can like members be recruited? Are members' special skills being utilized, and how can the expertise of talented members be tapped so that they are motivated to stay? Are assignments distributed equitably and properly? Are meetings well planned, and is the committee structure workable? Are evaluation procedures in place?

Boards are sometimes accused of being too narrowly focused on questions about finances, but certainly a fundamental concern of every board must be the long-range financial stability of the institution. The first questions asked are often, Who pays to keep the theologate operating? What proportion of funding comes from tuition, from endowment, from annual fund-raising, from dioceses or religious orders, and from contributed services? How do these proportions compare with proportions at similar schools? Is the development office functioning as expected, and are its energies suitably directed? Does tuition reflect costs, and how does it compare with that of other theologates? How well are finances and investments monitored? One question rarely asked by a board is whether enough money is being spent, for example, on scholarships that will attract certain categories of students, or on faculty sabbaticals which, if available, will affect the quality of faculty available for hiring, or on technology that will save money and personnel time in the long run.

The area of personnel and students raises another series of questions. A major responsibility of the board is to select the rector/ president, and it must reflect on how well it performs this essential task. What expectations does the board have of the rector/president, and what procedures for evaluating him are in place? How does the board demonstrate its support for the rector/president to prevent his untimely departure? What provisions are made for orderly succession? Concerning other administrators, does the rector/president have adequate administrative assistance? What long-range plans have been made to ensure a sufficient pool of viable candidates for future administrative openings? Is the relationship of the board with the faculty good enough to maintain adequate communications and morale? Is the board aware of the number of faculty? their status with respect to rank and tenure? their capabilities, aspirations, and limitations? How difficult is it to recruit faculty with characteristics that are preferred by the school? Does the mix of men and women, clergy and lay, young and old, meet the requirements of the school? Are benefits and salaries sufficient to attract and retain superior faculty? Does the apportionment of faculty time among teaching, writing, research, and formation responsibilities reflect the priorities of the theologate? Are the opportunities for direct communication with faculty satisfactory?

Regarding the student body, what changes are occurring in its composition? Are the quality and quantity of applicants sufficient? Do admissions policies and procedures and recruitment practices make it possible to select students who are suitable for the institution? What are the obstacles to recruiting students? Does the student body as presently constituted contribute to a positive environment at the school? How are students evaluated, and what are the procedures for dismissing those who fail to meet the standards of the school?

The quality of programs is a third area of consideration for boards. Do the personal and spiritual formation, academic, and pastoral programs correspond to the requirements delineated in the *PPF?* If there are discrepancies, what are the reasons for them and how do they compare with variations at other schools? How well are standards for accreditation being maintained, for example, those of the ATS? Are program staffs both qualified and competent in the execution of their respective responsibilities? Should new directions be taken in programming, and should any programs be eliminated? How do programs address the changing needs of the Church? How are outcomes of the formational and educational process monitored?

Undoubtedly one of the significant responsibilities of boards is to set goals and plan for the future. Are these goals attainable by the institution and coherent with its history? Are directions intelligible and identifiable? What evidence is there that an organized planning process is in place? Are the appropriate constituents contributing to the planning process? Does the process take into account available resources? Does planning move beyond theoretical abstractions to implementation? Do adequate and appropriate data substantiate the decisions being contemplated, for example, data on the climate outside the institution, internal strengths and weaknesses, key personnel, and institutional values? Are periodic and suitable evaluations occurring in all areas?

Issues for the Future: In order to gain a better understanding of collegiality and the collaborative role of boards, relationships between boards and administrations will have to be continually clarified. The consistent and appropriate functioning of boards depends greatly on the confidence the board has in the institutional leadership. If it is satisfied, the board will probably restrict its activities to the policy level, and will not interfere with day-to-day operations; but if it loses confidence in the rector/president, it will tend to intervene at every level.

When rectors/presidents were asked what they will most require from board members over the next five years, they responded that they expect members to guide the direction of the theologate by setting priorities, to make policy, to see to funding, and to evaluate the performance of the rector/president. In turn, board members said that they expect rectors/presidents to articulate a vision, to implement policies and programs, and to keep the board informed. Some experienced board members also expressed a desire to examine the basic structure of theologate boards, which they believe is complicated by being modeled too closely on the structure of university boards. In their opinion, a new model uniquely suited to theologates may evolve, the shape of which is still undetermined.

C. Finances

OVERVIEW STATEMENTS

The dioceses and religious orders that sponsor theologates pay a high price to maintain these schools because of the low tuition relative to the cost of theological education. The sponsors hope to move toward equity in funding by increasing charges to cover a higher percentage of costs.

Concern about financing theologates is intensifying as costs rise without corresponding increases in tuition; in several large dioceses where theologates are highly endowed, however, finances are not a major issue.

More than half of the theologates are planning to initiate or expand financial development programs, in large part because ordinaries are urging administrators to hold down costs for the sponsoring diocese or religious order. Over the past ten years almost every theologate has improved its financial planning and accounting policies and procedures, but most are continuing to work toward achieving even better control of finances.

A high proportion of seminarians pay little or no tuition because the cost of their theological education is financed by their religious order or diocese. At theologates that enroll seminarians from several dioceses, differences in the financial support given to students by their respective dioceses have created discontent among the less supported.

Scholarships for lay students are minimal at every theologate, and as a result many Roman Catholics are pursuing their theological education at Protestant seminaries, where scholarships are often available or even abundant.

1. INSTITUTIONAL FUNDING

Present reality: The cost of providing theological education is enormous, and the financial responsibility is unequally shared by the dioceses and religious orders that depend on theologates to prepare their candidates for ministry. The administrators we interviewed contended that those who do not sponsor their own theologates usually pay considerably less for the education of their seminarians than the sponsors pay. On the average, tuition covers only about one-fourth of the cost of one person's theological education; the remaining costs are covered by the contributions of the sponsors. But in view of the intense competition to recruit students, neither the sponsors nor the administrators want to risk losing students by raising tuition too much. Since almost no theologate is operating at full capacity, it seems preferable to recover at least some of the costs by enrolling more students who are paying low tuition than to drive away students by charging more for tuition than competing institutions do. Religious orders that run theologates are especially concerned about the financial burden on them because of the decline in the number of men religious who provide contributed services. But even as the disparity between costs and charges grows, most sponsoring ordinaries consider education for priesthood such a high priority that they continue their financial support.

Because of the shortage of priesthood candidates, every effort is made to provide funding for potential seminarians, lest cost become a deterrent to their pursuing priesthood. In the past, charges were not a major consideration when ordinaries and vocation directors deliberated about where to send their seminarians for theology. Recently, however, administrators have become alert to the fact that tuition and other expenses are taken into account when theologates are chosen for seminarians.

The research completed by a national task force and entitled "A Study of the Fiscal Resources of Catholic Theology Schools 1975-1983" was an important step toward a clearer understanding of what is needed to ensure a stronger financial basis for theologates.[1] The study provided the means of evaluating resources, costs, and charges. On the issue of institutional funding, for example, it noted that ordinaries who are "sending their personnel to seminaries they do not own and operate should realize their obligation in justice to pay a larger amount of the per student costs over and above tuition

---

[1] *Planning for the Future: Catholic Theology Schools/Formation Houses 1975-1983* is "A Report on National Policy by the Task Force for the Study of the Fiscal Resources of Catholic Schools of Theology/Houses of Formation," conducted by the Center for Applied Research in the Apostolate (CARA) under a grant from the Lilly Endowment, Inc., and published in 1980. It is commonly referred to as the "CARA/Lilly Study."

and room and board than is the common practice today."[2] The task force also made recommendations regarding other areas of fiscal responsibility, which are noted when appropriate in the following sections.

Issues for the future: As concern about the cost of theologates continues to grow, closer attention will be paid to finances. Administrators are tightening financial controls and looking for new ways to fund their programs. The task force report suggests that "theology schools must look to a multiplicity of resources" to meet their financial needs. To take advantage of available resources, they are urged to establish development programs, a topic considered in section 5 below. These and other recommendations in the task force report have been carried out with varying degrees of success.

Individual theologates are making efforts to stabilize their financial status and to plan for the future, but little cooperative financial planning is being done between theologates and dioceses, especially between theologates and nonsponsoring dioceses. Religious orders are demanding stricter accountability from their theologate administrators because of higher costs in both dollars and personnel. Diocesan rectors/presidents also observe greater interest in fiscal matters on the part of ordinaries, and they expect continued pressure from ordinaries, who want to ensure that appropriate fiscal controls are in place. A long-range goal is to relieve some of the financial pressure by equalizing responsibility for finances.

2. BUSINESS PRACTICES AND FINANCIAL PLANNING

Present reality: Administrators commonly reported to us during interviews that accounting practices, budgeting procedures, and reporting of expenditures have improved significantly over the past five years. Previously the responsibility for finances was largely the rector's, and he usually had a secretary to assist with basic bookkeeping. Since expenses were considerably lower and enrollments generally higher, the per-student costs were much less. Contributed services provided a high proportion of theologate revenue, though

[2] Ibid., 23.

this source of income was often not taken into account or recorded. Academic programs were more limited, and personal and spiritual formation programs less developed, so that total expenses were not as high. Because routine fixed costs occupied much of the budget, financial planning was not as crucial as it has subsequently become.

As seminarian enrollment began to decline, theologates made several changes that affected finances. Academic programs were expanded to attract students who were not seminarians, resulting in additional personnel costs but at the same time increasing tuition income. Meanwhile, the proportion of revenue derived from contributed services declined. These changes led to a demand for better fiscal accountability. Rectors/presidents needed to know more precisely the costs of various programs and departments, and so within the past ten years almost every theologate has hired a business officer to monitor the financial condition of the school.

Issues for the future: To ensure fiscal responsibility, business officers will continue to develop sound budgeting, investment, and financial-planning policies. Internal financial accountability will remain important to individual theologates, but larger regional and national policies will affect them in ways beyond their control. Regional planning and cooperation among dioceses, religious orders, and theologates could influence enrollment and per-student costs in significant ways. It is generally perceived that joint planning will not take place unless it is mandated; however, no central body has the authority to act on this issue.

The almost complete autonomy of individual dioceses or religious communities that operate theologates may be counterproductive with respect to both meaningful cooperation and decisions on the number and quality of theologates. Meanwhile, per-student costs continue to increase. The call for good stewardship issuing from several recent national meetings demands that the cost to the Church of the whole seminary system be considered, not just the welfare of individual theologates. Equitable funding and the effective use of resources are paramount questions of justice. With improved fiscal control and enough data to make strategic planning a reality, the next step is to seek agreement on national policies that will positively affect the future.

3. COSTS AND CHARGES:
TUITION AND OTHER EXPENSES

Present reality: The CARA/Lilly Study reports that in 1978-79 the average total cost per student in theology was $10,082 and the average student payment was $2,779 (28 percent of the total), leaving a deficit of $7,303 per student.[3] On the basis of these figures, and assuming an inflation rate of 10 percent compounded annually, the average total cost in 1986-87 would equal $21,613, while the average student payment was actually $6,630[4] (31 percent of the estimated cost), leaving a deficit of nearly $15,000 per student.[5] If tuition and fees alone are considered, the average cost in 1986-87 would equal about $13,000, while the average student payment was actually $3,386 (26 percent), leaving a deficit of $9,614 per student. The current cost-charge differentials are thus enormous.

The following tables give an indication of the distribution of charges at the theologates that reported these figures in 1986-87.[6]

Dollar Amount	*Tuition Charged*		*Total Charged*	
	Number of schools[7]	Percent of schools	Number of schools	Percent of schools
Under 2,000	1	2.8	-	
2,000-2,999	8	22.2	1	3.7
3,000-3,999	17	47.2	1	3.7
4,000-4,999	7	19.4	1	3.7
5,000-5,999	3	8.3	5	18.5
6,000-6,999	-	-	10	37.0
7,000-7,999	-	-	6	22.2
8,000+	-	-	3	11.1

[3] Ibid., 22.

[4] This item is comprised of an average of $3,386 for tuition, $107 for fees, and $3,137 for room and board.

[5] The CARA/Lilly Study projections were based on a 12.5-percent annual rate of inflation, which would bring the present costs to over $27,000. Recent experience of a considerably lower inflation rate suggests that a projected rate of about 10 percent would yield a figure closer to reality. For purposes of comparison, if the inflation rate had averaged 7 percent, the current cost would be $18,533. It is generally agreed that the average inflation rate since 1978-79 has been higher than 7 percent.

[6] The data are taken from the CARA Seminary Directory 1987.

How are the deficits made up? The CARA/Lilly Study and the ATS Fact Book for 1986-87 provide some data in answer to this question.

Source of Revenue	CARA/Lilly, 1978-79[8]	ATS Fact Book, 1986-87
Contributed services	25 percent	18 percent
Subsidies	24 percent	
Gifts and grants	10 percent	36 percent[9]
Endowment	5 percent	14 percent
Other	7 percent	6 percent
Tuition	28 percent	26 percent

Two significant shifts occurred between 1978-79 and 1985-86: Contributed services dropped from 25 to 18 percent, and endowment income increased from 5 percent to 14 percent. During the same period, the proportion of revenue from tuition dropped by 2 percent, while the combination of subsidies, gifts, and grants increased by 2 percent.

Increases in tuition are not keeping pace with corresponding increases in costs, and the current tuition deficit of nearly $10,000 per student is more than double the 1978-79 deficit. The low tuition charged by theologates (less than that charged by almost any other postbaccalaureate program) can be credited to several factors: Ordinaries do not want candidates for the priesthood to be deterred from their vocation on the basis of the cost of theological education; administrators are convinced that theologates with lower tuition will

[7]Some theologates report tuition, room and board, and fees separately, while others give only the total cost. Institutions that do not provide room and board report only tuition and fees. Because of the different ways of reporting, the number of schools represented in these statistics is forty.

[8]Although the CARA/Lilly Study has not been updated, its data seem comparable to the ATS data.

[9]In the "Analysis of Revenues" (audited 1985-86) reported in the ATS *Fact Book,* it appears that the category of gifts and grants includes "subsidies," which are separate in the CARA/Lilly Study.

be selected by potential students; and, given the long history of low tuition, it is realistic to raise tuition only gradually. These factors impact negatively on the finances of all theologates. Religious orders that sponsor theologates largely for diocesan candidates are particularly affected, because diocesan subsidies are not available to them and for that reason their tuition charges are usually slightly higher.

Issues for the future: Each year most theologates are raising their tuition charges incrementally, but the costs are escalating more rapidly than the amount raised from added tuition. As awareness about costs grows, it can be expected that some effort will be made to alleviate the burden of the sponsoring dioceses and religious orders, but progress in this direction has been slow. National funding for theologates is suggested as one possible way to equalize costs. Clearly such a policy would have both benefits and liabilities, which should be explored before action is taken. The experience of Protestant seminaries that are nationally financed could provide information about the advisability of pursuing this kind of funding.

The gap between costs and charges continues to widen. Many administrators believe that policy changes will have to be made so that tuition begins to cover more of the actual costs of theologate education. The main deterrent to higher tuition seems to be fear that if some schools raise their tuition while others keep it low, enrollment in the former will suffer. The only solution may be for all rectors/presidents to agree simply to raise tuition by a prescribed amount, for example, one thousand dollars. University-related programs would be exempt, since tuition at these schools is already substantially higher. Other means of raising money must also be investigated.

4. SCHOLARSHIPS

Present reality: Scholarship support and financial aid are readily available to most priesthood candidates either from their own dioceses or from individual sponsors, especially as they near ordination. Members of religious orders who are aspiring to priesthood have already taken the vow of poverty, which means that their expenses are paid by their orders. We learned from interviews that the amount paid by diocesan seminarians varies widely, depending on the policies of the home diocese. The most generous policy applies to a small proportion of seminarians who pay none of their expenses—no tuition, fees, room, or board—and, in addition, are given a monthly stipend and other benefits like health insurance and a car. More commonly, diocesan seminarians pay no tuition, but they do pay their other expenses. This policy applies in four or five dioceses that operate their own theologates and have large endowments, and in small dioceses with only a few seminarians. In other instances, seminarians pay a decreasing amount each year as they approach ordination. Still others are expected to pay a sizable share of their expenses. To cover costs, these students take out loans and work full-time during summers and part-time during the school year, usually in work-study programs.

In theologates where seminarians come from a number of different dioceses, the discrepancy in financial support creates some discontent among those who receive minimal support; it also causes concern among formation directors, for example, when excessive work hours interfere with field education or other aspects of formation. Nevertheless, it seems that in general only a few seminarians have serious financial problems, and these usually occur in cases where the diocese does not substantially assist students or previous debts remain to be paid. Repayment of college loans is the major financial problem for about 20 percent of theology students.

On a related topic, some business officers noted that most seminarians have not had to deal with finances in any serious way and yet in a few years many of them, especially those from smaller dioceses, will be serving as pastors with major responsibility for the business affairs of a parish. Since the already crowded theology curriculum rarely touches on parish finances, business officers believe that the subject should be a standard component of the continuing education curriculum for priests.

Issues for the future: Financial support for individual seminarians is likely to increase, especially if their number remains low. As dioceses and religious orders experience the shortage of priests, it appears that every effort will be made to assist seminarians in pursuing their theological education.

Because scholarship support and financial aid for lay students is minimal, many Catholic lay students are shopping for low tuition. They often find more support at Protestant or nondenominational seminaries; consequently, a large number of Catholic lay students are studying theology and preparing for ministry at non-Catholic institutions. The ramifications of this trend are of concern to future employers of lay ministers. To what extent will those who have been educated in non-Catholic settings be able to minister in Catholic contexts? If the intention is to encourage lay students to prepare for ministry at Roman Catholic theologates, more financial support will be required.

5. DEVELOPMENT PROGRAMS AND ENDOWMENT FUNDS

Present reality: In 1987-88, twenty-two theologates had hired development officers who were responsible for fund raising and for public relations. Development programs were being planned at about ten others. Most administrators realize that costs will increase significantly as the amount of contributed services continues to decline. With fewer priests who are appropriately educated and available for faculty and administrative positions, more lay people and others who cannot contribute their services are being hired. As noted, the proportion of revenue deriving from contributed services has dropped by 7 percent in less than ten years; in an effort to make up the difference, development programs are being enhanced or initiated.

One of the major assignments for development offices is to build endowments for faculty chairs, student scholarships, and other regular expenses. The endowment funds at the disposal of theologates range from none at all to substantial sums, several in the millions of dollars. Most administrators are looking for ways to increase these funds for the sake of long-term financial stability.

Issues for the future: In the future a higher percentage of revenue will come from development, but the expected proportion varies widely, and in most cases a set percentage has not yet been determined. About ten theologates are likely to inaugurate development programs within the next five years, and the other twenty-two will expand their existing programs. Gifts and grants are expected to increase as more personnel are hired to do fund raising. Future development efforts will focus not only on the collection of annual contributions but also on the enhancement of endowments through trusts, bequests, and deferred giving.

The extent to which theologates can rely on endowment income is not yet known. One theologate leader identified changes in sources of revenue as shifts in "tones of support." He maintained that Roman Catholic theologates have not yet begun to tap many potential financial resources for theologate education. Development officers also report that in fund raising it is popular to appeal for financial support for the education of future priests. In the next decade many development officers expect that, with the assistance of rectors/presidents, gifts and grants to theologates will at least double. If this amount of new support can be generated, it will go a long way toward providing financial stability for theologates.

Part III

Personnel and Students

A. Administrations

OVERVIEW STATEMENTS

The administration of theologates has changed, in most cases, from a simple system in which a rector was responsible for virtually all aspects of the school to a more complex and expanded administrative structure involving many more individuals.

During the process of change in administrative structures, the role of rector/president has seen the most extensive redefinition. It has evolved from a largely internal and comprehensive role to one in which internal responsibilities have been delegated to others and the rector/president himself has assumed more external responsibilities.

In most schools the role of administration is becoming clearer, and carefully defined job descriptions are helping to clarify the responsibilities of a new echelon of trained and effective middle management.

Though some tensions exist, relations between the administrations and their boards and faculties are being worked out successfully.

There is a rapid rate of turnover among major administrators, especially academic deans but also rectors/presidents. This is a matter of general concern, since the consequent lack of continuity is surely detrimental to the functioning of the schools.

Difficulty in recruiting rectors/presidents and academic deans is growing for several reasons, including lack of support on significant issues from ordinaries/religious superiors, and the extensive expectations placed on major administrators by superiors, faculty, and students.

1. CURRENT CONTEXT

Present reality: As the discussion of mission shows, theologates have changed and developed significantly over the past twenty years. Administrators and faculty have experienced new challenges and expanding roles accompanying the changes in mission, in large part because of the growing diversity and complexity of theologates. Some fifteen to twenty years ago the "administration" of seminaries was, in effect, the rector. He may have had a secretary or clerical staff to assist with registration and other paper work, but the management of the school was chiefly his responsibility. In that era, the curriculum of the seminary was a "given," the role of academic dean was not considered necessary, and the need for other administrative positions had not been established.

After Vatican II, new ways of providing seminary education developed. Programs of study were reviewed, changes in curriculum became common, and the position of academic dean evolved accordingly. At about the same time, enrollment of seminarians began to decrease sharply and recruitment efforts became necessary, sometimes involving the addition of a staff person. With the admission of lay students, personnel were needed to provide student services, and as new programs were adopted directors were appointed. Financial obligations skyrocketed because of increased personnel and the inflation of the 1970s. Many development programs were initiated and business offices established. Within a short period of time, administration and staff jumped from two or three individuals to as many as ten or twelve at some schools.

During these years of expansion, which were paralleled at institutions of higher education, changes in administration were rapid. Only recently have administrations been stabilizing, and in the process administrators are developing a better sense of their roles and are improving management practices such as budgeting, organizing, and planning. In fact, some are now reluctant to relinquish their authority to boards or faculties. As the role of administration in relation to these groups evolves, new patterns of communication are being established and new styles of management developed. As one seasoned rector put it: "We are beginning to learn effective management. A new echelon of trained and effective middle-management people are moving into position. This forces rectors/ presidents to attend to what is proper to their role."

Not all schools have changed at an equal pace. In some seminaries the life of the school still seems to depend on and revolve around a few key administrators, especially long-term rectors/presidents who still "run the school" and have little reason to consult with others. At other schools administrators are perceived and function more as figureheads, while the direction of the school is largely determined by a bishop or the board of trustees. In a few places the faculty seems to have more strength than the administration, with a history of involvement in the management of the school. The role of such a faculty in administration usually concerns academic matters, and in a sense parallels other administrative structures. At smaller institutions the complexity is not so great, but even there it is not surprising to find persons engaged full time in development, business management, or student services especially in relation to recruitment. Owing to a number of different factors, administrative styles vary considerably from place to place.

Issues for the future: As schools adapt to internal and external changes, effective management will depend to a large extent on the willingness of institutions to invest in qualified administrators. To the extent that these positions, beyond those of the rector/president and dean, are regarded as "secretarial," administration of the schools may be in jeopardy. The rectors/presidents and academic deans have sometimes inherited situations in which willing, dedicated, and hard-working but unqualified second-level administrators have managed the day-to-day operations. The top leaders have assumed responsibility for virtually all decision making, and little collaboration is evident.[1]

A point of argument at some schools is determining who is

---

[1] At colleges and universities presidents may not have background in management, but many of those working in other administrative areas do. These administrators complement the chief executive officer, whose function often revolves around public relations. The size of theologates is usually so small that this secondary level of management is thin or nonexistent.

included in "administration," that is, how far down the line does it go before it becomes "staff"? This issue has gained importance at a few schools where questions of decision making, authority, and salary are determined by a person's designation as administrator or staff. As the number of laity working in theologates increases, even more attention will have to be paid to this issue. One comment by a priest in administration is indicative of the problem: "The Church really doesn't know how to deal with lay people working for the institution. The problem is heightened when administrators are not part of the hierarchy. How do management decisions relate to obedience when the managers are not clerics?"

Unfortunately, a genuine sense of call to administration is rare, though not unheard of. Many in administration speak of "putting in time" for the sake of something they believe is important, but not out of a desire to be administrators. Ironically, administration is not often recognized by the ordained as a charism of service. The few nonordained persons in high administrative positions in theologates are often eager to do the work because they see it as long-term ministry. If theologates can resolve issues of salary and authority they will gain access to a valuable source of personnel among such dedicated individuals.

As schools search for administrators, questions frequently asked are: What constitutes good managers/administrators? Is it natural talent, or can they be "made" by attending some school for management training? If the latter, is anyone being prepared for the future administration of our seminaries? In other words, who will wish to undertake the administration of theologates in the future?

2. ROLE AND STATUS OF KEY ADMINISTRATORS

Rectors/Presidents

Present reality: In the past the role of rector was understood as broad and comprehensive. The priest in this position was not only the chief executive officer for the seminary, but he was also responsible for personal and spiritual formation and for the academic and pastoral programs. According to most current rectors/presidents, that role focused more on internal matters than its present-day counterpart does. Major shifts in the composition of student bodies and in programs have resulted in altered job descriptions for the chief executive officer (CEO). The main alteration has been an expansion of the rector's role to include significant external responsibilities, such as development and fund raising; recruitment of students; maintaining the reputation of the school with bishops and religious superiors; and involvement in cooperative efforts with national organizations, professional groups, and other theologates. Paralleling this reorientation of efforts has been a transfer of internal responsibilities, largely through delegation, to academic deans, formation directors, and other administrators.

Though some changes in the responsibilities of rectors/presidents have occurred at virtually every institution, the conception and implementation of the changes have varied. Differences relate in part to the type of institution, ranging from freestanding to university-associated, from independent to collaborative. The title assigned to rectors/presidents often indicates just how the position is conceived. The simple title Rector is used fifteen times; in addition, one person is Rector-Dean and another Rector/Vice-President. The title President is used at fourteen schools. A total of seventeen schools use a combined title—President-Rector in ten instances, and Rector-President in seven. At Catholic University, the person in charge of the theology program is called Chair of the Department.

When rectors/presidents were asked how their titles had been chosen, about half said with deliberation and the other half said by custom. Those holding only the title Rector are in ten out of fifteen instances (66.7 percent) the chief executive officers of diocesan seminaries. For the most part these schools are freestanding, and the rector is closely connected with the total formation program as well as with the general administration of the school. The energies of these individuals tend to be internally directed. Of the remaining five rectors, one is at a seminary operated by a religious order with mostly diocesan candidates as students, four are the rectors of formation programs attached to a university (the rector of the Theological College would add a fifth), and the rector-dean and rector/vice-president are both associated with universities. The simple title Rector, then, does seem to connote closer involvement with the everyday internal operations of the school.

The title President is held in all cases by the CEOs of religious order schools, twelve of them operated mainly for religious and two mainly for diocesan candidates. These schools are of several types.

Most are related to consortia or unions. Some are fairly large, and most include a mixture of seminarians and lay students. At these schools personal and spiritual formation is largely the responsibility of houses of formation, with academic deans administering the academic program. The president usually has significant external responsibilities, and in that regard resembles a typical college president.

The titles that combine Rector and President represent positions that try to encompass both internal and external responsibilities, with varying degrees of emphasis on one or the other. The functions of those who carry the title President-Rector tend to be more externally oriented, particularly in regard to fund raising. That title is used four times by diocesan seminaries, four times by schools operated by religious orders mainly for diocesan students, and twice by religious order schools. Those with the reverse title of Rector-President often function in a largely internal role that carries broad responsibility. This is the title of four diocesan CEOs, two religious CEOs serving schools mainly for diocesan candidates, and one religious CEO at a theologate for religious.

Who are the CEOs? The present group comprises twenty-seven men religious and twenty-two diocesan priests. The academic credentials of forty-three of them were identified as follows in catalogs:

Degree	Number	
S.T.D.	16	
Ph.D.	11	
D.Min.	2	74.4%
Dr.Theol./Dr.es Sc.Rel.	2	
S.S.L.[2]	1	
S.T.L.	5	
Master's	5	25.6%
S.T.M.	1	

The proportion of rectors/presidents who hold doctoral degrees (74.4 percent) is slightly higher than for the faculty as a whole (67.4 percent). Twenty-two rectors/presidents (51.2 percent) have pontifical degrees. The fields represented by rectors/presidents, when

---

[2]The S.S.L. is regarded as a doctoral-level degree by accrediting agencies, and is treated as such in this analysis.

specified, are as follows:

Field	Number
Pastoral	12
Systematic	11
Moral	3
Scripture	2
Theology (unspecified)	2
Other (Education, Anthropology, Sociology/Psychology)	5

The academic rank of rectors/presidents is identified in twenty-four instances, and it is most often at the level of professor or associate professor. The higher ranks reflect both the status of the position of rector/president and the relatively long association these officers have had with their institutions. The ranks are distributed thus:

Rank	Number
Professor	9
Associate Professor	13
Assistant Professor	2
Rank not given[3]	25

Issues for the future: Of special concern for the future is the question who the rectors/presidents will be. A religious superior expressed this concern in the following way: "It is excruciating to try to find a rector for our seminary. Our ranks are depleted, just like those of diocesan priests, and we simply don't have men who are prepared and willing to serve in that capacity." In answer to the question why it is so difficult to find seminary leaders, most respondents cited lack of professional support for and acknowledgment of the position. Some rectors/presidents identified the problem largely in terms of relationships with colleagues at their schools. Since the role involves evaluation of the work of others, when rectors/ presidents make negative assessments they may be resented. In other cases it is simply a matter of faculty not understanding the im-

[3]Sixteen of the eighteen CEOs who do not have an academic rank are at schools where rank is not given to anyone. The other nine are at schools that rank faculty but not rectors/presidents.

portance of administration in general, and as a result failing to cooperate with or appreciate the person in leadership. Some respondents mentioned the lack of support they feel from their ordinaries and boards of trustees. At times of tension or crisis, for example, when enrollments decline or when it is difficult to find suitable faculty, several rectors/presidents indicated that the problem was regarded as totally their own responsibility, even though they really needed assistance. Others experience a lack of encouragement and understanding from fellow priests who work in parishes and other ministries. These men often remember negative personal experiences from their seminary days, and still relate to the schools they attended from this biased point of view. According to some priests who are currently working in theologates, many priests in other ministries do not realize that theologates have changed. More planned interaction and information sharing between priests who work in theologates and those who work outside would be fruitful, it seems, both for morale and for future vocations.

Academic Deans

Present reality. The position of academic dean is relatively new in theologates, which means that the precise role—the job description—for the position is still evolving. Is the academic dean the dean of faculty or student adviser, the academic planner or general administrator, or a combination of all these? The response depends in part on the background and interest of the individual. The role of a few deans is even limited to something akin to a record-keeping function, as if the dean were the registrar. In such situations the school must be concerned about the extent to which academic planning is being done, if at all, and how faculty are being led and brought together. "In order to achieve clarity in the role of dean, the management role of administrations and of faculties needs to be made clear. The principle of subsidiarity needs to be invoked, and the specific tasks need to be defined," is the kind of statement that summarizes the concern of many deans.

Since the role lacks definition, many schools complain of difficulty in finding persons who will serve as dean and, once "co-opted," of having them stay for a reasonable length of time. Among administrators, it is especially academic deans who prefer teaching to administrative work and who often try to do both. The consequences are early burnout, frequent turnover, inadequate academic planning, and overwork.

The ultimate negative result is that deans stay in office for a very short time. Using 1983-84 as the base year and tracing the changes in deanships up to 1985-86, the records show that twenty-five schools changed deans during this period, two of them twice, yielding a total of twenty-seven changes. Fifty percent of the theologates changed academic deans within a three-year period, and the rate of turnover continued at an even faster pace during 1986-87. As one faculty member remarked: "Priests, understandably, are not eager to do a job with few 'perks' and lots of headaches. For diocesan seminaries, a long-term, well-paid lay dean may be an excellent investment for continuity, but I'm not sure we're ready for that step either." And a dean commented: "Respect for the vocation of administration is still low. You would think St. Paul had never mentioned it in I Corinthians."

Who are the academic deans? The present group includes twenty-four diocesan priests, twenty-one men religious, one woman religious, and three laymen. The academic credentials of the forty-nine deans are as follows:

Degree	Number	
Ph.D.	20	
S.T.D.	13	
S.S.L.	4	
S.S.D.	1	81.6%
Th.Dr.	1	
J.C.D.	1	
Master's	5	
S.T.L.	2	18.4%
J.C.L.	2	

Forty (81.6 percent) of the academic deans hold doctoral degrees, a considerably higher percentage than for the faculty as a whole (67.4 percent). Twenty deans (40.8 percent) have pontifical degrees. Of those whose academic fields are indicated, the distribution is thus:

Field	Number
Systematic	12
Scripture	8
Church History	5
Theology (unspecified)	5
Liturgical/Pastoral	4
Moral	3
Church/Canon Law	3
Other (Religious Education, Psychology, and Education)	3

The academic dean often speaks in the name of the faculty, and in both theory and practice it is understood that this officer should have at least some theological education and an appropriate degree, if the role is to be fulfilled effectively. Some believe that it is equally important for deans to have pastoral experience. Since deans are in a unique position to give future direction to theological education, much is to be said in favor of the viewpoint that both credentials are desirable.

The academic rank of academic deans reflects the high level of their preparation and often their long-term commitment to the school, though not usually to the dean's role.

Rank	Number
Professor	11
Associate Professor	12
Assistant Professor	7
Others ranked, but not the Dean	2
Ranks not given by the school	17

Issues for the future: Since a major concern regarding academic deans is their frequent turnover, a goal of many schools should be to determine how to choose and then support deans so that tenure in the position will last longer. In my conversations with deans, two recommendations were commonly made: First, individuals who have theological degrees and show an interest in administration should be given the opportunity either for an internship or for advanced study in management to test their potential for service. Second, job descriptions should be written so that the dean's task is not so overwhelming that theological research becomes impossible. If these recommendations were heeded, two of the greatest deterrents to effective deanships could be obviated: lack of preparation, which leads to frustration in the job; and lack of the time deans need to remain current with their theological discipline.

Academic deans are encouraged by two activities that they feel should be further developed. One is the opportunity for professional advancement in administration through conferences like the Institute for Theological Education Management (ITEM). Another is the establishment or continuation of regional deans' meetings, where issues and concerns peculiar to the role can be discussed. Without these supports and others still to be considered, the pattern of "revolving deanships" will continue to the detriment of academic programs as well as whole institutions.

3. RELATIONS BETWEEN ADMINISTRATION AND FACULTY

Present reality: The attitude of faculty toward administrators varies significantly from place to place. In some settings the professional credentials of all administrators, not only rectors/presidents and deans, give them the background and expertise to function as co-professionals with faculty. In other settings administrators are underqualified, and hence unable to function on an equal basis with faculty. In certain cases faculties seem reluctant to support professional administration, and tend to view added administrators as an unnecessary expense. Since few faculty have worked in other academic institutions, their experience with professional administrators is limited. For these reasons administrative and faculty roles are not clearly differentiated at many institutions, and the value of administration is only beginning to be understood and accepted by faculty. It is not uncommon for faculties to perceive administrations as much larger and more controlling than the reality appears to warrant.

Issues for the future: As administrative positions become more established and faculties mature in their own positions, the definition of specific roles should become clearer. Theologates have undergone tremendous upheavals in recent years, so that both faculties and administrations have had to adapt to new circumstances. Both have new expectations to meet, and both are still in the process of negotiating an appropriate place for themselves at their schools. The transitions have generally been smooth. If resources tighten, however, financial considerations could lead to competition for funds within institutions and thereby to potentially unhealthy relations between administrations and faculties. The dilemma for faculty is whether to dissipate their energies by engaging in more administrative tasks themselves, or to support the hiring of administrators to perform tasks that would otherwise be assigned to faculty. Each institution is in the process of deciding this question. Above all, trust on both sides is required if fruitless confrontations are to be avoided.

4. TURNOVER, CONTINUITY, AND THE FUTURE OF ADMINISTRATION

Present reality: One of the key concerns regarding administration is the rapid rate of turnover, especially at the level of rectors/presidents and deans. This pattern affects potential planning and contributes to the weakening of institutions. In order to plan effectively, leaders need to have both experience and the expectation of remaining in their positions for at least four or five years so that they can begin to implement plans. The problem of overextension among administrators is universal. In some instances it is related to increasing institutional complexity, and in others to the desire of administrators to teach several courses. It also arises from imprecise job descriptions. In part, administrators are motivated to perform many tasks because they sense the need to "prove" their worth to faculty and boards. The perception of administration as a valued ministry is still not prevalent in theologates. Instead, administration is often viewed as "filling in" by performing unrewarding but necessary tasks. The real work of the school is often regarded as teaching; therefore, many administrators want to do both. Common results are overwork and the lack of a feeling of accomplishment or satisfaction with the management of the school.

Another reason for high turnover rates among administrators may be the trend toward "term contracts," which though renewable often provide the occasion for resignation from the position. This practice is not entirely negative and has evolved in response to the high demands associated with administration. An individual who cannot conceive of extended service in one of these positions may be willing to assume a term of two or three years. But some leaders suggest that it is the short length of many term contracts that poses the problem. If contracts were routinely written for five or six years, the incumbent could achieve some long-term goals and provide continuity. Given the fact that people change positions so often, the alternative of longer-term contracts might actually enhance stability by ensuring that the incumbent would stay in the position for at least several years.

Finally, it seems that more direct accountability and thorough evaluation of administrators is important. When job descriptions are vague and objectives unclear, the tendency is for the management of the school to drift. If boards were able to define more carefully what direction they want their institutions to take, administrators could implement plans to reach those goals. Suitable evaluation would then make it possible for boards to affirm and support the work that is being accomplished. Unfortunately evaluation, especially in theologates, is regarded as negative and disapproving; it is associated with lack of trust, instead of being seen as an opportunity to learn and progress as well as to be appreciated.

Issues for the future: In order to establish a pattern of continuity, it is important to assess carefully the administrative needs of a school so as not to overburden top administrators and thereby cause early resignations. When asked about problems relating to administrators, one seasoned faculty member replied: "Where will good priest-administrators come from? Church leaders—bishops and religious superiors—must be made aware of how devastating frequent turnover in top administration is. If priests are to serve in theologates in the future they must be trained—but it seems there is no planning."

Concern about replacing persons in administrative positions is considerable. At schools operated by religious communities, a few talented individuals are called upon to carry the burden of administration when often they would rather teach or work in other ministries of their communities. There are exceptions to this attitude and some, though few in number, are totally dedicated to administration in this context. Diocesan seminaries are faced with a similar dilemma: As the number of priests available for parish work decreases, fewer men are being designated to earn the advanced degrees requisite for working in seminaries. And only a fraction of those receiving advanced training are willing or able to be administrators. "Administration has few rewards; battles are large and resources small," said a tired dean.

To forestall future problems, good administrative policies, adequate personnel, and "administrative teams" will be required. As one seminary leader stated: "The day of the 'lone ranger' is over. We are focusing now on providing continuity through cooperative management, but we are paying the price of a decade of ignoring replacements—an incredible lack of ecclesial policy, not bad will."

B. *Faculty*

OVERVIEW STATEMENTS

The role of faculty has expanded from a focus on teaching, often in combination with some aspect of spiritual or ministerial formation, to responsibility for administrative tasks and curriculum development, including multiple committee assignments and program administration.

It is becoming increasingly difficult to recruit the kind of faculty needed by the schools, that is, individuals with preparation in personal and spiritual formation and with an academic degree in theology.

Due to the many role expectations imposed on theologate faculty, only a small minority are able to give priority to research and writing, which has the long-term effect of jeopardizing the quality of teaching and professional reflection appropriate to theologates. An increasing disparity in this regard is developing between freestanding diocesan seminaries and other theologates.

In the recent past, faculties consisted almost entirely of priests, but the composition of faculties has become more diverse since then, with women religious, laymen, and laywomen comprising about one-fourth of those now teaching.

Although more women have been hired to fill positions in teaching and administration, developments in the Church over the past decade concerning their role in theologates are leading many women to reconsider their commitment to these institutions.

The influx of priests into the job market after the closing of many religious order seminaries in the late 1960s meant that for about ten years it was relatively easy to hire faculty. But now that this source has been depleted and there are fewer priests adequately prepared for seminary teaching than before, the task of hiring in the future is expected to be much more difficult.

Although most faculty members expressed great satisfaction with teaching and were deeply involved in and dedicated to theological education, many also voiced fears that the future might bring retrenchment, outside control, and diminishment of academic freedom, which would be detrimental to their profession.

1. VOCATIONAL STATUS AND DEGREES OF FACULTY

Vocational Status

Present reality: The faculty of every seminary and school of theology is central to its mission and goals. The future of the schools and the future of education for ministry depend essentially on the quality and dedication of faculties. A survey of the current catalogs indicates that 898 full-time and hundreds more part-time faculty members teach at the fifty institutions included in this study.[1] The average number of full-time faculty is nearly eighteen per school; seven schools have fewer than ten full-time faculty members; fourteen have from ten to fourteen, eleven from fifteen to nineteen, ten from twenty to twenty-five, and eight more than twenty-five.

Among the 898 faculty members, men religious make up the largest number: 392 (43.7 percent). Diocesan priests compose the second largest group: 292 (32.5 percent). These 684 priests constitute 76.2 percent of those who teach in seminaries. Women religious number 93 (10.4 percent), laymen 88 (9.8 percent), and laywomen 33 (3.7 percent). Thus the total number of individuals teaching in theologates who are not priests is 214 (23.8 percent).

Issues for the future: Most of those interviewed believe that being able to find and afford faculty will become an increasingly acute problem. Contributed services will diminish, for example, among women religious, and among men from religious communities if the theologate does not belong to their congregation or if the size of the congregation continues to decline. The large number of men religious teaching in theologates now is probably related to the dispersal of faculties when the unions were established in Washington and Chicago in the late 1960s. Many men were prepared to teach in

---

[1] The 898 full-time faculty are individuals listed as regular faculty, i.e., not adjunct, visiting, or part-time. Rectors/presidents and academic deans are always listed with faculty; so even though their teaching responsibilities are often limited, they are included in this number. Other administrators, such as librarians, registrars, treasurers, and development officers, are sometimes listed and sometimes not, so they are not included in this number, except in rare cases when they are specifically identified as teaching faculty.

seminaries for their own communities at that time; then with the amalgamations a large number of faculty were not needed by the unions and so were free to move to other theologates. Such a large reservoir of educated men is unlikely to become available again.

Sources of faculty for the future are uncertain. Some theologates depend on dioceses to prepare and place priests in seminaries but, as the general shortage of priests makes itself felt, seminary leaders fear that the supply of priests for future faculty positions will surely diminish. The need to identify prospective faculty members is a growing concern, especially in light of Vatican directives suggesting that virtually all faculty members should be priests.

Degrees

Present reality: The academic preparation required of faculty members in seminaries is mentioned in the *PPF* (pp. 66-67, #241), which refers the reader to *Sapientia Christiana,* where the issue is discussed in sections III and VII.[2] The latter document states that permanent faculty must have, among other qualifications, "a suitable doctorate or equivalent title or exceptional and singular scientific accomplishment," and that "these requirements for taking on permanent teachers must be applied also, in proportionate measure, for hiring nonpermanent ones" (section III, article 25, 1:2 and 2).

The number of current faculty with doctoral degrees is 574 (63.9 percent).[3] Of these, 251 hold the Ph.D., 201 the S.T.D., 61 other doctorates such as the Dr.Sc.Rel. or D.Phil., 35 the J.C.D., and 26 the D.Min. The proportion of men religious with doctorates is highest at 72.7 percent; laymen have the next highest proportion of doctorate holders at 65.5 percent. Nearly equal proportions of diocesan priests, women religious, and laywomen hold doctorates (55.5, 53.8, and 54.5 percent, respectively). In addition, 31 faculty (3.5 percent) hold the S.S.L., which is regarded by accrediting bodies as a terminal teaching degree and thus can be classified as doctoral-level

---

[2] Although the *PPF* does not itself list the qualifications stipulated for faculty, it says, "The training of faculty is further specified by *Sapientia Christiana*" (p. 67, #241). This would seem to imply that the qualifications listed in *Sapientia Christiana* apply to all theologate faculties, not just ecclesiastical faculties.

[3] See table below.

Faculty: Degrees and Vocational Status

	Diocesan	Men Rel.	Women Rel.	Laymen	Laywomen	Total
Doctorate						
Ph.D.	45	115	41	37	13	251
S.T.D.	81	111	2	6	1	201
Dr.Sc.Rel.et al.	13	31	1	15	1	61
J.C.D.	15	17	1	1	1	35
D.Min	8	11	5	–	2	26
Total	162	285	50	59	18	574
Percent	(55.5)	(72.7)	(53.8)	(67.0)	(54.5)	(63.9)
S.S.L*	12 (4.1%)	19 (4.8%)	–	–	–	31 (3.5)
S.S.L. &						
Doctorate	174	304	50	59	18	605
Percent	(59.6)	(77.6)	(53.8)	(67.0)	(54.5)	(67.4)
Licentiate, Master's, Bachelor's						
S.T.L.	48	30	1	2	–	81
J.C.L.	9	3	–	–	–	12
Th.M.	4	4	1	–	–	9
M.A.	29	31	38	21	15	134
M.Div.	26	19	2	3	–	50
B.A.	2	1	1	3	–	7
Total	118	88	43	29	15	293
Percent	(40.4)	(22.4)	(46.2)	(33.0)	(45.5)	(32.6)
Vocational Status:						
By number	292	392	93	88	33	898
By percent	(32.5)	(43.7)	(10.4)	(9.8)	(3.7)	(100.1)

*S.S.L. degrees are considered terminal teaching degrees by accrediting agencies and so are separately identified.

preparation. The S.S.L. is held by 4.1 percent of diocesan priests and 4.8 percent of men religious.

Among the theologates, the proportion of faculty with doctoral-level degrees ranges from 26 to 100 percent. At eleven schools (22 percent), more than 75 percent of the faculty hold a terminal degree. At the other end of the spectrum, at fourteen schools (28 percent) the doctorate is held by a maximum of 50 percent of the faculty. At the remaining twenty-five schools, between 51 and 75 percent of the faculty hold doctorates. Obviously, these statistics document significant institutional differences in the preparation of faculty and in the quality of teaching and scholarship.

Degrees at the master's or licentiate level, or below, are held by 293 faculty members (32.6 percent) of theologates. The S.T.L. is held by 81 faculty, while 134 have an M.A. or equivalent degree. Fifty hold the M.Div., nine the Th.M., and twelve the J.C.L. Seven persons are listed with a B.A. degree, usually in music. Many of those with a master's degree work in field education and pastoral formation. Notwithstanding the great differences in the academic qualifications of faculty, administrators are generally satisfied with their degrees. In practice, the master's degree is considered acceptable, though it appears that *Sapientia Christiana* calls for all theologate faculty to hold doctoral degrees.

Faculty have degrees from a variety of universities. At some schools nearly all faculty members have pontifical degrees, while at others there is more variety, including degrees from secular universities. The figures for all faculties are as follows:

Source of Degrees	*Percent*
Roman Pontifical Degrees	25.7
University of Louvain Degrees	5.1
Other European University Degrees	9.7
Catholic University of America Degrees	11.6
Other American Catholic University Degrees	30.0
Non-Catholic American University Degrees	18.0

The emphasis on pastoral programs, counseling, and psychology has created a pressing need for faculty with preparation in these areas, according to deans and faculty. Some areas of competence are more common among older faculty members, especially Scripture, systematic theology, and moral theology, but fewer older faculty have professional preparation in pastoral areas. As programs change, the preparation of faculty will also necessarily change.

Issues for the future: Since pontifical universities do not have programs to prepare people in certain pastoral specializations, diversity of faculty backgrounds is expected to continue in the future despite the call for pontifical degrees. Maintaining the proper blend of degrees is a challenge. Faculty in pastoral areas question how appropriate and realistic the requirement in *Sapientia Christiana* is that all permanent faculty earn pontifical degrees. Some bishops are concerned about where future faculty members are being sent to study, according to the reports of at least ten seminary leaders. Tension exists between the real needs of theologates and the Vatican directives concerning the source of faculty degrees.

2. ROLE OF FACULTY

Present reality: The role of faculty has changed in recent years. Many institutions, particularly those educating diocesan candidates, expect faculty to function both in spiritual formation and in an academic role. It is difficult to combine these tasks, especially since professional training for work in formation is becoming more common and necessary.

Faculty have also expanded their role by taking on some administrative tasks. In previous years they had little reason to be concerned with program structure, since the curriculum was set. More recently the role of faculty as distinct from administration has come under scrutiny, and the issue of faculty identity is surfacing at several theologates. Schools seem to pass through stages of development regarding faculty involvement with administrative tasks and committees. Whereas some schools have virtually no committee structure, others have begun to add a few committees, and still others have a large number of them. Some schools are now in the process of paring down the number of committees by streamlining and combining their functions. After extensive experimentation, a better evaluation of activities that are appropriate to faculty on the one hand and administrators on the other is beginning to emerge.

Issues for the future: It will become increasingly difficult to recruit the kind of faculty that is often perceived as needed by the schools, that is, persons with preparation in personal and spiritual formation and with an academic degree in theology. The question of what preparation faculty who are priests should have is often raised. Not everyone can do everything, and distinctively different qualities and qualifications are required for the two functions of personal-spiritual formation and teaching. Priests who can successfully combine scholarly work and formation are not easy to find.

As the number of diocesan priests declines, there will be fewer priests serving as role models. Already many faculty members reject the notion that role models are important at this stage in the life of seminarians. They believe that during the years of theology seminarians should develop their capacity for critical self-reflection, and should take responsibility for their own judgments and decisions. One priest suggested that the role-modeling issue is misplaced in the seminary; real role-modeling occurs before a candidate decides to enter the seminary. Professors may be scholarly eccentrics who perform their academic function effectively, but at the same time they may not provide an ideal or even adequate role model. "Should they be barred from teaching on that account?" this respondent asked. Another person summed up the issue this way: "People will be trained academically, but as role models for priestly formation they may be lacking a sense of priestly spirituality and identity. How can we discover ways to forestall this?"

Inability to hire and retain a competent faculty, and consequently to provide a sound academic program, is the major reason why some schools are presently considering either merging or closing, according to the report of a person who is in contact with virtually all schools that are facing the possibility of closing or have recently closed. "An overall shortage of personnel who are able to teach and do formation work is the number one difficulty in this decade for our theological seminaries," he stated.

Concerning involvement of faculty in administrative tasks, the consensus of faculty is that they do not want to discontinue committee work, other administrative tasks, or formation responsibilities. Rather, they believe, these tasks need to be balanced with the central role of teaching. The goal expressed by many, and summarized by one faculty member, is "to maintain enough involvement in the operation of the school so that faculty are not separated and alienated from setting the direction and creating the vision for the school."

On the basis of discussions about the role of faculty that I heard during interviews, I propose that models be developed for different types of faculty positions, so that the proportion of time designated for teaching, research, formation, and other kinds of services could be indicated when new faculty are hired. By allowing some choice regarding how different members of the faculty will serve, the possibility of attracting capable individuals with varied interests will increase. In general the role of faculty is still evolving in theologates, and new ways of designing their services should be explored.

Administrators and faculty are faced with the task of clarifying faculty identity, while at the same time preserving the integrity of the school as a working whole. Most seminaries are so small that they may need to have the whole corps of personnel working cooperatively. In practice, faculty and administrators seem to relate effectively, even though the relationship is quite often described as strained, and faculty tend to see themselves as over against administration. With the growing complexity of administration, more differentiation may be inevitable. Warding off the negative consequences of such differentiation is a worthy goal for both faculty and administration.

Both administrators and faculty reflected on how to guarantee quality in the effort to maintain the generally high level of teaching competence. A degree in theology does not ensure that the recipient is suited to teach on a theologate faculty. Schools will have to determine more specifically the responsibilities of each faculty position, and then seek to recruit persons accordingly.

3. HIRING

Present reality: In the past, most theologates had little difficulty in hiring faculty for most disciplines. This situation is changing, however, and even though it is easier to find faculty for some positions than others, extensive searches are needed to hire new faculty. The positions most readily filled are in Scripture and church history, and in some branches of systematic theology. Many schools mentioned great difficulty in finding teachers of moral theology and pastoral theology, including preaching but especially pastoral counseling. Individuals with a knowledge of Hispanic ministry, particularly those of Hispanic background, are in very short supply. Several outstanding representatives of this group stated in interviews that they are called upon constantly to articulate the needs of the Hispanic community. As the Hispanic population grows, faculty who understand how to teach others to minister in Hispanic parishes will be in great demand.

At many theologates considerable effort is given to careful hiring. Because these schools seek a large pool of candidates for most positions, the person who is finally hired is usually better suited to the job. This hiring procedure contrasts with instances in which minimal time and effort is put into the process, so that the final selection is made from a small pool of candidates. Those responsible for hiring cite as their most important criterion the potential faculty member's enthusiastic agreement with the mission of the school.

Several schools are electing to have more women on their faculties, in some cases because of special competencies that they bring, and in others because no priest is available for the position. At the same time, some women who are currently teaching in theologates speak about resigning because of the perceived problems of working within a hierarchical model where they are not regarded as equals, especially in the area of spiritual formation. This issue has been greatly exacerbated as a result of the visitations to theologates mandated by Pope John Paul II. Dissatisfaction about the situation of women in theologates is expressed not only or even primarily by the women involved, but rather by other faculty who oppose what they perceive as inequitable treatment based on a preference for clerical over lay status. During the past two or three years, the effects of what are widely perceived as unjust policies toward women have already reduced the number of women working in theologates.

Issues for the future: Given changes in the Church, such as the steadily decreasing number of seminarians and the increasing need for priests, and changes in theologates, such as demands on faculty who must fulfill several roles and an unwelcoming attitude toward lay faculty, there is widespread concern about where faculty will come from in the future. It seems obvious that a smaller number of priests will be available, both diocesan and religious. Among young priests who potentially could teach in theologates, many prefer other ministries and do not want to be involved with the seminary system. Some who currently work in seminaries feel that the climate is difficult because of the internal tensions in the Church at this time. All these factors point to a reduced number of potential faculty members.

Various external forces, especially decisions by religious communities, and bishops, have an impact on faculty quality, continuity, and composition. Since faculty are so vital to the future direction and vision of the schools, it is crucial to know who will be eligible and available for appointment to faculty positions. Many faculty and administrators believe that they could be effectively excluded from hiring decisions if appointments are made by ordinaries, or if so few potential faculty are available that there is almost no choice among candidates. Clearly stated and well-developed policies about hiring and terminating faculty should be adopted. Carefully delineated grievance procedures are also need by most schools for the protection of both the institution and the individual.

4. SCHOLARSHIP

Present reality: At six or seven institutions, research and writing are given high priority. Faculty teaching loads at these schools are usually lighter—two courses per semester rather than three. Potential faculty members compete strenuously for positions at these institutions and, if hired, are expected to publish regularly. Such faculty are engaged in major research efforts in theology, and offer the valuable perspective of those who combine academic theology with an understanding of ministry. These settings would be desirable for more-established theologians than can currently be recruited, if money were available to hire them. But few schools have the endowed chairs or other funds that would make that possible. Consequently, many prominent Catholic theologians are being attracted to Catholic graduate schools and to secular universities, where salaries and benefits are considerably better.

Apart from the few schools where publishing and writing are expected, scholarship in the theologates is extremely limited, and faculty feel overwhelmed with the multiple tasks they are asked to perform. The problem is especially acute for those who live in self-contained seminaries, where duties tend to be comprehensive and time-consuming, leaving little energy for scholarship. Many regret the lack of time for research and writing, because they realize that these activities have positive effects on teaching. The large number of highly qualified faculty who are pastorally sensitive tend to devote their time to pastoral work. Motivation for doing scholarly work is often low; the tangible rewards are almost nonexistent, funding for sabbaticals is usually not available, and there is little expectation at most schools that scholarly writing will be done.

Issues for the future: The long-term effect of burdening faculty members with multiple tasks is that the interest in and potential for scholarship will continue to decline. The thoughts of many interviewees are summarized in the words of one priest: "If the present trend continues, it will be necessary to go to a secular university to find good 'published' Catholic theologians." A recent survey documents this alarming trend at both Protestant and Catholic seminaries. The survey shows that a decreasing proportion of articles in scholarly journals is being published by theologians on seminary faculties as compared with those on university faculties. Recent controversy concerning the role of theologians and the issue of dissent adds another unknown to the future of scholarship in the Catholic seminary. This situation will affect, in particular, writing on sexual ethics and certain aspects of ministry. A commonly expressed sentiment was that "we should not expect scholarship from seminary professors in the future, in part because the Church tends to give people multiple tasks under one label, leaving little time for study, but even more because of fear of publishing on controversial topics."

5. MORALE

Present reality: Morale among faculty varies considerably from place to place and probably from time to time. In many schools the feeling of camaraderie is high, and a strong sense of mutual respect is present. Most faculty mentioned positive relationships with students as their main source of satisfaction. Many spoke of the rewards of teaching in a seminary setting. Those who teach a diverse student body were especially emphatic in identifying teaching as their greatest morale booster; they further specified the opportunity to meet and influence people from all over the world who will minister in many varied situations in the future.

Another source of satisfaction to faculty members is the personal and professional interaction they enjoy with their colleagues. This interaction could be further enhanced, they feel, by events such as luncheon seminars for discussion of ongoing research combined with an opportunity to socialize, and other planned occasions for participating in professional development.

Some faculty were concerned, however, about the quality and number of students at their schools and even their schools' survival. The possibility that their schools might close overwhelms them at times. An equally important concern was fear of losing academic freedom and the ability to exercise the ministry of teaching in a way that is consonant with their beliefs; this concern included the prospect of being required to use specific texts.

Issues for the future: Administrators will need to take more responsibility for facilitating ongoing professional development for their faculties. High morale may be more difficult to maintain in the light of heavy demands, less perceived prestige, disagreements about the direction of programs, and confusion about ecclesiological questions. As formulated by one astute observer of theologates, the issues are, Who is discussing the cumulative effects of the morale questions relative to overwork, dissent, tenure, and job satisfaction? Should some policies be recommended at a level beyond the local theologate?

6. RETENTION AND TURNOVER

Present reality: The rate of faculty turnover differs considerably from place to place. Too much turnover can have negative repercussions, since programs never have a chance to stabilize and teaching methods become eclectic and lack integration. Roughly one-third of the faculties expressed serious concern about too much turnover. When as many as one-third of a faculty changes every year, program continuity is difficult to maintain. About half of the schools were satisfied with the length of service of their faculties, and only a few believed that too little turnover was a problem.

A small number of schools have clearly articulated policies relating to both rank and tenure. Seventeen schools do not differentiate faculty by rank, and very few have tenure. According to a deans' report in one region, resistance to tenure is based on the view that it is not necessary and, in some cases, might even create dissension. Some schools have not instituted tenure because of financial and programmatic implications. Changes could be costly, and a tenure policy reduces flexibility in terms of hiring future faculty.

Other faculty and administrators noted the advantages of a tenure policy, remarking that it can generate a sense of affirmation and promote stability in a rapidly changing situation. One experienced faculty member who supports tenure said: "A good retention and turnover policy can strengthen faculty—for example, when tenured, a person feels he/she truly belongs—and it can force a school to evaluate faculty more carefully and get rid of 'dead wood' early. Otherwise mediocre people can stay on for a long time without the issue being forced." An intermediate solution adopted by some schools is to have term contracts for a period of three to five years, after which the faculty member is reviewed and a decision about continuation is made.

Issues for the future: To retain able faculty members, schools will have to work toward providing a better reward system, which may include a rank and tenure program as well as adequate benefits. Concurrently, an effective evaluation process must be put in place to determine the recipients of these rewards. In close communities such as exist among most theologate faculties, evaluation is rarely undertaken with vigor. Objective evaluation is inhibited by the fear both of losing members who would be vulnerable to a critique and of risking personal relationships through critical comments. The result is that highly competent faculty experience little institutional affirmation, and those with inadequacies continue without challenge or improvement.

A particular concern regarding the retention and turnover of able nonordained faculty members was raised by a significant number of those interviewed: If the role of nonordained faculty becomes more constricted, especially in spiritual formation, some administrators fear that they will choose not to remain in a two-tiered system. In that case a crisis could ensue, given the diminishing number of priests available for seminary work. The questions often asked were, What is the future of those who are not priests on seminary faculties? What effect will the exclusion of the nonordained from spiritual formation have on the mission of the church in general in the United States? These questions have no immediate and obvious answers, but the long-term implications of a dwindling supply of faculty are serious.

It is generally projected that the rate of faculty turnover will continue to be high at about ten schools where this problem has recurred year after year. At some fifteen other schools, administrators are expecting an increase in turnover. Religious communities and dioceses find themselves forced to recall good faculty for "their own ministries," which range from administrative to parochial assignments that require the special expertise often possessed by well educated faculty members. Sometimes other ministries are viewed as more important. As one seasoned participant in the seminary world observed: "With a low respect for theological learning in the U.S. Church, there is too often little sense of a theological seminary as a theological resource for the Church. The approach remains consistently that of a purchase of services, not a valued ministry. Greatness does not flow from this. It is at most a pedestrian practical approach."

C. STUDENTS

OVERVIEW STATEMENTS

Considerable differences in opinion were expressed about the overall quality of students—their academic ability, personal maturity, and suitability for ministry. About half of the respondents believes students are as qualified as ever, while the other half believes they are less qualified.

Students studying in theologates today compared with twenty years ago are about five years older, their values are negatively affected by the environments from which they come, and their backgrounds lack a fundamental understanding of the Catholic faith.

The perception of a majority of those interviewed suggests that a conscious choice of celibacy is central to the commitment of about half of the seminarians; in light of the broad concern about sexual issues, formation directors are providing programs to help students understand their responsibility to live a chaste and celibate life.

Student attitudes toward social justice suggest diminished interest in serving the poor and marginalized members of the Church.

Considerable differences in opinion were expressed about the overall quality of students—their academic ability, personal maturity, and suitability for ministry.

Many faculty believe that the same proportion of "excellent students" no longer enters seminaries as did fifteen or twenty years ago, the time at which many faculty members were in seminary. "The top has been cut off," was a common judgment.

The need for careful selection and high standards of admission is crucial in view of the pressure to accept unqualified candidates that is exerted by the decreasing number of applicants.

The ministry goals of many students focus on their desire to work in situations with individuals, but the needs of the Church are more often calling for group leadership and administrative skills. An individual's wish to minister in a particular way is sometimes inconsistent with the needs of parishes and other ministry settings.

In contrast to the nearly all-seminarian composition of student bodies twenty years ago, student bodies are currently composed of

about 60-percent seminarians and 40-percent women religious and lay students. Integration of the two groups varies; women religious and lay students feel fully included in some cases but only nominally so in others.

Transition from a relatively structured and enclosed seminary to active ministry is often difficult, and new ways of facilitating the change are being explored.

INTRODUCTION

In the 1980s more research on seminarians who are currently preparing for priesthood is being done than on any other aspect of theologates. Comprehensive self-reported data, based on questionnaires sent to all seminarians, are available in three published works: *Seminarians in Theology* (1986), and *Seminary Life and Visions of the Priesthood* (1987), both by Eugene F. Hemrick and Dean R. Hoge; and *Seminarians of the Eighties* (1985), by Raymond H. Potvin. These studies are concerned with the backgrounds and characteristics of seminarians; they give no comparable data for students enrolled in theologates who are not preparing for priesthood. Another recent study, *An Academic Profile of Catholic Seminaries* (1987), by Bernard J. Rosinski, S.C.J., provides initial information about the academic backgrounds of all students in theologates, including some who are not seminarians.

In this chapter, the data from these recent studies is supplemented with several other sources of information. Among the latter are the findings from interviews with over one hundred students, informal interaction with hundreds of other students, and interviews with three hundred faculty and administrators who offered their perceptions of students. In addition, 229 vocation directors responded in the spring of 1986 to a questionnaire that requested information about vocations, the screening of candidates, and the selection of theologates for candidates. With all of this information, a fairly complete profile of students emerges.

It is advantageous, we believe, to be aware of the characteristics of those enrolled in theologates so that environments and programs can be adapted to their needs. In other words, their backgrounds should influence the type of formation that is offered. Attitudes and perceptions about students on the part of faculty and administrators affect both the way faculty and administrators work with students and how programs are structured. If students are regarded as mature and capable, a different living situation and formation program will be designed for them than would be if they were considered immature and unprepared for an adult experience of graduate theology. The composite profile of students that is presented here can assist in determining their formational requirements during theological studies.

1. BACKGROUND AND PROFILE OF CURRENT STUDENTS

Present reality: In recent years, between 1985 and 1988, just under 4,000 seminarians were enrolled full time in theologates, along with approximately 2,500 other full-time and over 500 part-time students. From the detailed information compiled about seminarians, we know that on the average they are about thirty years of age, almost five years older than seminarians of the late 1960s. The average age of other students (women religious and lay women and men) is thought to be about the same, though their age distribution is slightly different, that is, proportionally more are slightly older and more are slightly younger than seminarians.[1] The personal and spiritual values of students entering theologates reflect those of contemporary society, and are sometimes in conflict with the values traditionally considered desirable for future priests and other professional Church ministers to have. Since most current students were born after 1955, few have a lived sense of the pre-Vatican II Church, a factor that may contribute to what faculty characterize as "neo-conservatism." Further, compared with twenty years ago, surveys show that fewer seminarians have studied at Catholic institutions at any level; thus they lack fundamental knowledge about the Catholic faith. These factors, which are described in more detail below, point to the need for careful selection, high standards of admission, and a pretheology program or comparable preparation for some. Whereas

---

[1] These perceptions are confirmed in part by Ellis L. Larsen and James M. Shopshire in *A Profile of Contemporary Seminarians*, 10-34.

students enrolled in theology who are not seminarians share many of the traits of their counterparts, they often exhibit fewer conservative tendencies, and this difference frequently becomes a source of tension when the student body is mixed.

Family Background and Social Context: The survey of seminarians reported in *Seminarians in Theology* (p. 77) shows that they continue to come from families representing traditional structures, 75.2 percent have two parents living and residing together, one or both parents of 18.6 percent are deceased, and only 6.2 percent have parents who are separated or divorced. Yet our interviews with students show that their families otherwise reflect the less stable conditions of contemporary society. For example, the occurrence of alcoholism is reported to be high, and stress over job security and finances is prevalent. Although very few incidents of drug addiction were mentioned, many formation directors and some students observed that a small percentage of students are known to have experimented with drugs. Formation directors also noted changes in the ways families interact: Since families spend less time together, limited opportunities for growth in interpersonal relationships are available. This pattern, they believe, results in lack of self-confidence and diminished ability to function effectively in groups. They also observed that seminarians from more fluid family environments are likely to view lifelong commitment as negotiable.

Compounding the difficulties of somewhat unstable family systems, the social fabric of this country has also contributed to changes in the backgrounds of seminarians. Since the early 1970s, certain American cultural trends have had a considerable impact, for example, greater mobility causing lack of rootedness, emphasis on materialism and individualism, delayed vocational commitment among young people, and the privatization of religion. Theological education is in many ways affected by such cultural trends, and those responsible for preparing individuals for ministry find that they must shape their programs to counteract some of these negative influences.

Age and Personal Maturity: Hemrick and Hoge's study *Seminary Life* (p. 11) indicates that the median age of students preparing for ordination and enrolled in theologates in 1986 was 29.95, as compared with 25.20 in 1966, an average of nearly five additional years. The same study (p. 11) also gives the percentages of students from different age groups at different years:

Age	1966 (%)	1984 (%)	1986 (%)
20 to 25	72	36	36
26 to 30	20	34	31
31 and older	7	30	33

The changes that have occurred over this twenty-year period are highly significant, especially in the youngest and oldest groups. The proportion of those aged between twenty and twenty-five decreased by exactly half from 1966 to 1986, and during the same period those thirty-one and older increased almost fivefold, from 7 to 33 percent. Moreover, in 1966 no seminarian was over fifty, but now 4 percent of all seminarians (about 160) are over fifty. The middle group increased less substantially, by about 10 percent. The range of ages enhances the dissimilarity of backgrounds to which formation programs must adapt.

Of interest as well is the difference in ages of religious and diocesan seminarians. In *Seminarians in Theology* (p. 30) Hemrick and Hoge report that in 1984 the median ages of the two groups were respectively 30.7 and 29.1, a span of nearly two years. The percentage differences between the two groups are even more pronounced:

Age	Diocesan Seminarians (%)	Religious Seminarians (%)
20 to 25	42	20
26 to 30	31	41
Over 30	27	39

Religious order seminarians aged twenty to twenty-five number less than half of diocesan seminarians in the same age group. This phenomenon exists in large part because religious seminarians precede theological studies with a year or two of novitiate and often some ministerial experience. In the other two age-group categories, there are about 10 percent more religious than diocesan seminarians. Among those in the over-thirty group, however, the 4 percent who are over fifty are mostly preparing for diocesan priesthood. Religious orders have been reluctant to accept candidates who are over fifty, so the increase in age of their candidates can be attributed to the fact that students across the board are a few years older.

Concern about older candidates was highlighted in Cardinal William Baum's 1986 report on freestanding seminaries, which makes the following statement: "There is sometimes the mistaken presumption that simply because a man is older he is necessarily more mature. We have advised a number of seminaries to be alert to what has been called the mid-life crisis, to the motives of older candidates, and to their special circumstances." These older men are accustomed to independence and have often established set patterns of behavior, which raises questions about whether they are flexible enough to change their life-styles in the process of formation. Some formation personnel view older students quite positively, however, noting that they are often more mature, able to be outgoing and compassionate, and more serious about their futures. Those in religious orders may come with international mission and ministerial experience, and most older candidates have considerable social and business experience. Faculty and formation personnel observed that their participation in classes and activities improves the quality of discussion and interaction.

The comparative findings reported in *Seminarians of the Eighties* (pp. 5-17) indicate many signs of personal maturity among current seminarians: Fewer are indecisive, report discomfort with superiors, feel interpersonal inadequacy, or admit symptoms of psychopathology. They enjoy higher morale and appear better adjusted than their counterparts in 1966. This positive profile was generally supported by our research. Certainly the perceptions of faculty and formation directors suggest that students now are more "streetwise," more aware of their sexuality, less threatened by authority, and have manifestly higher morale than students twenty years ago. Many of those interviewed asserted that present-day students are as mature, intelligent, and well intentioned as students have ever been. Respondents described them as quite stable, responsible, and highly motivated, as well as hardworking and sincere. Though adolescence often starts earlier and ends later, the basic personality profiles have remained about the same, they affirmed.

A significant minority of theologate personnel believes that this positive assessment must be qualified. They reported a decidedly low level of confidence in many students, despite an honest desire to do good for the Church. They also noted a lack of academic and pastoral zeal, commenting that more students seem passive, dependent, and less able to deal with ambiguity than before. As Potvin suggests, such inadequacy may result from an overprotective mother, from lower achievement scores, or from a host of other factors relating to development. We found that the perception of interpersonal competence overpredicts the reality as perceived by formation directors. What students sometimes view as interpersonal competence, others describe as a tendency to form protective partnerships characterized more by dependence than by freedom. Although there are differences in perception about personal and human development, it was agreed that these areas need more attention, especially the development of self-confidence and relational skills.

Religious and Educational Background: Since most seminarians today were born after 1955, they have experienced far less "Catholic culture" from which to derive an understanding of traditions and norms. One of the reasons for this is that the extent of previous education in Catholic schools has decreased substantially; 95 percent of seminarians in 1966 had received all their college education at a Catholic institution, compared with only 56 percent of seminarians today. Only 25 percent of the latter attended college seminary for four years. The absence of Catholic elementary and high school backgrounds is even more prevalent; less than half of current seminarians received all their early education in Catholic schools, compared with 70 to 80 percent in 1966 (*Seminaries of the Eighties*, p. 10). The decline in Catholic education has resulted in limited exposure to a Catholic tradition that in previous years could be taken for granted. The cultural and spiritual Catholic heritage as perceived by students may manifest itself in traditional forms, including stylized and ritualized manners that are without substantive symbolic meaning.

Faculty are looking for ways to supply the composite Catholic culture that was previously learned and experienced over many years through dogma, doctrine, ritual, and practice. They find that they need to adjust both the content and methodology of their courses to meet the needs of students, while at the same time challenging them to move beyond the stereotypes of their time and culture. Several faculty report that they have resorted to protracted or remedial formational and academic programs in order to "get a student through." Students, for their part, prefer consolidation and clarity to analysis and critique in their studies, and they are disturbed by faculty in dialogue about the tradition of the Church. For most students today, Vatican II is a historical event rather than part of their experience; thus their understanding of ecclesiology is very different from that of previous students and of faculty who grew up in the pre-Vatican II Church.

In our study, faculty cited an increasing tendency toward the pious external practices of faith that characterized the 1950s more than the immediate post-Vatican II years. Respondents commented that present-day students are quite conservative liturgically and show more interest in habits, vestments, Church paraphernalia, traditional music, and devotions. Among some younger candidates, an increasingly reactionary stance toward moderate views on authority and liturgical law has appeared. Some students feel it is their responsibility to hold in check both faculty and other students with regard to ritual, dogma, and ecclesiastical prescriptions.

We observed that the tendency to embrace the more hieratic dimensions of office and priestly roles is curiously juxtaposed to a small but vocal group that fosters justice and social awareness with the same degree of passion. The former group would contend that they champion the orthodoxy of the gospel, while the latter, represented more often by religious order seminarians, is equally convinced that the orientation toward societal issues is the correct one. At theologates where sizable groups of each persuasion are found, considerable energy is spent in promoting one or the other viewpoint, much to the detriment of maintaining a collaborative environment.

Church Authority and Moral Values: Most of those interviewed affirmed that students seem loyal to the Church, and desire to grow in their knowledge of Church teachings and in their life of faith. Although they tend not to be confrontational about Church issues in classroom settings, in other contexts they question the validity of certain positions taken by the Church and are selective in their acceptance of ecclesial authority on moral questions. The result is cognitive dissonance, the state that arises when moral beliefs and moral actions are not integrated. Formation personnel believe that overly restrictive environments intensify this effect. "Students who fear authority put undesirable behavior on hold until they are ordained," they said; and then it is too late to confront behaviors and beliefs in a developmental environment.

At more progressive theologates where traditional students are in the minority and at more conservative theologates where liberal students are in the minority, such students acknowledged that they tend to keep their views to themselves until after ordination. The words of one seminarian speak for more than a few students: "The message is to play the role until you are ordained, and then you can really express what you believe." The life-style of the seminary and the private beliefs of individual seminarians are sometimes in conflict. "There are times when one must obey one's own conscience rather than the teachings of the Church," was an attitude expressed often. Faculty repeatedly remarked that in the lives of seminarians there is a complex interaction between liberal and conservative views, between personal conscience and objective morality, and between existentialism and essentialism.

Attitudes toward Priesthood and Celibacy: Considerable data on the attitudes of seminarians toward priesthood and celibacy have been made available through recent surveys. In *Seminarians of the Eighties* (pp. 31-42), Potvin compares the attitudes of seminarians in 1966 and 1986 with those of young priests in 1970. Among seminarians today, celibacy appears to be more clearly understood and valued rather than merely endured, and priesthood is seen more as a lifelong and full-time commitment. Whereas a part-time priesthood was considered acceptable by 79 percent of young priests in 1970, today only 27 percent of seminarians see it that way. Likewise, today only 50 percent would accept resignation from priesthood as a wise and mature choice in many cases, whereas 71 percent would have seen it that way in 1970. Although papal pronouncements declare that women cannot be ordained, 54 percent of all seminarians believe that ordination of women should be an option, compared with 47 percent of the Catholic population. This question was not asked of seminarians in 1966 or of young priests in 1970.

According to Potvin's findings (pp. 36-38), the proportion of those who believe that celibacy is meaningful increased from 54 percent in 1966 to 63 percent in 1984. Today 58 percent say they would not marry even if allowed to, compared with only 40 percent in 1966. The view that diocesan priests should take a vow of celibacy was expressed by 44 percent in 1984, and the view that religious should do so by 70 percent. For diocesan seminarians, celibacy is more important than religious perceive it to be in the lives of diocesan priests. These expressions of stronger commitment to celibacy stand in contrast to the responses in the survey of vocation directors, who consider willingness to be celibate on the part of candidates a low priority.

The sexual values and sexual behavior of students is of concern to faculty and formation personnel, with reference to both homosexuality and heterosexuality. In formation programs considerably more instruction is given on sexuality and on the obligation of priests to live a chaste and celibate life than in previous years. Extensive publicity about the sexual misconduct of a few priests and growing concern about legal implications have changed the attitudes of many about the necessity of careful formation in this area. In relation to both homosexual and heterosexual behavior, consideration must be given to appropriate boundaries within the role context of the priesthood. The discrepancy between public commitment to celibacy and private behavior that is not in keeping with the vow is being challenged.[2] Only a few theologate leaders believe that sexuality and celibacy are not problematic issues; most believe that the questions surrounding these issues are of grave concern for the Church. Open discussion is encouraged as a means of helping students to integrate their sexuality with their ministerial life. Many of those interviewed stated that reluctance to discuss sexual matters can no longer be tolerated, and formation directors believe that in this respect attitudes have changed significantly. Their goal, they explained, is to prepare ministers who have chosen celibacy out of a desire for that way of life, and unless seminarians understand the meaning and purpose of celibacy they will not be able to live out a commitment to it.

---

[2]A discrepancy between belief and actions is called cognitive dissonance. This theory is based on the assumption that individuals attempt to live in a balanced state of consonance. Discrepant cognitions create tensions that the individual will attempt to reduce. Attitudes are inferred from behavior: "I did this; therefore, I must believe in it." Dissonance is generally resolved by altering beliefs to correspond to actions rather than by altering actions to correspond to beliefs. For example, the celibate student who finds himself sexually involved with someone will say, "I did this; therefore, either I don't believe in celibacy or I believe that celibacy allows for sexual experimentation." In the former statement ("I don't believe in celibacy") there is consistency between his actions and beliefs. In the latter, he changes his attitude to correspond to his behavior. This experience of cognitive dissonance can lead to increasing personal and social deception, rationalization, scripted living, and moral renunciation.

Students preparing for ordination tend to reflect society in its more conservative stance on religion and social issues, but not on sexual and personal morality. Although Potvin observed that students in 1984 had fewer problems with authority figures, we perceive that this is true only within a limited framework. Students selectively moderate the influence of ecclesial authority. With respect to issues of sexual orientation, alcoholism, and the honest revelation of personal needs, many students remain unconvinced that they will not be expelled for revealing such matters or, alternatively, that revealing them will be helpful in dealing with the issues, since many "authorities" are themselves unable to discuss such problems.

Concerning social justice, faculty and administrators' appraisals of students are mixed. About half of those interviewed believe that students are less concerned about the problems, needs, and anxieties of people in American society, and more concerned about their individual ministries and their own well-being. The other half believe there is a growing awareness among students of the role the Church must play to alleviate social injustice and inequity. The commitment of the latter group to social justice is perceived as more thoughtful than the progressive stances of the 1960s. Especially among religious order theologates, considerable energy and time are put into work for the needy and those who are on the margins of society.

Many students are deeply concerned about the role of women in the Church, but others are threatened by the emergence of women's issues. About half of the seminarians we interviewed expressed a growing sense of distress about women being excluded from ordained ministry and other liturgical roles in the Church. Faculty also reported this feeling among many students; in their opinion the exclusion of women causes some seminarians to leave theologates and other potential candidates not to consider priesthood. On the other hand, faculty stated that up to one-third of their students have little desire to work collaboratively with women in ministry.

Academic Backgrounds of Students: Until recently, comprehensive information about the academic status of students in theology was lacking. But in 1987 *An Academic Profile of Catholic Seminaries*, by Bernard Rosinski, S.C.J., was published, providing base data that will prove invaluable for future comparisons. Rosinski's findings reveal that 95.2 percent of students in theologates are college graduates with an average grade point average of 3.11 (B). His research also shows that, on the average, seminarians took thirteen hours in religious studies or theology before beginning graduate theological studies; 75.5 percent of seminarians and 40.6 percent of other students took twelve or more hours. Twelve hours are prescribed in the *PPF*.

Greater importance is accorded the study of philosophy. The *PPF* states that if a student's undergraduate field of concentration is other than philosophy, "their pretheological studies must include the equivalent of two years of studies of a particularly philosophical nature" (#416), and that "the intended purpose of introducing philosophy into the curriculum cannot reasonably be fulfilled in less than eighteen semester hours of strictly philosophical study" (#417). Seminarians took an average of nineteen hours in philosophy, but only 71.1 percent took the prescribed eighteen hours or more. The philosophy background of students other than seminarians was less adequate, with only 18.7 percent having taken eighteen hours or more.

Yet the majority of faculty respondents observed little difference in classroom performance between those who had more background in philosophy and those who had less. As one faculty member explained: "Having taken courses does not assure that students will be able to think philosophically or apply previous course work to theology. Some individuals who have little background but more natural ability in this area often exhibit greater understanding." Faculty also noted that seminarians who had taken all their philosophy in one year in a pretheology program seldom absorbed as much as those who had taken it over a period of years. Such concentrated study does not always enable students to conceptualize in philosophical terms, and therefore is not especially helpful for the study of theology.

In situations where both ordination candidates and other students are studying together, it is nearly unanimously agreed that the quality of nonordination students equals and often surpasses the quality of ordination students. Faculty consistently remarked that the level and quality of interaction in classes has improved with the addition of lay students and women religious. Yet others expressed a preference for the exclusive presence of ordination candidates, because it then becomes possible to focus more intensively on questions related to priesthood.

The consensus of faculty who were interviewed is that the overall academic quality of students preparing for ordination is somewhat lower than previously, but they also pointed out that within a student body the range of talent is wide. Faculty who teach religious order seminarians, for example, maintained that their students are more academically oriented now than in the recent past even though they have less adequate background in philosophy, languages, and basic doctrine. Others portrayed the change in academic ability as "the top being cut off," meaning that the quality of most students remains about the same but the top 5 to 10 percent of the students of ten years ago is missing from the profile. Yet a significant minority believe that students have changed little over the past twenty years.

In our research we found a high degree of satisfaction among students with the way courses are taught, with faculty competence, and with overall intellectual standards in the schools. However, the later study by Hemrick and Hoge shows that only half (51 percent) of the students surveyed there consider course work to be of "high importance" in their total formation program.[3] The much higher ratings for spiritual formation (76 percent) and pastoral field experience (64 percent) suggest some discrepancy with the apparently high evaluation of courses given by our respondents. While our research does not contradict Hemrick and Hoge's findings, it does highlight a question raised frequently by faculty, and to a lesser extent by students: Does the particular set of courses now required effectively prepare students for ministry in the Church in the late twentieth century? Many faculty believe that some changes are needed. For example, they feel that present curricula do not deal adequately with the need for evangelization or for serving the Hispanic community and the elderly. Many faculty noted the absence of courses that consider ministry in a collaborative context, or that deal with conflict resolution or methods of working with groups. These shortcomings may signal part of the reason for the quite moderate importance that students attach to course work as preparation for ministry.

Summary: The responses of faculty and administrators represent a continuum of judgments about the quality of students. Whether those who are enrolled in theologates in the 1980s possess abilities that are adequate to the demands of future ministry is a topic that

---

[3] *Seminary Life and Visions of the Priesthood*, p. 15.

has generated considerable discussion and debate in many quarters. Ordinaries and vocation directors, as well as faculty and administrators in theologates, diverged in their responses to two questions regarding present students: What are the appropriate criteria to be used when assessing students, and what is the actual quality of students? Depending on the particular emphasis of those making the judgments, opinions about the extent of personal, spiritual, and intellectual development among students varied. Some, for example, are more concerned with personal piety and so are not disturbed when students exhibit minimal academic potential. Others who believe that intellectual capability is basic to professional ministry, look first for measures of academic achievement. Emotional maturity might be seen by yet others as the key ingredient.

Regardless of the order of criteria, ambivalence about students characterized the responses of those interviewed. They typically reported that while students today possess many positive qualities, certain negative qualities are also prevalent. Attitudes ranged from defensiveness on behalf of students to extreme criticism of them. The consensus of opinion is that students are different from, but not necessarily better or worse than, their counterparts in previous years. Much of the self-reported data in the studies cited above is more positive, however, and the same observation can be made about the results of the academic profile. The societal and family context from which students come, their age and level of maturity, and their previous educational and religious backgrounds all affect their approach to theological education and to future ministry.

Issues for the future: Student populations will be increasingly heterogeneous—by culture, age, family complexity, and personal-relational competence. Formation programs will be required to address individual needs regarding personal and spiritual development, academic and pastoral preparation, group dynamics, and cultural diversity.

Multifaceted programs that offer these dissimilar students some measure of stability will have to be maintained. Individualized programming is needed in some instances to provide more awareness of societal and cultural trends, knowledge about various forms of addiction, and assistance in dealing with the complex dynamics of interpersonal relationships. One of the most difficult areas in formation is how to manage personal relationships, especially in relation to a homosexual orientation and appropriate boundaries within the role context of the priesthood. More attention is expected to be focused on the development of human and relational skills, for example, by designing living units that focus more on the quality of interpersonal relationships, like the one at Mundelein Seminary.

A second concern is associated with celibacy. Though the official discipline of the Church seems unwavering in this regard, many individuals privately believe that the Church will change and permit a married clergy when the number of priests drops even lower. Opinions differ as to whether a married clergy of men only or the addition of celibate women clergy will come about first, but the belief that some change will occur is pervasive. This belief is reinforced by the fact that some Episcopalian priests who are married have been admitted to Roman Catholic priesthood. All of this contributes to complications for formation directors, who are charged with the responsibility of instructing men in the discipline of celibacy.

Continuing attention will have to be focused on the religious and educational backgrounds of students, since fewer and fewer grew up in a context where participation in church activities was central to their families and friends. In view of the fact that students do not share the same background, respondents asked if there is some way to supply the composite Catholic culture that comes from years of learning dogma and experiencing ritual.

Formation faculty also questioned the motivation of some priesthood candidates. Although students appear to desire to serve the Church, there is concern about the self-interest that dominates the drives of some men toward priesthood. The reasons why candidates choose priesthood is an matter of enormous concern, and careful selection procedures must be employed to ensure that the vocational call is understood as a call to service.

In light of the now older student body, teaching methods need to be reevaluated and thought given to developing an adult learning model, incorporating experiential learning. The assessment of older candidates must be done carefully, since they bring so much history to this final stage of preparation for priesthood. Last but not least, specialized programs and training for the considerably older student seem desirable.

2. SCREENING AND ADMISSION OF STUDENTS

Present reality: A review of the admissions policies and procedures of the fifty theologates included in this report shows considerable variation in requirements for enrollment. Some of this variation can be explained by the range of students who enroll; diocesan candidates, lay students, and members of religious communities are subject to different admissions requirements even when they apply to the same theologate. Ecclesiastical documentation is not required of those who will not be ordained, nor are they in most cases expected to present psychological reports. Academic standards are usually the same, and letters of reference are required for all, but the sources specified for the recommendations differ. The type of school also affects policies; thus freestanding theologates differ in their requirements from university-related and collaborative schools. Not only is different information required for admission by different types of schools, but institutional policies and procedures are not uniformly and comprehensively stated in the documents of most theologates.

The requirements for admission listed in catalog and policy statements vary from minimal to extensive, but generally they fall into three clearly identifiable categories. The first area concerns spiritual and personal background, including ecclesiastical documentation— a baptismal certificate, confirmation certificate, and parents' marriage certificate; the approval of an ordinary; psychological tests; a health examination; and a statement written by the applicant. The second area relates to academic background, including college and graduate degrees, transcripts, and grade point averages; educational testing; and specific area prerequisites such as philosophy, theology or religious studies, and English proficiency. The third area concerns other information, including letters of reference, signed statements of intent, Armed Services discharge papers, and photographs. Personal interviews might also be compulsory, but in many cases because of distance the interview is optional.

Some admissions statements describe the preferred characteristics of students the school wishes to enroll, which is useful information for potential applicants who are investigating the most appropriate setting for their own ministerial preparation. A particularly well-developed example is one taken from the catalog of The Athenaeum of Ohio, Mount St. Mary's Seminary of the West (pp. 19-20). The desired qualities listed are "a. A knowledge of and a fidelity to the

Word of God and the authentic teaching of Christ's church; b. Charity, zeal for souls and lifelong commitment to the priesthood, including celibacy according to the tradition of the Western church; c. Competency in pastoral skills, especially in the proclamation of God's Word and in leading divine worship; d. A sense of responsibility and commitment to the people entrusted to them and an ability to communicate with them; an interest in the universal work of the church and a commitment to the mission agencies which help that work; e. Personal initiative and capacity for courageous leadership, together with prudence and decision in action; f. Willingness to subordinate personal preferences in the interest of cooperative effort; and g. A commitment to the promotion of justice." Further specifications about academic preparation are also given: "The college work of the student should result in the ability to use certain tools of an educated person . . . in increased understanding of the world in which we live . . . in a sense of achievement."

A profile like this describes clearly the type of student the school hopes to enroll and would give potential applicants, who depend so heavily on the "reputation" of a school in making their selection, more adequate information.

The form and nature of many policies and procedures suggest that students are expected to have attended college seminaries, a situation that is no longer the case for a growing proportion of students. Many theologates rely heavily on dioceses and religious orders to prescreen candidates, but few indicate how the interaction or contact with these agencies should take place in the process of admission. It is implied by the minimal documentation required by seven or eight theologates that screening and evaluation of students is done elsewhere. One statement summarizes this approach: "It is the responsibility of the various superiors and pastors to ascertain eligibility of the candidate with regard to his social, psychological readiness for the seminary." Fewer requirements are specified for the admission of students who are not preparing for ordination. Generally only academic records are required, and in a few instances an interview is recommended, but little inquiry is made into the suitability of individuals for ministry.

In order to maintain enrollment, a majority of faculty and administrators believe that admissions standards have been lowered. Because of competition for enrollment, almost all admissions personnel acknowledge that on occasion they accept candidates against their better judgment. In the interest of enrolling the qualified students from particular dioceses or religious orders, they feel forced to admit candidates from those dioceses or religious orders who do not meet admissions standards. Nonetheless, admissions committees are determined to maintain relatively high standards. They try to correlate admissions requirements with the type of ministry to which individuals believe the Church is calling them. Candidates for religious orders, for example, may need to be examined on whether they are aware of being called to the charism of a particular order. If screening in religious orders or dioceses is minimal, it is incumbent on the theologate to do an even more careful assessment.

A central issue in the admission of students to theology is the meaning of "vocational call." It is a spiritual and theological reality that is not only an individual decision, but one that must be confirmed by the community of the Church. One seminary leader expressed it this way: "I believe this concept has to be reevaluated—something that has not been done since the 1920s. We need a better way to help people discern their inward call to ministry by discussing with them their gifts in relation to the needs of the Church."

Issues for the future: Admissions procedures and selection processes have improved remarkably over the past two decades. A primary goal for admissions committees is to maintain high standards for admission by making better use of the selection research that is available. Accurate and careful screening of potential students is crucial to future ministry, both for the ordained and for other professional ministers. Several important questions must be kept before admissions committees: How can a vocational call be discerned? Does the individual possess the qualities that are needed for professional ministry today? How can consistency in standards be achieved when screening students?

One model for the future that has been suggested is to develop national criteria and national screening centers. The greater expertise of interviewers who specialize in interviewing candidates could ensure consistency and help prevent the mistaken acceptance of students who are inadequate. Sensitive questioning of potential candidates in difficult areas such as suicide attempts, drug use, and sexual activity might be done more successfully by individuals who are specially trained in interviewing techniques. In the questionnaire answered by vocation directors, many indicated that they need and would appreciate assistance with selection. Objections to this centralized model have been raised, however; it has been suggested that professional interviewers would not know enough about the ecclesiologies of individual theologates or of the dioceses to which graduates would return. The possibility of using such a model has been proposed, but many interested parties, including vocation directors, are opposed to screening on a level where the selection seems to be out of their hands.

Short of a national screening center, theologates can improve their admissions standards by reviewing their practices in relation to these recommendations:

a. Policies and procedures should be inclusive and clearly delineated in public documents, that is, in catalogs and other admissions brochures, so that ordinaries, vocation directors, and potential students will be better informed as they choose a theology program.

b. Policies and procedures should be reviewed on the basis of how effectively admissions requirements enable school officials to select candidates they wish to enroll, and to screen out those who are not suitable.

c. A health examination should be required as part of the admissions process, and policies on sensitive health issues, in particular the handling of AIDS, should be developed.

d. At theologates where lay students are admitted, policies and procedures for their admission should be clearly defined.

e. A specific request should be made for information from any seminary formerly attended by a candidate, since candidates who have been dismissed from one school frequently seek to enroll at another. A national "clearing house" for keeping records of students who have been enrolled in seminaries might be considered.

f. Though not immediately involving admissions standards, appropriate policies and procedures for the dismissal of students should be discussed by responsible authorities.

The following additional suggestions might also assist theologates in improving their admissions practices:

a. Each theologate should review its policies with the goal of acquiring whatever information is needed beyond what has been gathered by religious orders or college seminaries, so that an accurate assessment of the candidate can be made. Admissions committees should become thoroughly familiar with the testing and screening that has been done in each diocese or religious order, so that where standards are not equivalent to those of the particular school additional inquiry can be made.

b. Theologates enrolling lay students should reevaluate the nature of the requirements for their admission, and consider additional documentation that might be helpful in assessing their suitability for professional ministry.

c. Theologates should use data available from psychological testing in ways that are helpful as the student enters the formation process, while at the same time guaranteeing confidentiality. Competent interpreters of psychological tests should be available to consult with admissions committees during the screening process, to assure that correct interpretations are made and that the value of what can be learned from the tests is not overlooked.

d. Attention should be given to more consistent gathering of information in several areas, for example, previous Church ministry experience or community service; whether an individual is a convert and if so for how many years; and if an applicant has been married, whether annulment papers are available. Personal statements by applicants about their motives for entering theology might include these areas, and should be universally required. A more specific description of the nature of the essay the school expects to receive from the applicant should be provided.

e. Whenever possible, personal interviews should be conducted, since many of those who screen candidates believe this to be one of the most effective means of evaluation.

3. MINISTRY GOALS

Present reality: Seminarians readily identify with what they consider will be the central priestly role in their future ministry. During interviews, when asked how they envisioned their future ministry, almost all responded that it would be largely liturgical (including preaching) and sacramental. They further commented that in a short time they will be responsible for the administration of a parish, which few anticipate with enthusiasm. Those from rural dioceses especially, recognize that within a few years they will probably be pastors. They express the ambivalence of wishing to "be in charge" and yet wanting to avoid administrative tasks.

The survey of seminarians reported in *Seminary Life and Visions of the Priesthood* indicates similar trends. This study found that seminarians focus more on personal spirituality than on some communal expressions of prayer, and that they foresee their ministry largely as celebrating the sacraments, giving homilies, and ministering to individuals rather than as developing Christian community, enabling lay ministry, and performing administrative tasks. Faculty expressed concern about the desire of most seminarians to work with individuals rather than with groups, fearing that the lack of time for personal counseling and other one-on-one ministry may prove frustrating to the newly ordained. Of fundamental concern is whether attitudes and orientations toward different types of ministry are compatible with the anticipated needs of the Church.[4]

Other major insights into how seminarians view their future ministerial roles are set forth in the same study (pp. 23-39), which employs a new approach to understanding differences in how seminarians perceive the future. The model used by Hemrick and Hoge identifies two dimensions: the Institutional Orientation versus the Communal Orientation, and the Social Leadership Tendency versus the Personal Witness Tendency. As students locate themselves on this dual continuum, a clear image of how they see their future roles as priests emerges. The new model produces, in effect, a classic description of seminarians as traditional/conservative or progressive/liberal, terms that are now assiduously avoided. It helpfully incorporates the content and context of old concepts and articulates well some basic perspectives on Church and ministry.

An important aspect of the Institutional versus Communal Orientation dimension is how future priests perceive themselves in relation to Church structures and lay people. At one extreme end of the

---

[4]A clear and authoritative statement about the changing role of pastors can be found in *A Shepherd's Care* (Washington, D.C.: United States Catholic Conference, 1987).

spectrum are those who see themselves as representing the official Church "over and against" lay people; at the other extreme are those who see themselves as having virtually no role distinction. These extremes are represented by only a few seminarians, and most are struggling to find a suitable place somewhere closer to the center of the spectrum. During our interviews, students expressed views that suggest the same kind of diversity as found in the *Seminary Life* study: About one-third tend toward the side of distinction and separation from lay people, and about two-thirds tend toward collaboration and sharing of functions. The faculties of theologates see it as a crucial part of their task to present an understanding of the needs of the Church that will help students reflect on the most appropriate role for themselves once they are ordained.

The second dimension, that of the Social Leadership Tendency versus the Personal Witness Tendency, relates to the institutional versus communal orientation in important ways. A congeries of "traits" is associated with each of the two sets of orientations. Personal and spiritual formation personnel were especially aware of the differences in types of students. They commented frequently that seminarians who see themselves as "set apart," with a serious responsibility to be witnesses to lay people, are often the same students who envision their ministry as "going it alone." On the other side, seminarians who stress unduly the social leadership role sometimes fail to understand that their future ministry requires a kind of public religious leadership that does set them apart in some ways. Formation directors consider it an important goal to help seminarians recognize the necessity of collaborating with and enabling lay people while also exercising their own distinct role as liturgical and spiritual leaders.

The findings in the earlier study by Hemrick and Hoge (*Seminarians in Theology*) corroborate other responses from our interviews as well. When asked, "If your bishop or superior assigns you to parish work, which function of your role do you consider will be most essential?" the reply of 50.8 percent was liturgy and sacramental ministry; 32.5 percent said teaching and preaching. A much smaller percent said counseling (8.6), a few chose organizing lay groups (5.5 percent), and a tiny minority (1.6 percent) named administration (*Seminarians in Theology*, p. 87). An extremely low valuation was given to administration by the seminarians we interviewed, even though they recognize that this function will absorb much of their time in the future. Of special concern to some diocesan candidates, and to some in religious orders, was the decreasing number of priests, which will make it nearly impossible for them to consider specialized ministries. Some are struggling with the notion that for the rest of their lives they will be doing virtually the same ministry, with little anticipation of variation in their routines. Many are interested in ministry to individuals, which they believe will not be considered essential in the future.

Issues for the future: Students ask, "What will I do in a complex future that is very uncertain?" Ministry that involves collaboration with women religious and lay women and men is of concern to most students. For some there is excitement and enthusiasm about the prospect of working with a diversity of people, but for others the changing role of priests is threatening. The stages of development on this issue are not unlike those in the Church as a whole and even throughout society, and theologates will be increasingly called upon to accommodate their programs to these demands.

Other implications for theologates arise from the ways in which students see themselves ministering in the future. All aspects of formation must be directed toward educating seminarians who know their own identity but do not consider themselves an elite group— separate from and above the people they both serve and serve with. Awareness of the changing context of priestly ministry in the next decade is a prerequisite for determining the content of formation programs. Collaboration is desirable, even inevitable, given both the smaller number of priests and the desire of lay people to work in and for the Church in new ways. The new structures require that future priests have a clear sense of how integral to their ministry is their ability to work effectively with others. Enhancement of the priestly role is inextricably linked with enhancement of the role of lay ministers.

4. CHANGING COMPOSITION AND INTEGRATION OF STUDENTS IN THEOLOGATES

Present reality: About 60 percent of the students currently studying in theologates are preparing for priesthood, and about 40 percent are preparing for other professional ministry roles. The quality of integration among these two different types of students, where both are present, varies considerably. At some schools both attend the same classes, while at others they do not. Common liturgies and social interaction are in some cases part of the program, and in others they are not. Models of effective ways to achieve healthy integration are strongly desired at schools where different types of students are enrolled. Since many theologates provide housing only for ordination candidates, others are commuter students and the desired integration is even more difficult to achieve. Commuter students are negotiating an unfamiliar system and moving into areas of service in the Church that are only beginning to be understood. At times they appear as a threat to seminarians and are made to feel quite unwelcome. In other instances, where formation personnel have made a concerted effort to use the environment as part of the entire learning process, all types of students benefit. Students then see the situation as reflective of the actual ministry settings in which both priests and lay ministers will eventually serve.

It is commonly agreed among faculty who have had the experience of a mixed student body that such a composition raises academic standards. The caliber of lay students is high, which can spur either interest or defensiveness on the part of seminarians. Lay students often judge seminarians harshly; they believe that many have not dealt with difficult human issues. According to a seasoned professor of Old Testament: "A mixed group in the classroom clarifies what each is about. Four or five years ago there was violent opposition to having lay students present, but the anger is diffused now, and the real value of sharing viewpoints is becoming clear." Lay students generally want a high degree of involvement in their schools, but many of those interviewed said that inclusiveness is on paper only. They still feel the tension of being in a seminary setting. Some locate this tension more between lay and religious than between men and women, but whatever the causes it is clear that issues of ministerial roles and vocational identities will continue to arise as the Church moves toward new forms of ministry.

Issues for the future: All but six or seven theologates enroll some students who are not seminarians, though several of them do not report the numbers in official documents or surveys such as the CARA Seminary Directory. Having a more diverse student body is a stated goal for some theologates. Several reasons for this change are given. Some believe that sexuality and interpersonal relationships can be dealt with more realistically in a mixed setting. Others state frankly that, given the limited number of seminarians, the survival of theologates depends on their ability to attract women religious and lay students. Still others believe that the optimum educational environment for future ministers should include students who represent different viewpoints and goals. But this diversity may be obtained through cooperative programs rather than by enrolling a nontraditional student population, especially women.

As theologates strive to develop more effective education for ministry, the Church continues to define the role of lay ministry. As long as creativity and innovation are accepted, these simultaneous trends can lead to better pastoral service for the people who depend on the Church for their spiritual sustenance. Ecclesiastical structures and financial limitations still inhibit the full development of education for lay ministry. A few bishops are responding to the need for more professional ministers by sponsoring lay students, and it is expected that this practice will grow.

5. TRANSITION

Present reality: Transition to a professional ministerial role in the Church is difficult for all students. Seminarians find that the move from a relatively structured and enclosed theologate to a parish rectory is often stressful and unsettling. Aware of these transitional adjustments, many pastors and associates are beginning to work with theologates to provide appropriate supervision and consultation. When this kind of support is made available, the new minister is able to adjust and mature in responsibility and judgment. When such support is lacking, the Church is faced with young priests who may become discouraged and uncertain of their future in ministry.

Among the problems resulting from the stress of adjustment, alcohol abuse is one of the most serious, especially as it affects the newly ordained. As seminarians and young priests move into parishes where support structures are absent and companionship limited, alcohol abuse often becomes acute. Seminarians working in parishes during field education or for a diaconate program are not infrequently confronted with an alcoholic pastor or associates. Knowing how to react to such situations requires assistance from experienced people who can recommend an appropriate response.

Lay persons who begin working for the Church for the first time in a professional capacity face transitional problems as well. Many of them are moving into situations where they will be the first lay person to hold a position in the parish or diocese. Resistance to changes of this nature is often high, and anticipated ways of serving the Church sometimes need to be adjusted. Among other difficulties, financial constraints are usually severe, and opportunities for promotion are almost nonexistent. Like seminarians, lay ministers miss the companionship of their peers that they enjoyed during theological studies. As the Church moves into the twenty-first century, concerns like these will have to be addressed.

Issues for the future: Theologates, dioceses, and religious orders are all looking for structures to facilitate the transition from theology to active ministry. Programs for continuing formation are in the planning stages at many schools, and at a few initial efforts to provide continuity have been made. Even more support is needed, though, including assistance with serious personal problems as well as with spiritual and social growth. Some theologates invite young priests and other graduates back to the school for a week or more for several summers after ordination and graduation. Most find that this opportunity is of critical importance in helping to sustain individuals in ministry. Theologates are attempting to incorporate opportunities for supervision and for enhancing pastoral skills into these sessions as well.

Part IV

Formation Programs for Future Ministers

This part of the report concerns three distinct but interrelated elements of formation in theologates—personal and spiritual, academic, and pastoral. These elements were typically defined, described, and distinguished by respondents, and they correspond to the outline in the *PPF*, namely: "Development of the Seminarian: Personal and Spiritual," "The Academic Program," and "Pastoral Formation." In freestanding theologates, all three dimensions of formation are under the auspices of the school; but in university-related and collaborative schools, personal and spiritual formation is the responsibility of a religious community or a diocesan formation team that conducts the program in separate houses. However the formation program is structured, all three areas of formation are integral to preparation for priesthood and other professional ministry. Although the *PPF* addresses itself to priesthood candidates only, many schools have adapted these three basic components for other candidates for professional ministry. The emphasis in this report is on formation for priesthood; nevertheless, many comments apply to education for ministry in general, and specific reference is also made to formation for lay ministry.

During interviews for this study, questions were asked about the goals, programs, personnel, and concerns associated with the three areas of formation. Virtually all respondents spoke of two interrelated but distinct goals of the formation process: It involves the development of the personal and spiritual life of the candidate; and it seeks to prepare the candidate for public ministry, with an appropriate life-style for such ministry. These two strands of formation are defined in the *PPF* as *objectives* that emphasize the deepening of faith and commitment to service on the one hand, and an understanding of the nature of priesthood on the other. They are to be achieved "through critical theological reflection in the light of the magisterium of the Church" and through "a vital integration of their theological understanding and their life in Christ"(*PPF*, p. 15). Though the process of formation is lifelong, these special objectives are set out for the years of study in theology.

To achieve these objectives every theologate attempts to integrate, with varying degrees of success, the three principal components of the program: "spiritual and personal formation through community life and worship and personal spiritual guidance; academic preparation through humanistic and theoretical studies; and pastoral training through supervised practical experience" (*PPF*, p. 16, #39). Although these three areas of formation are part of the preparation undertaken by all students, the spiritual and personal area is commonly called "the formation program," and the other areas are referred to as "the academic program" and "the ministerial program," or "the pastoral field education program." Following is a discussion of the specific purposes of the three programs, the content of the programs, the backgrounds and qualifications of personnel with major responsibility for the programs (except faculty, who are covered in a separate section), and the concerns associated with each as described by the respondents.

A. Personal and Spiritual Formation

OVERVIEW STATEMENTS

Emphasis on personal and spiritual formation has increased significantly in recent years, and much work has been done to develop effective models of formation.

The qualifications and preparation of directors of formation are not always specifically related to the role they are called upon to fulfill; the result is that some programs lack organization and cohesion, while others need experienced spiritual directors.

Variations on two distinct models, one focusing on integration and the other on identification, are used in personal and spiritual formation.

Elements common to most formation programs include spiritual direction and faculty advising, a class program covering various topics, common prayer and other larger community events, and special events and opportunities. Spiritual direction is regarded by students as the single most important aspect of their personal and spiritual formation.

The major issues that are confronted in personal and spiritual formation are understanding the identity of the priest as public minister and formation for celibacy, developing a prayer life appropriate to the ministry, working to improve an underdeveloped self-image, resolving questions of deference and obedience to hierarchical authority, and becoming responsive to the needs of the church.

The goal of achieving integration of moral beliefs and moral actions, so that private beliefs are consonant with public behavior, is primary in formation. Adaptation to the priestly role is linked to this process.

Members of religious communities often have far more formational opportunities before theology than do their diocesan and lay counterparts. These differences can produce tensions when different groups are studying together.

At virtually every theologate visited, concern about defining the role of women and incorporating their expertise in the formation process was raised.

INTRODUCTION[1]

Almost every person interviewed stressed the centrality and importance of the personal and spiritual formation of students. Faculty and administrators often noted that, without a certain level of growth and maturity in these areas, the study of theology and the experience of pastoral field education could not be undertaken effectively. This viewpoint was expressed by those at institutions that

---

[1] I am indebted to David Nygren, C.M., for much of the conceptual material in this chapter, especially pp. 147-155, section 3.

provide for this aspect of formation, as well as by those in situations where it is provided by separate communities or institutions.

The same viewpoint is also expressed in the *PPF.* Quoting from the Second Vatican Council's *Decree on the Training of Priests,* the *PPF* states that "the whole training of the students should have as its object to make them true shepherds of souls and after the example of Our Lord Jesus Christ, teacher, priest, shepherd (n. 4). Spiritual formation should be closely associated with the doctrinal and pastoral, and, with the assistance of the spiritual director in particular, should be conducted in such a way that the students may learn to live in intimate and unceasing union with God, the Father through His Son Jesus Christ, in the Holy Spirit" (n. 8; *PPF*, p. 18, #47). Spiritual and personal formation is identified as central to education for ministry. This part of formation, it is emphasized, must be integrated with the academic and pastoral components.

1. GOALS AND PURPOSES OF PERSONAL AND SPIRITUAL FORMATION

Present reality: In light of the context described above, interviewees were asked to elaborate on this broad question: "What provisions are made for the personal and spiritual formation of students?" At every theologate, most of those interviewed indicated that spiritual and personal formation is being stressed more now than in the recent past. Many spoke of the significance of the transitional years in theology. Typical entering students are in their mid-twenties, an age at which transition to adulthood ordinarily is coming to completion. The observations of formation personnel correspond to theories of development, which suggest that it is during these years that individuals shift their focus from themselves to others, modify expectations of perfection in themselves and in others, and integrate personal idealism with the realism of the work world; at the same time, they regard responsibility more seriously.

On the level of faith, formation directors commented that appropriate growth at this stage calls for a transition from uncertainty about, and lack of knowledge of, the faith to the attempt to understand and recognize God's revelation in one's own life and in the experiences of others. Within the context of ecclesial formation, appropriate growth in community at this phase requires an increasing desire to be part of the public ministry of the Church. The integration of personal and spiritual dimensions is both the context and one of the significant goals of formation during theology.

Formation directors responsible for program development and implementation gave detailed information about the nature and purpose of their work. The three areas that they considered most central to the process of personal and spiritual formation were helping the student to (1) develop interior values and habits of prayer appropriate to priesthood; (2) come to an understanding of the meaning of the priest as public minister; and (3) be able to respond to the needs of the Church.

Regarding *interior values and prayer life*, formation directors see as a primary goal the development of an active faith-life and habits of personal prayer. Students need to learn to engage in personal prayer that will enable them to live out of their own interior life and sense of mission. This kind of prayer not only involves individual piety, but also serves as a source of apostolic effectiveness. Interior values must reflect gospel values. Living a simple life-style, showing concern for the poor and for the cause of justice, and willingly embracing celibacy and chastity are outward manifestations of these values. Formation directors see these as foundational values that are an essential part of any program designed to prepare effective ministers for the Church.

Both in individual interviews and in the Hemrick and Hoge study reported in *Seminarians in Theology* (1985), students expressed a strong desire to develop their prayer life. When asked what were the most important qualities for anyone engaged in religious ministry, being prayerful was the first or second choice of 84 percent of the respondents. The focus on interior personal growth is clear. However, the same convergence of values is not so evident from the results of interviews for this study. The students we interviewed tended to identify prayer with "individualized spirituality" rather than with a spirituality that incorporates ministry. Moreover, this evaluation is corroborated by most theologate personnel, who lament the lack of connection between interior values and lived spirituality, especially when it entails minimal interest in the broader mission of the Church and in social justice concerns.

Regarding *public ministry in the Church*, theologate personnel have tried to implement programs that prepare the student to be a religious leader, able to experience and express the spiritual life. Their goal is to promote growth that will make it possible for the future minister to relate to people in parishes and other ministerial settings in a way that enables them to become actively involved themselves in the life of the Church. One of the desired ecclesial outcomes, according to formation directors, is that "our students be able to get others actively involved in the life of the Church—the parish, the school, wherever they are. Formation should prepare each of them to be a minister of ministers—collaborative, account-able, enabling. They should also be leaders in the sacramental and prayer life of the Church, and provide the experience of community for people in the Church."

Students, too, value highly the ability to build community, which according to Hemrick and Hoge's survey they view as the most important activity for religious ministry. Yet formation personnel see a gap between this ideal and reality. Personal and spiritual formation are directed toward helping individuals achieve a balance between liturgical presence and personal piety, communal accounta-bility and personal integrity, ministry to a single individual and to the larger demands of a congregation, but that goal is achieved only after years of active ministry. Usually in the beginning years of ministry, the tendency is to be preoccupied with personal piety and ministry to individuals rather than with broader communal concerns. Formation directors are trying to shift the balance as students progress through theology, so that even in the early years of ministry personal and communal demands are balanced.

Regarding formation in relation to *the needs of the Church*, a key goal is to help students develop a keen sense of how to promote the mission of the Church. "They need to see what difference the Church makes in the world, and they have to recognize how important others are in spreading the gospel. Sometimes the personal agendas of those in ministry cause them to lose sight of real needs," com-mented one formation director. The challenge is to encourage stu-dents to focus on the needs of the Church and the people, not on their own wishes to minister in a particular way. As one rector said, "Real leadership means that priests or other professional ministers don't have to do it all, but they do have to serve as catalysts in the community and parish." This understanding diverges from that of many students who emphasize interpersonal and one-on-one ministry to a much greater extent.

For seminarians who are moving toward priesthood, another aspect of relationship to the Church is becoming part of the presbyterate serving the local church or doing the work of the religious community. "It is important to develop a sense of being connected with other priests, but the dilemma is that the nature of the work often requires independence and initiative. Finding ways in formation to establish a sense of belonging without making students dependent is difficult," remarked one diocesan formation director.

In summary, the goals of personal and spiritual formation programs are almost always defined in relation to three areas: personal development of values and prayer life directed toward service to the Church—an apostolic spirituality; public ministry, with the focus on a ministry of leadership that at the same time enables others to minister; and attention to the needs of the Church, with an understanding of the role of the Church universal and the difference the Church makes in the world. Not all directors spoke of these areas in exclusive categories, but the essential aspects of the nature and goals of spiritual and personal formation as perceived by formation personnel are represented in this outline.

Issues for the future: Strong emphasis on a program of personal and spiritual formation will continue as the role and functions of priests take on new dimensions. Of particular concern for the future is the fact that students now come to theology with vastly different backgrounds and preparation. A typical comment was: "Some of those entering theology come with a deep relationship to the Church, a good religious education background, and a history of service. They have a 'sense' of Church. But in recent years a greater proportion have come with little previous association with religious structures—no formal connectedness with the Church and even less knowledge of their faith." For formation to be effective, measures must be taken to meet individual needs. Some students will be helped by a pretheology program, while others will benefit from parish experience or stronger academic preparation.

Formation directors believe that more students will need individual attention not only because of increasingly varied backgrounds, but also because of the influences of a society whose values diverge significantly from gospel values. Summarizing a common sentiment, one director of formation said: "We are trying to do so much in such a short time, and everyone is vying for time. Because of the problems students bring to us, spiritual direction often consists of 60-percent counseling and 40-percent spiritual direction; spiritual directors are often not prepared to do counseling, but they are thrust into that role." Another observed that "vocation directors send strange people sometimes, and seminaries don't always have the personnel and time to deal with the problems." The problems identified range from unstable family backgrounds resulting in low self-esteem to pre-occupation with status and personal fulfillment without reference to the needs of the Church.

Some unanswered questions concerning personal and spiritual development were posed by respondents. Many asked for more discussion and consideration of these issues by theologians, especially theologians experienced in formation work. Regarding spirituality, questions like these were raised:

> What is an authentic holistic spirituality in our secular culture? Is there a countercultural spirituality that embraces peace and justice in a holistic fashion?

> Someone might try to demythologize the old "stereotype" of monastic spirituality and the new "stereotype" of pastoral spirituality by asking, What is authentic spirituality in the context of a secular culture? What is the vision of a holistic spirituality from the perspective of the Gospels?

> What psychological and developmental models of personal growth are authentically ethical in our secular and permissive culture?

Regarding priesthood, the following questions were among those asked:

> What is the specific identity of the ministerial priesthood vis-à-vis the universal priesthood?

> Will the role and functions of priests take on new dimensions? If so, will that mean a more refined or defined role, or more roles than priests have now? What will be emphasized? What changes in formation will be required as roles change?

What would be the effects of not clarifying the role, the spirituality, and the identity of the diocesan priest? What would this do to vocations, to the mission of the local church, and to the leadership of local bishops?

Regarding the Church in general, questions and comments concerned these areas:

Are we ready to demand a spirituality open to the Church universal? Will theologates be willing to take this responsibility? Strong backing from the Church for this approach seems to be lacking; there are words, yes, but not decisions to back them up.

Although commitment to celibacy is considered essential by ecclesial officials, in practice it is regarded as less central. Can we give celibacy a new and somewhat different value in the post-Vatican II Church? How can formation programs be adapted to face the challenge inherent in such a reappraisal?

2. PERSONAL AND SPIRITUAL FORMATION PERSONNEL

Present Reality: Of the fifty theologates included in our study, all except eight designate a person who is responsible for personal and spiritual formation. In situations where no one is listed, this aspect of formation is usually the responsibility of religious communities or diocesan houses of formation. In three cases, though the personal and spiritual formation directors are not attached directly to the schools, they are included in the statistics. These are Catholic University, whose diocesan priesthood candidates reside at Theological College, the Jesuit School of Theology in Berkeley; and Weston School of Theology in Cambridge, whose rectors are responsible for personal and spiritual formation. The number of directors included in the data below is forty-seven, with two schools having codirectors. Credentials and degrees are listed according to the information available.

Several different titles are used to designate the individual responsible for personal and spiritual formation. The most common is Spiritual Director, which is used at twenty schools, followed by Director of Spiritual Formation or simply Director of Formation, used at eighteen. Dean of Formation is used twice. Rector is used four times, and Spiritual Direction Coordinator, Seminary Dean, and Dean of Growth in Life and Ministry are used once each. The various titles are significant and seem to represent two different approaches to spiritual formation. Although there are exceptions, many Spiritual Directors tend to see their role as comprising one-on-one work with individual seminarians, whereas those who are Directors or Deans often hold a position that includes the planning and coordination of all activities encompassed by spiritual and personal formation. As noted above, the extent and development of these formation programs varies considerably.

The *vocational status* of the forty-seven formation personnel includes thirty who are diocesan priests and seventeen who are members of religious orders—four Jesuits; two Vincentians, Benedictines, and Dominicans; and one Holy Cross Father, Maryknoller, Franciscan, Oblate, Salesian, Sacred Heart Father, and Sulpician. The *degrees* of thirty-two, twenty of the diocesan priests and twelve of the religious, are identified. Of all these, thirteen (40.6 percent) hold doctoral-level degrees, including five with the D.Min.; five are diocesan (38.5 percent) and eight are religious (61.5 percent). The S.T.L. is held by three (9.4 percent), and thirteen (40.6 percent) have M.A. degrees, usually in addition to the M.Div. Two have an M.Div. and one a B.A. only. The *academic fields* of twenty-one are identified, including six in systematic theology, five in spirituality, three in pastoral theology, two in music/liturgy, two in theology with the field not specified, and one each in moral theology, psychology, and religious studies. About one-fourth of those interviewed for the study felt that they had been adequately prepared for the work they were expected to do.

Issues for the Future: A concern voiced often was how appropriate the preparation of those in spiritual and personal formation work is. Although a number of directors are currently enrolled in summer programs, it appears that a minority of those engaged in this work are not specifically and directly prepared in spirituality or psychology or both. Some argue that priests who have successfully engaged in ministry are the best persons to head formation programs, but those actually doing formation work generally believe that specific preparation is necessary. The skills required for directing a program are varied, ranging from administrative and organizational skills to spiritual direction and counseling skills. Directors who are prepared in either or both of these areas expressed considerably greater satisfaction with their work, and have experienced greater success.

Observations based on site visits and an evaluation of program goals and content indicate that more comprehensive and cohesive programs are in place at institutions where the director has been specifically prepared for formation work and has had several years to implement and refine a program. For the future, it seems reasonable to encourage those responsible for the selection and appointment of individuals to these positions to choose persons with credentials that directly relate to the tasks associated with formation. Almost no faculty member teaches outside his or her area of expertise, but a very high percentage of those in formation work have little or no specific preparation. Even rectors, who are occasionally prepared in matters of personal and spiritual formation, are often otherwise engaged in the management of institutions and so are not in a position to supply ongoing leadership in formation. The quality of formation in the future will depend significantly on the preparation of personnel whose responsibility it is to develop and implement formation programs.

3. PERSONAL AND SPIRITUAL FORMATION: MODELS

Present reality: To understand current formational concerns, it is important to examine the context of formation and the various models in use today. From interviews with formation directors and written accounts of formation programs, we observed that nearly all theologates are in a period of transition between the classical models of formation, drawn usually from either the seventeenth century or monastic traditions, and contemporary models that adopt a more apostolic and pastoral orientation. The tradition of internal forum and external forum as a means of structured communication for the seminary student remains more or less intact. Whereas the internal forum has taken on new dimensions with the addition of spiritual direction and psychological counseling, however, the criteria for external-forum communication are less obvious. Models of the past tended in part to rely on compliance as a measure of readiness for ministry, but current models emphasize internalization and integration as the chief measures of readiness. Yet how is authenticity to be measured? And what type of formation is more likely to produce the desired congruence between what one believes and how one acts? What factors contribute to a more institutional or communal orientation? Are environments shaping behavior, or are they shaped by individuals recruited into them? These questions are only beginning to be explored during the present period of transition in the formation process.

In our research we became aware of many operative models, either implicit or explicit, around which the theologates' philosophy of formation is structured. By way of example, I will cite two distinct models and their assumptions as they relate to congruence between behavior and attitudes. Although many variations of these two models are currently used, it is possible to contrast two distinct approaches to formation, one emphasizing integration and the other identification.

Integration Model. The first model assumes that students, with guidance, have the responsibility to integrate and internalize information and values as a basis for their identity and outlook. They need to develop a capacity for critical reflection on their personal values and the results of their ministry. The integration model is based on these assumptions:

1. The individual is motivated by a drive toward competence that develops as he or she moves from a state in which behavior is controlled by external forces to one characterized by internal choices. The internal exercise of control enables an individual to feel that he or she is responsible, instrumental, and an agent in self-development.
2. The ultimate goal of the integration model is an internalized locus of control where one realizes the effect of one's actions in relation to the larger public responsibility of ministry.
3. Contextually the integration model assumes that one's beliefs, attitudes, and behaviors are most appropriately formed in an environment that fosters private self-consciousness in dialogue with either a spiritual director or a formation counselor. The language most typically associated with this model includes descriptions of personal development, psychological strength, and extended discernment of vocation.

Problems with the integration model are expressed in these terms:

1. If the model is set in a relatively isolated or homogeneous environment, it can promote self-reflective narcissism that remains useful
   only in that environment.
2. If the integration process is not performed and perceived in both
   the internal forum and the external forum, it can lead to an
   individualistic and privatized spirituality.
3. If psychology is regarded as a substitute for spirituality, the model
   can be effective in only limited areas of personal and spiritual
   growth.

The integration model requires specialized programs and highly
trained personnel to facilitate the internalization of magisterial teaching, personality differences, and personal-growth factors. The model
appears to work successfully when students are involved in actual
ministry, which directs private self-consciousness toward reflection
on that ministry as well as on personal-growth issues. In a more
limited way, growth can occur in restricted environments where the
only content for reflection is the interpersonal interaction between
students without reference to lived ministerial activity.

Evaluation of the model's success derives primarily from personal
reflection on internal integration, but is also grounded and informed
by observations and reports of interactions in multiple settings and
circumstances.

Identification model. This model assumes that there is an objective
standard or priestly role against which the seminarian is measured.
The seminarian attempts to emulate a certain "model" deemed appropriate by seminary faculty. A "master image," often depicted by
the figure of "Christ the Priest," is assumed. Within this formational
context, criteria for ordination are most often behavioral, with
considerable attention paid to external adherence to role expectations
such as attendance at functions, perceived prayerfulness, or carefully
circumscribed behavior.

Although the concept of modeling is important in theologates, it
must be understood within the complex dynamic of freedom. The
locus of control must gradually move from outside oneself to inside.
Choice is the opportunity to make an uncoerced selection from
multiple options. Situations that limit choice often produce the

response of learned helplessness, which occurs either when individuals come to believe that their responses have little impact on outcomes or from the repeated experience of failure. The identification model can keep the locus of control outside the individual.

Problems with the identification model occur for three reasons:

1. Overidentification with a standard or role can lead to uncritical acceptance and foreclosure. This premature cognitive commitment to a role may render the individual ultimately incompetent by virtue of dependence on external factors that may or may not allow new information to penetrate personal awareness and adaptability. This phenomenon, sometimes referred to as the "retreat to commitment," may be less of a threat with older candidates than with younger ones.

2. Identification with the role of priest can lead to a kind of mindlessness in the pursuit of priesthood as a goal. As one student put it, "They want you to become a priest before you become a person." This reaction is most apparent in individuals who manifest a mechanical and impersonal attitude.

3. Identification can lead to self-induced dependence and the relinquishing of control. This behavior shifts responsibility for actions to others and creates distance in interactions.

The identification model may have specialized programs and well-trained personnel, but in its extreme form the focus of formation becomes the outcome of priesthood—a role without substance. To produce consistency in behavior, the model depends on social forces from groups within the theologate, for example, peer pressure or the demands of authority figures. With this model, individual differences in attitude are often obscured by the expectations associated with the role of the priest. For example, under the old "lock-step" approach to formation, individual exceptions to the standard track were made only for very serious, punitive reasons by the seminary authorities when an individual did not live up to behavioral standards.

The model appears successful when apostolic contacts are limited and when formation is defined principally as preparation for priesthood apart from direct apostolic service. Evaluation is focused on the individual's conformity to a role rather than on careful analysis of internal integration. This phenomenon is intensified by the distinction between the internal and external forums. Evaluation by faculty is based on inferential behavioral data observed in the external forum. Such data may or may not be confirmed by substantial attitudinal assessment or any systematic confirmation of integration.

To complicate matters further, our observations led us to conclude that either formation model can produce a kind of "institutional hypocrisy," that is, an inconsistency between attitude and behavior, when honest self-revelation is absent. At a later time the consequences for the Church and the individual can be devastating. Individuals who withhold information about known problems may engage in behavior that leads to misconduct and, ultimately, to litigation.

In fact, most models of formation now operative are located between the two extremes of integration and identification. The models are necessarily malleable in nature, since attempts must be made to adapt to changes in the Church. Likewise, the programs attempt to be responsive to change, but as a consequence they are generally not yet fully developed. Such malleability is particularly apparent when the essential mission of the school is undergoing transition and attempts are being made to meet the formational needs of the laity as well as of seminarians. In these contexts, formation personnel are searching for an integrated model of formation that distinguishes the proper ministry of the priest from that of the laity. The positive effect of such environments is that they force identity issues to the forefront, and require that the seminarian achieve a balance between the socially defined role of priesthood and the integration of his own beliefs in relation to the Church rather than apart from it. Lay students, too, can test their identity and role in situations that somewhat realistically reflect the ministerial settings in which they will later serve. In other words, service to the Church is enhanced when identities and roles are clarified, and when they can be tested even as they are being shaped in the formational environment.

Role Identity. One of the desired outcomes of the formation process is the development of individual candidates for ministry who willingly engage in an honest search for themselves in relation to God. They are discerning a vocation that has clear standards of behavior, which they are attempting to emulate. At the same time their psychological development, the social and cultural milieu of the

Church in the United States, their family backgrounds, and their previous relational experiences are brought to bear on that discernment. The formation process aims to develop individuals who manifest attitudes and behavior consistent with the demands of both hieratic office, to which they believe they are called, and personal integrity.

Another desired outcome of the formation process is that the person of the priest and the role of the priest become fully integrated. Within the social context the role of the priest requires behavior appropriate to its status as a profession, a leadership position, and an ecclesial office. Models of formation that emphasize these aspects of the role as the normative forces that control behavior may reinforce socially desirable behavior in situations where this is expected. In essence, such models induct the candidate into the culture of the priesthood enough so that he knows the behavior that is expected of him in social situations. The candidate may then appear to be the essence of what it means to be a priest. But the appearance of acceptable clerical behavior in social situations does not necessarily indicate attitudes consistent with that image. An important goal of formation is to bring about congruence between behavior and attitudes.

The role of the priest has personal dimensions that interact extensively with the social role. Conformity to the normative expectations of the social role may not signify integration as much as compliance. At some point in the formation process, most formation directors believe, the individual must be given the freedom and support to explore the meaning of the social role and its congruence with values, desires, and personal needs. Theologate personnel who participated in this study reported that some young priests find adaptation to the priestly role problematic. In some instances, their behavior neither matches the expected social behavior of a priest nor mirrors a clear sense of integration. The context of formation may negatively influence the process of integration, and inadvertently reinforce within the individual a discrepancy between attitudes and behavior that results in considerable pain for the priest in ministry as well as for those served. This is especially true in formation programs that emphasize conformity to prescribed behavioral standards as the principal criterion for ordination.

Such conformity to role expectations characterizes the identification model of formation in its extreme form. For example, formational environments that do not include routine interaction within a larger ecclesial context may so emphasize behavior associated with priesthood as to produce individuals who are not adaptive or able to interact with the Church body apart from the social role. In such situations, behavior observed in the seminary will not necessarily predict behavior after ordination.

Models that emphasize the integration of personal attitudes and behavior will likely be less governed by self-presentational concerns and role expectations. Critical self-reflection may minimize the detrimental effects of external social controls, and may also limit variability in behavior across situations. Thus the similarity of preordination and postordination environments may support attitude-behavior congruence. Models that emphasize critical self-reflection on occasion succeed in producing a highly individuated minister whose attitude is responsible and seemingly mature, though he may lack the appropriate behavioral mannerisms associated with priesthood.

On the other hand, behavioral compliance to a set of role expectations does not guarantee attitude-behavior congruence. There are many young priests who modeled exemplary behavior within the tightly governed social boundaries of the seminary but now refuse to allow lay people any liturgical role in the local parish, or establish protective or dependent partnerships with other men or women, or are depressed or even entirely dysfunctional. Faculties and ordinaries who are struck by the "inconsistent" behavior of such priests after ordination may find antecedents of the current difficulty in the formational context. Examples abound of the failure of current formation models to generate both the attitudes and the behavior that are required of a gospel minister.

This failure might be predicted of formation programs that are based on social roles alone, or of programs in which attitudes are formed without cross-situational validation of behavior or without adequate direct experience of actual ministry. Such a model can produce a role-appropriate individual for the Church only if public behavior is primary, but his attitudes and beliefs may remain unintegrated. In its most extreme form, the identification model creates a split between the public persona of the priest, which is governed by socially defined structures, and the private persona of the priest, which is confined to his own attitudes and needs apart from his role. The integration model demands that operative beliefs be tested against the reality of ministerial life.

A model that depends significantly on self-reflection within the context and activity of the Church seems most effective in achieving behavior-attitude congruence. The integration model is thus the one that appears to allow the theologate and the Church time to examine behavior-attitude consistency before ordination. The identification model, on the other hand, runs the risk of introducing ultimately irrelevant social influences that govern behavior within a particular context while obscuring the necessary attitude-behavior consistency required of an individual who is chosen by the Church to preach the gospel. Forced behavioral consistency within the limits of the theologate context may ultimately lead to inconsistency between behavior and attitudes, once an individual is ordained. Outside the supportive climate of the theologate, the issues or conflicts of the internal forum may become externalized as inappropriate behavior in the ministerial context.

Issues for the future: As theologates continue to investigate models of formation appropriate for the Church, the critical factor is the balance between the internal forum and the external forum, between behavior and attitudes, and between the public and private identities of the priest. An important goal is to develop a model that forms individuals whose behavior will reflect their deepest beliefs about the gospel, and that prepares them to serve accordingly.

What practices now present in formation programs should be more widely implemented so that individuals can gain a sense of control over their identities and behavior as public ministers? The following practices are recommended:

1. Increasing the opportunities for students to observe that actions have consequences that are proportional.
2. Reinforcing internalized values by providing multiple contexts in which to validate them.
3. Decreasing premature adherence to role standards expected of the priest.
4. Deliberately complicating the environment by allowing the student to interact with all levels of Church life and ministry while being formed to assume a specific role within the Church.
5. Accepting success and failure as equally worthy of discussion and

support, without fear of retribution that is either random or dis-
proportional.

6. Encouraging a self-directed view of formation and education that
is not "lock-step."

7. Building into the role identity of the priest a capacity for collaboration.

To the extent that formation programs incorporate some of these
practices, ministers will emerge in the future who have a method of
integrating the multifaceted public dimensions of priesthood with
correspondingly clear personal images.

4. CONTENT OF PERSONAL AND SPIRITUAL
FORMATION PROGRAMS

Present reality. Formation programs are structured in diverse
ways and consist of a wide range of elements. These include retreats,
conferences, andworkshops, as well as spiritual direction, which is
always a requirement for priesthood candidates and strongly encouraged for other students. Special programs, to be described later,
are designed for diocesan seminarians, for religious order seminarians, and for other students preparing for professional ministry. At
some schools, programs are well developed by directors of formation,
who often use a team approach in implementing them. In other
cases, spiritual and personal formation is carried out under the
leadership of the rector, with the spiritual director responsible mainly
for individual spiritual direction. Some programs have carefully
defined goals and concrete behavioral objectives, while others seem
rather ad hoc and are provided at the discretion of the rector. At
institutions with a loosely structured program, a more developed
and integrated set of experiences would be beneficial. Vocation
directors pay special attention to personal and spiritual formation
when they work with their candidates in selecting a theology school.
Diocesan directors consider the perceived quality of formation to be
the most significant criterion in the choice of a seminary; 77 percent
of them ranked it either first or second.

As noted, the organization and content of personal and spiritual
formation programs differ radically from one theologate to another,
but certain elements are generally included. These are spiritual direc-

tion and faculty advising; a group or class program covering a variety of topics; larger community events, especially the Eucharist and Liturgy of the Hours; and special events such as days of prayer, retreats, and the sacrament of reconciliation. Some institutions more than others stress the formational value of participation in the community life of the school, that is, the influence of the total environment. Each of these components is described briefly below.

a. *Spiritual Direction and Faculty Advising.* In nearly every conversation with students, they emphasized that spiritual direction was fundamental to their formation. Likewise, the results reported in Hemrick and Hoge's *Seminarians in Theology* indicate that 61.9 percent of all respondents find spiritual direction the most satisfactory means of helping them to maintain their commitment. Interviews with spiritual directors revealed various approaches to providing spiritual direction and different understandings about its nature. The experienced and professionally prepared director helps the student to identify the movement of the Spirit by reflecting on his or her faith life and commitment to ministry. In dialogue director and student clarify and interpret areas of growth and areas of resistance. Those who use this more personal and individual approach are usually assigned a smaller number of students for direction, and they meet with them more frequently. Others who view spiritual direction more as a group function conduct an occasional spiritual conference, supplemented by even less frequent individual meetings. The number of formation programs adopting the latter practice was diminishing until recent enforcement of the Vatican policy of having only the ordained provide spiritual direction reversed the trend, according to about ten formation directors. The lack of available and trained directors who are ordained has meant that theologates are resorting to assigning priests the role of spiritual director, whether or not they are inclined or prepared to undertake the task. As one director stated: "It is not well understood by some of those who make policy about spiritual directors that this role requires specialized training. They operate under the illusion that by virtue of ordination one is capable of providing sustained and formative spiritual direction. Our students suffer when they are assigned a director who sees his role as primarily one of confessor."

The issue of who may serve as spiritual directors has proved to be divisive. Theologate personnel sometimes disagree among themselves or with those in authority about the appropriateness and effectiveness of removing the nonordained, particularly women, from the role. Generally the women who were serving as spiritual directors were professionally as qualified as, or more qualified than, the priests who are taking their places. Priest faculty, more often than the women who have been dismissed, have protested the way in which the policy enforcement was handled. At almost every school where a change in spiritual directors has occurred, faculty and formation directors expressed concern over the failure of administrators to voice their objection to the policy. Some theologates are circumventing the directive to eliminate the nonordained from doing spiritual direction by assigning the student an "official" spiritual director who is a priest, in addition to a spiritual adviser who may or may not be ordained. The official director meets once or twice a year with the student to monitor his progress, but the spiritual adviser provides frequent, ongoing direction.

Of concern to those who must ultimately recommend candidates for priesthood is how to preserve confidentiality without sacrificing adequate evaluation of all dimensions of behavior that pertain to public ministry. The public and private worlds of individuals must be integrated, and evaluation must be thorough even while respect for privacy is maintained. In response to this need, the role of faculty adviser (external forum) is being developed more fully. Most schools assign a faculty adviser who meets regularly with students;they discuss community life, academics, courses, ministry, relationships, and other ministerial issues and concerns. These conversations and interactions are part of the evaluation process. Establishing appropriate use of the internal and external channels of communication is a special challenge to formation directors.

b. *Class Program.* Virtually every formation program includes a series of events for class groups, comprised of spiritual conferences, prayer, reflection, and discussion. The best programs use a developmental approach, according to which students move from foundational material on prayer and commitment, to a consideration of discipleship and the personal qualities necessary for those who will serve the Church, and ultimately to the meaning of public ministry. In the early phases, planning is done largely by the school; ideally in the third and fourth years, the programs are planned and implemented by students. Methods include lecture presentations, group discussions, journal keeping, theological reflection, and shared prayer.

One example of a well-developed class program is described by Mundelein Seminary in a publication entitled "Formation Program." The entire booklet concerns formation, with one section devoted to the class program (pp. 17-23). The program is designed "to offer the opportunity for support and encouragement, for mutual sharing, especially among peers, and to foster systematic planning of personal and professional goals in light of the needs of the Church." Different themes are assigned to the different years of the program: the first year focuses on personal discipleship so that the student can come into contact with his identity as a person of faith; the second year focuses on lived discipleship so that the student can understand and appropriate the calling to love and serve the Lord; the theme of the third year is priestly ministry so that the student can better understand and live out the call to discipleship in light of his identity as a diocesan priest; and the fourth year returns to the theme of priestly ministry, seeking to prepare the seminarian for ordination and public ministry in the Church.

Unfortunately such a carefully structured plan, with regular analysis and evaluation of goals and objectives, typifies only a few programs; more commonly a series of worthwhile presentations and events is offered each year, but acknowledgment of the developmental needs of students as they move toward active ministry is not evident. Few programs manifest program development adequate to the expectations that are espoused as required for ordination. In fact, many faculties and formation directors state their preference for the integration model without developing programs under that rubric. What then emerges is a reductive emphasis on outcomes and behavior that parallels the identification model.

c. *Prayer and Other Activities for the Whole Community.* In addition to events that are directed toward students in a particular class or at a particular level, some elements of formation are designed for the whole community. The most significant of these is participation in the daily Eucharist, a practice that is urged in every setting and compulsory at a few schools where absences must be excused. Morning and evening prayer is variably encouraged, but a significant minority of formation directors remarked that in contrast to the situation a few years ago, when less emphasis was placed on these common prayers, they are now more likely to be widely attended. Religious order formation houses and schools almost always build common prayer times into the horarium. At diocesan seminaries two schools of thought are current, and about equal numbers subscribe to each. Some formation directors believe that regular common prayer raises unrealistic expectations about having prayer companionship with other priests after ordination. Not many of the newly ordained will move to rectories where priests pray together, and in a few years many will be living alone in a rectory. Other directors hold that establishing a pattern of prayer is important and that, by requiring students to pray together, directors can be assured that students are at least present. They feel that students benefit from support groups, especially in times of transition, and need to be convinced of the necessity of prayer. In fact, all schools sponsor at least occasional prayer services, for example, Common Vespers (Liturgy of the Hours), but the degree of emphasis on common prayer varies considerably from place to place.

An issue related to prayer life concerns the dual nature of prayer— liturgical and devotional. In a few notable cases, directors spoke of the formative power of the liturgical life and how their whole program of prayer is built around the seasonal themes of the Church year. They believe that the liturgical leadership role of future priests is absolutely essential, and that every effort should be made to acquaint students with the richness of the liturgical tradition. In a different vein, at a significant minority of schools, directors mentioned the great interest shown by students in rituals and devotions, such as Benediction and the rosary, novenas, and litanies. The responses of formation directors to the practices of these students varied; some urged students to broaden their understanding of prayer and to become more aware of liturgical directives given by the Church since Vatican II, whereas others regarded emphasis on personal devotions as an acceptable way to grow in prayer. At a third small group of theologates, personal devotions were acknowledged as part of the rich tradition of personal spiritual development, though always in relation to the sacramental and liturgical structures of a post-Vatican II ecclesiology.

The occasions that most frequently bring the whole school community together are prayer services, but other activities like weekly spiritual conferences, regular retreat days, and scheduled discussion groups, especially for theological reflection on apostolic experience, serve as points of community focus.

d. *Other Events and Opportunities for Formation.* Many other occasions for personal and spiritual development are made available by theologates. The nature and scope of these activities vary with the size of the school, its location, its articulation of the integration and identification models, the forms of ministry and life-style anticipated for its students, and its underlying ecclesiology. Usually, implicit objectives determine how programs are put together and how the outcomes are evaluated.

Most schools sponsor lectures, workshops, or short seminars on a series of topics such as peace and justice; celibacy and sexuality; alcoholism and other addictions; and specialized areas of ministry, for example, to families, to the physically and mentally challenged, and to youth or the elderly. Annual retreats, either preached or directed, are required of all seminarians, but the degree of involvement and seriousness with which retreats are approached varies. Whereas some see them as days of relaxation away from academic and pastoral work, others view them as important occasions for spiritual growth.

An aspect of formation that is sometimes overlooked, yet considered valuable especially at freestanding theologates, is the environment of the school. The intense focus on preparing for ministry in the Church unites the community, and relationships with teaching and formation faculty as well as with other students who have similar goals, are sources of encouragement and challenge. One school's catalog summarizes clearly the positive dimensions of this informal formation: "Total community environment has an important role in supporting development toward ordination. Students and resident priest faculty share the fellowship characteristic of the priesthood." Support also comes from students' bishops, the clergy of their dioceses, and vocation directors, in addition to pastors, lay ministers, and congregations in settings where students do field placements. The same catalog identifies other aspects of formation: "Finally, our programs bring priests, deacons, religious, and laity to campus so priesthood preparation occurs in a manner that reflects the Church renewed by the Second Vatican Council. This model engages varied ministries in collaboration to advance the gospel, and it recognizes the specific contribution each makes to building the total Christian community" (St. Paul School of Divinity, *Catalog*, p. 7).

e. *Special Focus: Personal and Spiritual Formation for Diocesan and Religious Order Seminarians.* In settings where students are being prepared for diocesan priesthood, considerable attention is given to what is appropriate spirituality for a diocesan priest. This was often articulated as being either an apostolic or a Eucharistic spirituality, with several common elements identified by these typical remarks:

1. Spirituality begins with the interior journey, and private prayer time is essential so that one walks with God through the day; this stance helps feed into ministry.
2. The interplay between ministry and prayer leads to deeper awareness of the priest as an instrument of God; ministry is not just an emptying but also a receiving from the Lord; and personal prayer is nourished by bringing concrete issues from ministry to it. Private devotions should be channeled to nourish the interior life, which finds its expression in the activity of ministry in Christ.
3. Opportunities for communal prayer—the Office, the Eucharist, and others, including spontaneous prayer and shared prayer—are needed for sustenance. If there is a community that provides support, personal difficulties such as alcoholism are not as likely to become major problems.

Spirituality for diocesan priests centers around the capacity for solitary prayer, daily Eucharist, and common worship, all performed in relation to ministry, with openness and sensitivity to the mystery of God in the people. Without prayer and solitude there is no mystery, and without mystery there is no prayer and solitude.

The basis for the spirituality of religious orders is usually the tradition and charism of the founder. A challenge for religious communities is to help seminarians integrate the charism and tradition of their community with the role of priest. In some religious orders expectations converge readily, but in others students struggle with the meaning of priesthood in the context of a particular ministerial focus. As John O'Malley, S.J., indicates in Part Ib of this study, documents on priestly formation neglect any description of religious order ministry suggesting models, goals, settings, or persons ministered to that differ from those of diocesan clergy. Hence the burden of supplying this aspect of formation is left to the religious institute.

At schools attended by both religious order and diocesan seminarians, the presence of some distinctive elements in the formation program is helpful. Religious order students have all experienced at least a year or two of novitiate and have received instruction in the spirituality and prayer of their congregations, whereas diocesan students come with more diverse religious backgrounds. Those who have been in college seminaries are at a different level from those who have not. These heterogeneous backgrounds can become a source of tension at theologates where differences are not taken into account. In a discussion of formation with several groups of students, some expressed concern about being "held back" by those who had had no previous seminary or religious-life experience, while others felt that they were always trying to "catch up" with the more experienced students. In either case, the wisdom of providing for the needs of students at different levels seems obvious. Creative interaction between those who are more experienced and those who are less well versed in the spiritual life is beneficial to both groups.

f. *Special Focus: Personal and Spiritual Formation for Other Students.* Interest in developing programs of personal and spiritual formation for students preparing for professional ministry other than priesthood has intensified over the past five to ten years, as the number of these students enrolled in theologates has increased. According to the 1987-88 CARA statistics, all except six theologates enroll at least some lay students and women religious on either a full-time or a part-time basis; twenty-two enroll more than fifty students who are not seminarians, and ten of the twenty-two enroll more one hundred such students. Most formation programs for these students are still in their infancy, and several issues remain unresolved. Among them are questions about what the goals of the programs should be, what elements of formation should be included, what distinctions should be made in the respective requirements for lay students and women religious, whether participation should be required or voluntary, and how to staff the programs. As understanding of lay spirituality evolves, effective ways of attending to the needs of these students will be found.

At some theologates where lay students and women religious have been enrolled for a number of years, formation-program goals and content are well developed. Generally the programs at these schools are designed to promote spiritual growth, to further personal maturity, to encourage commitment to Christian service, and to assist students in integrating learning on intellectual, spiritual, emotional, and pastoral levels. The content of the programs is not unlike that of programs for priesthood candidates. Spiritual direction, retreats, workshops, group and individual meetings, and prayer sessions are usually components. Nonordination students are also encouraged to take advantage of the theologate's other spiritual resources and to participate in its liturgical life. When feasible, these students join with seminarians in activities to enhance collaboration between lay ministers and clergy. The more developed programs also include periodic evaluations and seminars on formative spirituality. Approximately ten theologates have a distinct and well-developed program staffed by trained personnel for lay students and women religious, but only two or three require that they participate. It was reported, however, that voluntary participation is high and that students in most cases are seeking formational opportunities.

To distinguish between formation for lay students and formation for women religious, separate programs seem advisable, but they are not yet available. Women religious, who are usually older, have often lived ten or more years in community and have almost as many years of experience in ministry. They tend to be well grounded in prayer and in basic doctrine and faith; thus their needs for spiritual growth are likely to be met through spiritual direction and peer-group interaction. Few are interested in a required or more extensive program. With the primary focus on seminarians and the new demands of preparing lay students for ministry, it is not uncommon that providing for the spiritual needs of women religious is given low priority.

Issues for the future: Most schools regard personal and spiritual formation as integral to the total formation of students. With programs continuing to take shape, formation directors highlighted several areas that need to be augmented: the identity of the priest and formation for celibacy, development of a prayer life appropriate to ministry, working with those who exhibit signs of an underdeveloped self-image, resolving questions of deference and obedience to hierarchical authority, and reducing anxiety about evaluation so that honest self-revelation can lead to necessary growth and development. Concern about students covering up serious personal problems out of fear that revealing them will lead to expulsion is an issue for those who must recommend students for ordination and ministry positions.

Students identified parallel challenges that they expect to face in the future: embracing Church discipline with regard to celibacy while developing healthy relationships, learning how to be a friend and to be intimate without being possessive; continuing growth in prayer and spiritual life by working through difficulties in prayer, learning to accept both dark periods and periods of consolation and intimacy with God; establishing a positive self-image in ministry, so that involving lay people and especially women will not be threatening; and remaining faithful to the Church despite fear of retrenchment from Vatican II teachings and a perceived repressive response to certain theological positions.

A separate concern involves defining the boundaries between the internal forum of spiritual direction and the external forum of faculty advising. This distinction remains blurred, especially at freestanding theologates where personal and spiritual formation personnel have dual roles as faculty, and students sometimes lack the trust required for genuine accountability. The dichotomy of roles is less problematic when students have spiritual directors who do not take part in public ministry evaluation, though the same person would never serve in both capacities for the same student. With fewer available personnel and the policy restricting those who can serve as spiritual directors to the ordained, it seems less likely that the discrete role of spiritual director at freestanding seminaries will be easily filled. In the future it will be important for more priests to be specially trained in spiritual direction, a point made by Cardinal Baum in his letter on freestanding seminaries.

Another area that was identified as needing attention is the integration of academic and pastoral programs with spiritual and personal development. Theoretically, the different programs are viewed as separate entities in only a few cases; but in practice, theologate personnel have not determined clearly how to help students apply their academic knowledge to pastoral situations or to their interior life. The aim is to move, through theological reflection, toward an inclusive ecclesial spirituality that can be applied to ministerial situations. Supervised ministry is the vehicle that bears much of the burden for achieving this integration, but most faculty realize that applications must also be made from the beginning in course work and in personal and spiritual formation programs.

Finally, at theologates where students who are not ordination candidates are enrolled, there is a strongly perceived need for the development of formation programs for these students. To achieve this goal, a commitment of both personnel and financial resources will be required. Whether the desire to implement appropriate programs is strong enough to overcome current resistance in some settings has yet to be determined. Many of those interviewed believe that a positive response to this need will be of enormous benefit to the Church in the future.

B. *Academic Formation*

OVERVIEW STATEMENTS

The academic requirements for the M.Div. degree in theologates generally correspond with the broad outlines in the *Program of Priestly Formation (PPF)*. Vastly different ways of constructing and implementing the curriculum are operational at the various schools, however.

In virtually every interview with faculty and academic deans, the conclusion emerged that the M.Div. curriculum will not change substantially over the next five years or so, until the roles of priests and the roles of other professional ministers are clarified and differentiated.

Determining what the role of theologates in contributing to the education of lay ministers in the Church should be, and what the nature of that education should be, is a point of considerable disagreement among seminary leaders.

Whereas programs of preparation leading to ordination are with few exceptions four years long, at fourteen schools the M.Div. degree can be earned in three years, which is the required professional standard.

Many theologates are reviewing the length and structure of programs in light of the changing demands of ministry and changes in the student population, which includes seminarians from diverse backgrounds and a growing number of lay students, but few schools have made substantial changes in programs during the past few years.

The greatest variation in curricular requirements occurs in the pastoral area, with respect to both the number of credits required, which ranges from nine to thirty-eight, and the extent to which pastoral concerns are integrated into other courses.

Several adjustments in the curricula of most schools that are generally recommended by faculty include more emphasis on a theology of ministry that will clarify and differentiate the roles of priests and lay ministers, the incorporation of courses that will address foundational questions of collaborative ministry and leadership, and courses that

will enable understanding of the contemporary culture and society that is the context for ministry.

1. CURRICULUM IN RELATION TO MISSION AND CHURCH NEEDS

Present reality: The basic standards and patterns of curriculum are set out in the *PPF*. Within these general guidelines considerable variation in courses and requirements exists, and discussion during interviews frequently focused on the appropriate content of courses for those who are preparing to minister in the Church. Following is an analysis of the academic programs of theologates.

Of the forty-nine catalogs reviewed,[1] most state that the curriculum is designed to reflect the mission of the school. In all but a few cases, the *primary* mission of theologates is the education of priesthood candidates. Therefore, the curriculum is built around the M.Div. degree, with requirements attempting to reflect the anticipated future ministry of the ordained. But only rarely is a statement of the philosophy or purpose of the curriculum given. When it is, such a statement explains the unifying principles and the conceptual framework behind the curriculum. Explicit reference is often made to the *PPF*, indicating that this document provides the basis for the selection of courses and the determination of settings for pastoral field education.

Over the past ten years, many schools have made some minor revisions in their programs of study, with at least two distinct goals in view: bringing their courses into line with the *PPF*, and responding to changing needs in the Church. Church directives significantly influence curricula, and the prospect of the papal visitations to American theologates heightened awareness of the *PPF*. Directives from accrediting agencies like the Association of Theological Schools

---

[1] The forty-nine include all theologates in the continental U.S. that publish a catalog of their own or are associated with a university that does, and The American College of Louvain. Those theologates with systems not totally comparable, namely, CEDOC in Puerto Rico, the North American College in Rome, the Byzantine and Melkite seminaries, and the two Cistercian theology programs, are not included. The catalogs reviewed cover the years 1985 to 1987. For schools that publish a catalog annually, the latest one available was used. Since this analysis was completed, Holy Trinity Seminary in Dallas, Texas, closed its theologate, but its statistics are included here.

are also very influential. In the long run, such documents and agencies have virtually total control over the guiding principles and even some of the details of the curriculum. In the accreditation process, the nature of the curriculum and its appropriateness to the students it serves are central to evaluation. As a person experienced with accreditation of all types of seminaries noted: "Sometimes the Catholic theologates are not in the 'driver's seat' on this issue. There is still the sense that the program is 'given' to them. They feel excluded from the process of making significant decisions about the curriculum." This observation may help to explain why theologates have taken so little initiative recently to modify curricula.

The pastoral area is an exception, however, and has undergone considerable adaptation over the past ten to fifteen years. Impetus for change has come from increased demands in parishes for professionally prepared priests and lay ministers. Members of parishes expect that those who minister to them will be well trained in pastoral skills, which include the ability to preach and teach, to lead groups, and to counsel individuals. Schools have responded by incorporating experiences that will educate students in these areas. The introduction of theological reflection, for example, is designed to help students understand how various pastoral situations relate to theology and to the tradition of the Church. Supervised field placements, ranging from several months to a year, are being inserted into the program to provide the basis for theological reflection. Further, at a few schools new pastoral theology courses are being added in areas like counseling and group leadership.

Issues for the future: As theologates reevaluate their present mission statements and consider the needs of the Church, adjustments in curricula can be expected, especially as attempts are made to respond to the expanding mission of schools. The ministry of the Church must become a more significant driving force behind the rationale for academic programs, reducing the tendency to maintain the status quo. Many faculty and administrators believe that differentiation of the roles of priests and lay ministers is required before appropriate responses can be made. Several suggested that both seminarians and lay students would benefit from a course dealing explicitly with the theology of ministry, and covering the full range of service to be rendered in the Church. Since the total scope of ministry is seldom considered during theologate programs, misunderstanding about roles is prevalent. Summing up the comments related to role definition, one priest said, "If we continue to isolate individuals who perform roles and fail to promote understanding of the interrelationship between the varied gifts and varied ministries, we will not move the mission of the Church forward as a whole."

One striking aspect of the interviews was the uncertainty expressed by faculty about changing the academic program—the courses required, the methods used, and the arrangement of courses. Even when pressed on the topic, respondents were hesitant about making recommendations at this time, even though a large proportion of faculty see the importance of adapting to the changes that both lay ministers and priests will experience in public ministry. Most faculty feel that it is difficult to change curricular requirements without having a better sense of the kind of ministry that priests will be called upon to exercise in the future. Will it be almost entirely a sacramental ministry? Will priests continue to have heavy administrative duties? Will they almost certainly be engaged in collaborative ministry, given the reduced number of priests projected for the near future? Will ministry in nonparochial settings increase, especially to certain alienated or marginalized groups of people?

The large number of lay students enrolled in at least half the schools further complicates the issue of curricular change. Some faculties are eager to explore more effective ways of educating seminarians and lay students in common courses, while at the same time providing for the special needs of different ministries. The goal is to prepare individuals with different roles and different gifts to engage cooperatively in the common task of serving the people of God. Focus on the mission of the Church, said many of those interviewed, will help direct attention to the very reason for the existence of schools of theology—preparing those who will be in service to the Church.

Since the mission statements of many schools have recently been substantially reformulated, curricular change can also be expected at these schools. Many lay students are already studying for the M.Div. degree, and even more are working toward the M.A. or M.T.S. degree. Academic deans, who are primarily responsible for curricular development, frequently commented as follows: "Changes in curriculum will tend to come slowly because of limited resources and uncertainty about the nature of the ministry for which students are preparing, both those who will be ordained and those who will not. Though it may be five years before change happens on a widespread basis, it will happen." Yet about one-third of the faculty interviewed spoke of the urgency and importance of adapting to the needs of students, be they seminarians whose future role as priests is likely to be different from the role of priests now, or others in professional ministry whose roles are only beginning to take shape. Within theologates, much energy needs to be devoted to reshaping programs internally. These adjustments must be accompanied by significant dialogue with Church leaders and others outside the schools who will depend on the ministerial services of those now enrolled in theologates.

A related question frequently raised in a variety of contexts was, Should there be separate M.Div. programs for seminarians and for others preparing for professional ministry? Although this issue was addressed in the chapter on "Mission," it has specific ramifications for academic programs that need explication here. Opinions about the issue depend largely on the number and status of lay students enrolled at a given school. Among the thirteen schools enrolling only seminarians in their M.Div. programs, most take the position that the program for priestly formation would be diluted and limited resources drained if they had to teach other students. They believe that a significantly different orientation of the curriculum is appropriate for priesthood candidates, a sentiment sometimes echoed by students in those settings. The ten to twelve schools enrolling only a few lay students in their M.Div. programs express two intentions: Some plan to keep the number of lay students very limited and to make no special provisions for these students; others would welcome more lay students and may even depend on their presence for survival. The latter group of schools is eager to accommodate the needs of lay students. Finally, about twenty schools have a large number and proportion of lay students. For the most part, these schools are eager to explore more effective ways of educating seminarians and lay students in common courses, while still providing the specialization needed for different kinds of ministry. Finding models for collaborative preparation and collaborative ministry is a major goal for many of these schools. Other concerns focus on the type of courses, the kind of spiritual formation best suited to lay students, and the evaluation and eventual certification of lay students in these programs.

The question of mission is far from settled, and therefore questions related to curricular change are also undecided. Yet the very survival of at least ten to fifteen theologates depends on resolution of the issue of mission in favor of continuing to enroll lay students. At the majority of these schools, the manner in which programs are structured and integrated is in the process of being revised, sometimes by considered decisions, sometimes by default. Concurrently other decisions about where and how to educate professional lay ministers are being made, not by Church leaders but by the individual choices of lay students, many of whom have opted to study in Protestant seminaries or divinity schools. Will the curricula of these alternative schools enable their graduates to minister effectively in a Catholic context? Will negative attitudes toward the Catholic hierarchy and clergy develop more in Protestant settings than in Catholic theologates? It is my conclusion that dialogue about where and how to educate those who will serve as Catholic lay ministers must take place between theologate personnel and the broader Church if there is to be a creative vision for future ministry.

2. CONTENT OF CURRICULUM

Present reality: The question of precisely what should be taught to those who will minister in the Church was addressed by almost everyone who was interviewed. The core of theological education is often taken for granted and includes the obvious—courses in Scripture, systematic and moral theology, Church history, and pastoral studies. However, considerable discussion revolves around the allotment of credits to the various disciplines. Since the pastoral area, in its present form, is a relatively new discipline of theological education, it is the most controversial. With space and time being carved out of the more traditional disciplines, about 20 percent of the faculty talked about the regrettable "erosion of the academic." By this they meant that students are now spending more time in pastoral placements or "peripheral" courses, usually identified with the pastoral studies area.

Faculty find it frustrating to try to meet the multiple demands of preparing those who will minister in the future. They view as unrealistic the expectation that more courses or experiences be incorporated into the years of theology. A common sentiment was, "Not everything can be learned during theology. We need to decide on the basics and stay with them." The "basics" are usually defined as those areas that provide both an understanding of the tradition and the skills to communicate it. The consensus is surely that everything need not be crowded into the seminary curriculum, but determining exactly what is fundamental remains a problem. Although some believe that it would be desirable to build more choice into the curricular design, the difficulty of innovating and still fulfilling all of the requirements listed in the *PPF* is cited in response.

Course of study: Since the *PPF* serves as the guiding document for curricular design of theology programs, this section will compare the *PPF* requirements with the programs as they now exist. In chapter 3, entitled "The Academic Program," the *PPF* offers guidelines for the theological curriculum as a whole, beginning with basic principles. It states that "in the renewal of the theological curriculum must be a deeper appreciation of the meaning and importance of faith and its content, both for Christian living and theological understanding" (p. 36, #115). The document then notes the significant shift in the teaching of theology, which now stresses "the need to involve seminarians in the dynamic process of reflection" (p. 37, #119). In terms of method, courses must provide the opportunity "to learn and exercise the specific methodologies of exegesis, historical criticism, and systematic reflection, as well as the more practical methods related to the ministry itself" (p. 39, #129). The document states that historical and pastoral dimensions should pervade all courses. In general, the document's introduction to the academic program advocates integration of all courses and experiences that are to be part of the program. When determining the specific content of the curriculum, faculties are urged (in consultation with ordinaries) to establish programs appropriate to their own talents, the needs of their students, and the local situation. The document thus proposes that within broad guidelines each school is to establish a sound and practical curriculum, and one that is open to constant improvement.

Both from interviews with faculty and administrators and from a survey of the catalogs of the schools, it is clear that in most cases care has been taken to follow the general prescriptions set forth in the

PPF, but at the same time flexible interpretation is also evident. In chapter 3, five required areas of study are listed: Sacred Scripture, historical studies, systematic theology, sacred liturgy, and pastoral studies; and in another chapter under the heading "Pastoral Formation," the field education program is described. Most schools make two exceptions to this division of courses: They use a separate category for moral theology, and they incorporate sacred liturgy into systematic theology when the course is theoretical or into pastoral studies when it concerns application. The analysis that follows is done on the basis of the schema most commonly used: Sacred Scripture, historical studies, systematic theology, moral theology, pastoral studies, field education, and electives.

Overall requirements: A survey of the requirements for the M.Div. degree in the forty-nine theologates shows variation in the number of years required, the number of hours required, and the selection of courses offered. Through interviews, especially with faculty, it was possible to gain an understanding of the perceived strengths and shortcomings of each school's programs, how curriculum has changed, and what the major influences are that determine curriculum.

Forty-two schools list requirements according to semester credits, six according to quarter hours, and one according to units. For purposes of this analysis, all are translated into semester equivalents. On that basis, the average number of credits required is 101.5 for the M.Div. degree and 107.7 for seminarian programs. At nine schools, seminarians are required to take either more credits for the M.Div. degree itself or courses that go beyond the M.Div., which are sometimes applied to an M.A. or Th.M. degree. Twelve schools require field education that is not credited in the usual way. In some cases these credits are units, and in others a number of clock hours. Six of the twelve schools require a period of several months in internship, but without designated credits. The equivalent credits would add approximately six hours to each program.

The number of semester credits, or the equivalent, required by theologates for the M.Div. degree and for seminarians is as follows:

M. Div. Requirements	*Seminarian Requirements*
< 80 hrs. = 5 schools	< 80 hrs. = 3 schools
81-89 hrs. = 5"	81-89 hrs. = 2
90-99 hrs. = 8"	90-99 hrs. = 4"
100-109 hrs. = 12"	100-110 hrs. = 13"
110-119 hrs. = 15"	110-119 hrs. = 18"
> 119 hrs. = 4"	> 119 hrs. = 9"
Mean = 101.5 hrs.	Mean = 107.7 hrs.
Median = 104 hrs.	Median = 112 hrs.
Mode = 90 hrs.	Mode = 120 hrs.
Range = 72-139 hrs.	Range = 72-139 hrs.

The *PPF* outlines two different models, recommending 120 semester hours for each model, but as the document states, "They are not proposed as obligatory nor as descriptions of what is being done in any specific seminary" (p. 147, #551). The substantial variation in the number of credits required can be explained in large part by differing theories about the best way to prepare adult students for ministry. A school's underlying philosophy of course and credit distribution is reflected in the way it constructs its curriculum. Some schools require an average of four courses per semester, with intense and in-depth study expected; others require as many as seven or eight courses, which obviously affects the amount of time a student has to spend on a particular course. Faculty members who argue that fewer courses are preferable hold, by and large, that students gain more by intense study of carefully selected courses than they do by spending so much of their academic time in class, with little left over for research, reflection, and reading. On the other side, those who require many credit hours maintain that the longer time spent in class guarantees exposure to the different aspects of theology needed for ministerial service, which they believe is especially important now when students come with less philosophical and theological background than in previous years. The merits of these divergent approaches to theological education are debated at many of the schools.

The average distribution of credits by discipline or area of study is given in the table below. The number of credits and the concerns associated with each of the areas are discussed in detail beginning in the next subsection.

	M.Div. Requirements		Seminarian Requirements	
	Sem. Hrs.	% of Total	Sem. Hrs.	% of Total
Scripture	17.1	16.8	17.6	16.3
Historical Studies	8.1	8.0	8.6	8.0
Systematic Theology	23.9	23.5	26.6	24.7
Moral Theology	10.6	10.4	11.2	10.4
Pastoral Theology	23.0	22.7	23.9	22.2
Field Education	11.5	11.3	11.8	11.0
Electives/Other	7.3	7.2	8.0	7.4
	101.5	99.9	107.7	100.0

By way of comparison, the models proposed in the PPF distribute credits as follows:

	PPF Requirements Model A		PPF Requirements Model B	
	Sem. Hrs.	% of Total	Sem. Hrs.	% of Total
Scripture	18	15.0	21	17.5
Historical Studies	15	12.5	12	10.0
Systematic Theology	27	22.5	21	17.5
Moral Theology	6	5.0	9	7.5
Pastoral Theology	21	17.5	21	17.5
Field Education	7	5.8	7	5.8
Concentration	0	0.0	9	7.5
Philosophy	6	5.0	0	0.0
Electives/Other	20	16.7	20	16.7
	120	100.0	120	100.0

Several significant differences between the average actual requirements and the *PPF* models can be noted. On the whole, schools require fewer hours of historical studies, and many fewer credits are allowed for electives than either *PPF* model suggests. Further, neither a concentration nor philosophy is required during the theology program of any seminary. By contrast, theologates require more moral theology, pastoral theology, and field education credits than are allotted in the models.

Sacred Scripture: Among those interviewed who teach Sacred Scripture, virtually all have goals that include teaching methods of exegesis from a scientific viewpoint and helping students to make proper pastoral applications of biblical studies. In fact, the study of Scripture also forms the basis for systematic theology and other theological disciplines. The emphasis given to one or the other goal is quite varied, depending on the orientation of the individual teacher and of the school's programs. About one-fourth of the Scripture professors who were interviewed prefer a technical, scientific approach. These faculty lament the loss of language requirements, which makes it difficult to engage students in more scientific study. The majority, however, spoke of the necessity of teaching Scripture in a way that enables students to preach and teach effectively, using Scripture appropriately. This difference in method may relate to the years during which a faculty member was engaged in advanced study. Since about 1968 it has been possible to earn a licentiate in Scripture that is not a theological degree. The approach used in such a program may have involved historical and literary criticism, but not pastoral application or a theological orientation.

The number of credits required in Sacred Scripture indicates the considerable weight that is given to this area of study. Students most commonly begin their first semester with Introduction to the Old Testament and their second semester with Introduction to the New Testament. Beyond the first two courses, at least one additional course is ordinarily required in Old Testament, usually a choice between Psalms, Prophetic Books, and Historical Books. In New Testament, more commonly two additional courses are required, with the choices usually between the Synoptic Gospels, Johannine Literature, and Pauline Literature. The numbers of semester hours (or the equivalent) required by the schools are indicated below. At four schools, seminarians are required to take more credits in Scripture than their counterparts who will not be ordained. Both sets of numbers are given.

M. Div. Requirements	*Seminarian Requirements*
12 hrs. = 8 schools	12 hrs. = 6 schools
13-15 hrs. = 10"	13-15 hrs. = 9"
16-18 hrs. = 14"	16-18 hrs. = 14"
19-21 hrs. = 13"	19-21 hrs. = 15"
> 21 hrs. = 4"	> 21 hrs. = 4"
Mean = 17.1 hrs.	Mean = 17.6 hrs.
Median = 17 hrs.	Median = 18 hrs.
Mode = 16-18 hrs.	Mode = 19-21 hrs.
Range = 12-28 hrs.	Range = 12-28 hrs.

PPF Models = 18-21 hrs.

As the figures indicate, the vast majority of M. Div. programs (37; 75.5 percent) require from 13 to 21 hours, or 5 to 7 courses, with 17.1 being the average number of hours. For seminarians, the requirements are slightly higher, with 39 schools (79.6 percent) requiring from 13 to 21 hours and 17.6 as the average. The range of credits is significant and may be accounted for in several ways. Some schools require a relatively low number of credits in Scripture, as well as in other disciplines, making available a higher number of elective credits to spread over the various disciplines. Other schools require fewer courses overall and demand more intense work in each course. A small minority have very small faculties and cannot provide much variety in what is offered, so that the possibility of taking more courses does not exist.

Two major challenges in teaching are identified by most Scripture professors. One is how to help students apply Scripture properly to preaching and teaching. Given the strong fundamentalist influence in contemporary society, it has become increasingly urgent to familiarize students with the scriptural texts and to educate them in the use and misuse of Scripture. A second challenge, of less concern than the first, is how to teach Scripture when few students read the original biblical languages. Faculty who wish to inculcate the practice of a truly close reading of the text especially regret the absence of language requirements. Only at The American College of Louvain is language training required. One final observation about this area of study is that the number of scholars prepared to teach Scripture at the theologate level is sizable, and until very recently schools have had little difficulty in recruiting suitable faculty.

Historical studies: As with the study of Scripture, the *PPF* recommends that historical studies be integrated into all theological work; the value of historical studies is that they help students to "see that the past conditions the present and that present problems cannot be understood without a knowledge of the past" (*PPF*, p. 37, #121). It further suggests that all faculty be trained in historical methodology. Several history courses are recommended, including courses on the early, medieval, Reformation, and modern periods, as well as the history of the Church in the United States. The number of hours required by the schools in historical studies is as follows:

M. Div. Requirements	*Seminarian Requirements*
< 6 hours = 5 schools	< 6 hours = 4 schools
6 hrs. = 14"	6 hrs. = 12"
7-9 hrs. = 15"	7-9 hrs. = 15"
10-12 hrs. = 10"	10-12 hrs. = 13"
> 13 hrs. = 2"	> 13 hrs. = 2"
Mean = 8.1 hrs.	Mean = 6.0 hrs.
Median = 7 hrs.	Median = $\frac{7}{8}$ hrs.
Mode = 6 hrs.	Mode = 6 hrs.
Range = 2-15 hrs.	Range = 3-15 hrs.

PPF Models = 12-15 hrs.

Faculty instructors in Church history identified as their greatest challenge trying to teach the scope of Church history when students seldom have general historical knowledge. But most agree that, given the other requirements, it is unreasonable to expect students to take more than three or four history courses.

Systematic theology: In many ways systematic theology is the most complex of the theological disciplines. It is the area that "aims at helping the students analyze and synthesize their understanding of the Christian faith in continuity with the heritage of the past and in the context of the community of the faith today" (*PPF*, p. 44, #152). In some respects this discipline, because of its breadth and complexity, offers students the most significant encounter with their understanding of the Church and of faith. Although the *PPF* includes both dogmatic theology and moral and spiritual theology under the heading "Systematic," the schools more typically use two categories: systematic, which covers fundamental theology, Trinity, Christology, ecclesiology, eschatology, spiritual and sacramental and liturgical theology, et al.; and moral, which is distinguished by the specific way in which it demonstrates the relationship between belief and life. Some schools have a separate category for spiritual theology, but since most include these courses under systematics, spiritual theology credits are reflected in the figures below.

M. Div. Requirements	*Seminarian Requirements*
< 16 hrs. = 4 schools	< 16 hrs. = 3 schools
16-21 hrs. = 16"	16-21 hrs. = 11"
22-27 hrs. = 15"	22-27 hrs. = 16"
28-33 hrs. = 11"	28-33 hrs. = 15"
> 34hrs. = 3"	> 34 hrs. = 4"
Mean = 23.9 hrs.	Mean = 26.6 hrs.
Median = 24 hrs.	Median = 25 hrs.
Mode = 24 hrs.	Mode = 24/29 hrs.
Range = 8-47 hrs.	Range = 12-47 hrs.

PPF Models = 21-27 hrs.

In no other discipline of theology is there more diversity in the method and content of courses than in systematics. Some faculty approach the material mainly from a historical viewpoint, trying to help students reflect on doctrine as it developed over time. Others see the necessity of covering what they consider to be the essentials of the faith, viewed as a somewhat static and basically unchangeable body of doctrine. Still others seek to teach with a pastoral orientation, constantly considering the application of material to ministerial situations. Further differences are found in approaches to the subject matter of fundamental theology, Christology, Trinity, and the like—the focus may be on one or several authors, or on major themes, or refracted through a particular methodology, for example, philosophical, anthropological, or psychological. Though more courses are typically required in this area than in any other, the problem of covering the wide range of topics remains the greatest challenge.

It is noteworthy that ecumenism receives little attention at most schools, perhaps because of the multiple expectations of the curriculum. Some faculty explained the absence of courses on ecumenism by the fact that the use of Protestant and Jewish authors in many areas of theology already offers an adequate understanding of other faiths. Nonetheless, given the Church's strong emphasis on ecumenical concerns after Vatican II, many faculty would like to see more explicit ways of introducing students to the many facets of ecumenism reinstated.

Moral theology: The required courses in moral theology are usually in the areas of fundamental, personal, and social ethics. Just over half of the schools require a fourth course, often an elective. The *PPF* states that the goal of these courses is to move students toward a "prudential understanding of Christian life and decision making, both for the formation of their own consciences and for skillful teaching and counseling of others in the formation of their consciences in due obedience to the moral teaching of the gospel and of the Church" (p. 47, #161). The credit requirements in moral theology are as follows:

M.Div. Requirements	*Seminarian Requirements*
6 hours = 6 schools	6 hours = 6 schools
7-9 hrs. = 14"	7-9 hrs. = 14"
10-12 hrs. = 18"	10-12 hrs. = 16"
13-15 hrs. = 8"	13-15 hrs. = 6"
> 15 hrs. = 2"	> 15 hrs. = 6"
Mean = 10.6 hrs.	Mean = 11.2 hrs.
Median = 11 hrs.	Median = 11 hrs.
Mode = 12 hrs.	Mode = 12 hrs.
Range = 6-20 hrs.	Range = 6-24 hrs.

PPF Models = 6-9 hrs.

The majority of faculty and administrators who were interviewed identified moral theology as the most difficult area to teach because of present controversy in the Church surrounding some moral issues. At least half of the moral theologians interviewed voiced concern about their teaching being misunderstood by their students and these same students misrepresenting it to others. The following comment typifies the attitude that was expressed: "Let's be honest. Those of us who teach moral theology are afraid about what is happening to our profession. We are no longer free to be scholars. We are under constant scrutiny." It is no surprise, then, and perhaps a consequence of the present climate in the Church, that it is more difficult to find professors of moral theology than of any other discipline, a situation that seriously concerns academic deans and rectors/presidents. Another issue related to moral theology, and mentioned frequently by those teaching it, is the decline in interest on the part of students in courses on social justice. Several schools require a course with that title, and most offer an elective in the area, but few students see this study as urgent or central to the gospel message. The prevalence of such apathy concerns not only moral theologians but also many faculty and administrators.

Pastoral studies: In addition to recommending a general pastoral orientation of the curriculum, the *PPF* suggests that a number of special courses dealing with the principal areas of pastoral ministry be part of theological studies. The four areas listed are canon law, homiletics, religious education (catechetics), and pastoral leadership and counseling. At most of the schools liturgical courses oriented toward practice, such as presiding at Eucharist, leading prayer services, and administering the sacraments, are included in the pastoral section. Therefore, these credits are also counted in the numbers that follow.

M. Div. Requirements	*Seminarian Requirements*
< 13 hrs. = 5 schools	< 13 hrs. = 4 schools
13-18 hrs. = 7"	13-18 hrs. = 6"
19-24 hrs. = 17"	19-24 hrs. = 16"
25-30 hrs. = 10"	25-30 hrs. = 12"
> 30 hrs. = 8"	> 30 hrs. = 9"
47 schools[2]	47 schools

[2]Two schools list combined requirements for pastoral studies and field education at twenty-four and thirty hours. Since the numbers cannot be divided by area, they are not included in these totals.

Mean = 23.0 hrs.   Mean = 23.9 hrs.
Median = 24 hrs.   Median = 24 hrs.
Mode = 24 hrs.   Mode = 24 hrs.
Range = 9-38 hrs.   Range = 9-38 hrs.

PPF Models = 21 hrs.

As noted above, the range of requirements in pastoral studies is great, and the ways in which these credits are distributed varies considerably. All schools state that at least some pastoral courses must be taken, but not all designate courses in each of the areas recommended in the *PPF*. The range of elective credits in pastoral studies is between three and twenty-four, with the remaining credits assigned to specific courses.

In *canon law*, one course is required by fifteen schools, two courses by twenty-four schools, and three courses by six schools; four schools do not require any courses. Seven schools have slightly lower requirements for those who are not seminarians. Teachers of canon law remarked that in the short time allotted only the most basic concepts can be taught; thus they focus on applications to ministerial situations, especially the canons pertaining to marriage. The case-study method is used by many teachers of canon law, and students appreciate this approach because it allows for simulation of actual pastoral situations.

In *homiletics*, thirty-seven schools require two or more courses, six require one, and six do not specify a requirement. Since preaching is one of the most important duties of those who minister, the necessity of good preparation was stressed by many respondents. For teachers of homiletics, the lack of control that they have over the results of their teaching is frustrating. Some students have a natural ability to integrate their faith and prayer life in well-delivered homilies, while others struggle even with basic speech skills. Faculty often mentioned the great number of complaints they receive about the preaching of former students in parish settings, but most feel that only several years of training would help some students to improve and other students may always be inadequate homilists.

In *religious education (catechetics)*, twenty-four schools require from one to three credits, some of them in practica. Thus religious education is clearly a discipline that receives very little attention. If the future role of priests is to include work with Confraternity of Christian Doctrine (CCD) programs, some faculty believe that more courses should be available in religious education, but perhaps taken as a specialization after theology. Few seminarians aspire to work in religious education, which represents a significant shift from previous years, when most newly ordained priests did some kind of teaching.

Pastoral leadership and counseling is the heading designated in the *PPF*, but the schools almost always require courses only in counseling, and leadership as such is not mentioned. At least one course in counseling is required by thirty-three schools, and twelve schools require a second course. During interviews with those who teach pastoral courses, a concern frequently voiced was that, although much of what will be expected of priests and other professional ministers in the future revolves around group work (including staff collaboration and work with parish groups), few schools offer courses that cover these areas. The acquisition of skills in conducting meetings, resolving conflicts, and enabling others to become involved in caring for the needs of people is usually not addressed in a significant way in seminaries. The dichotomy between what students are prepared to do and what they actually do, once finished with theology, is particularly evident here. The implications of failing to address this issue, faculty believe, will seriously hinder effective Church leadership in the future. If the number of priests continues to decline, the need for both leadership skills and collaborative skills will become even more acute.

In *liturgical practice*, sixteen schools require one course, and twenty-nine schools require two or more courses. These courses are distinguished from courses in sacramental and liturgical theology, and are usually listed under pastoral studies. They prepare seminarians to celebrate the Eucharist and the sacraments; other students are instructed in leading groups in prayer and presiding at communion services and other liturgical functions. Occasionally the study of music and art are specifically required under this section, but on the whole little attention is given to the fine arts.

The strongest disagreement about curriculum occurs around the issue of how important and central pastoral studies courses are. A significant minority of faculty perceive that greater demands for spiritual and pastoral training since Vatican II have eroded the academic program. They believe that the essential task of theological education is to prepare seminarians intellectually and not to train them in ministerial skills. These skills, they believe, can be learned on the job or perhaps through a deacon internship. Other faculty assert that the academic program has been aided by the addition of pastoral studies, theological reflection, and field work. In their view the personal integration of the traditional course material through these experiences, and through personal and spiritual formation, helps students to apply theological principles in meaningful ways, thus increasing interest in, understanding of, and involvement with the academic subject matter.

As mentioned earlier, much concern about what to teach and how to teach it can be located in this area. Pastoral studies faculty are newer to the seminary and therefore have little authority or power to make changes that would give more status to their discipline. But the need for better preparation of students in pastoral studies surfaces often, especially among those who have recently graduated. Some schools have made much progress in resolving this issue, whereas others have not yet dealt with it. Continuing dialogue about it is needed. If graduates could somehow be evaluated on the basis of how effective their practice of ministry is, schools could more easily make decisions about how best to shape their programs.

Issues for the future: While it is clear that the general structure of the curriculum is set, a number of clarifications and adjustments must be addressed in the future. First, clear statements about the overall goals of the curriculum would allow teachers to relate what they teach to what others teach, and the faculty then to provide a comprehensive view of the tradition of the Church. The problem of the "crowded curriculum" is in part due to inadequate design, so that the content of some courses overlaps while other topics are omitted. A review of the responsibilities of each discipline and the content of each course would result in some realignment of subject matter, and would enhance the total academic program of most schools.

Second, in light of considerable discussion about priestly identity and the appropriate roles of ordained and lay ministers, a specific and explicit course on the mission and ministry of the Church is recommended by many faculty. Such a course, they say, should deal with the theology of priesthood as well as the theology of lay ministry. The changing needs of the Church would form the back-drop for the content of the course. The meaning of collaborative ministry and the exercise of leadership in a Church with changing parochial structures need to be understood by all who will work in ministerial positions. Training in group leadership and conflict resolution should be a required part of ministerial programs.

Finally, implicit in the discussion about curriculum is the desire to educate future ministers in such a way that the needs of the people they minister to are fully addressed. A notable lack of knowledge about contemporary culture and society makes it difficult for students to apply theological insights to their ministry. If the overall content of the curriculum is reviewed along the lines suggested above, space will be found for the study of social structures and influences. Without knowledge about the context in which people live, ministerial effectiveness cannot be expected. With it, not only will people's needs be met, but regenerated enthusiasm for service in the Church can be anticipated as a likely and healthy by-product.

3. THEOLOGICAL METHOD AND METHODS OF TEACHING

Present reality: When faculty discussed curriculum, they frequently mentioned the need for review of both theological method and methods of teaching. Confusion exists about the difference between the two. In the *PPF*, for example, methodology in one section refers to "the specific methodologies of exegesis, historical criticism, and systematic reflection, as well as the more practical methods related to the ministry itself" (p. 39, #129). In a different section, methods of instruction in theology are considered (pp. 50-51, ##174-187). Both of these concepts were discussed by respondents, and most suggested that clarification of the meaning of different understandings about method would be useful.

The *PPF* also advises that appropriate methods be used to achieve integration. For some faculty this means intellectual integration of course material, for example, from the scriptural, historical, and pastoral areas; for others it means something more personal, an integrated appropriation of values.

Some specific issues were raised about methods of teaching. As most theologians who were interviewed noted, since Vatican II Catholic doctrine has become less "dogmatic," that is, able to be reduced to agreed-upon statements, and more discursive, with emphasis on its dialogical and developmental nature. The *PPF* notes the shift and underlines "the need to involve the seminarians in the dynamic process of reflection on the problems of life and to instill in them a sense of the historical development of the Christian faith and the life of the individual and the Christian community" (p. 37, #119). The change in the nature of Catholic doctrine entails a reexamination of approaches to teaching. Currently, many faculty still prefer the lecture method. They observe, however, that in the past this method generated spirited and challenging class discussion. The growing inclination of students today is to absorb information rather passively and unquestioningly. This trend is disturbing to many faculty, some of whom believe that teaching methods should be reviewed and perhaps revised in the hope of engaging students in discussion and reflection. They point out that theology is not merely information to be memorized, but a living tradition to be understood in light of the Church as it exists today. Many faculty debate about the best way of teach effectively and would welcome ongoing discussion of teaching methods.

From a practical point of view, a major concern of academic deans and some faculty is the extent to which faculty members are willing to consider departing from their preferred method of teaching. While certain methods are more appropriate to some kinds of course material than others, some faculty seem reluctant even to entertain the possibility of anything other than the lecture method. Most were educated at a time when the accepted mode of learning was listening to lectures; thus they have not experienced newer methods, such as the use of case studies, student presentations in small seminars, team teaching, or the various forms of so-called experiential learning. Education on how to implement these methods is not usually made available to faculty. It cannot be assumed that a person who lectures effectively can easily switch to a different approach, and so a good lecturer hesitates to consider such a change. A comment made by one faculty member represents the consensus: "Even if we accept the premise that we should change the way we teach theology, we often do not have the confidence to carry it out. We have to be committed to change and then train full-time faculty in these new methods."

The inadvisability of adopting a set of textbooks that would be required by all theologates in certain courses was a practically unanimous sentiment. There is no enthusiasm for another set of manuals, yet some faculty and administrators sense growing pressure from a few in Church leadership who want all students to study from such required texts.

4. PROGRAM LENGTH

Present reality: Almost all programs leading to ordination are four years long and thus conform to the *PPF* (p. 147, #552), which states as the first of its "basic requirements" that "the four years of the theology program should normally involve approximately 120 credit hours." Only two schools require five years, in both cases because of an internship year; several others offer the option of an extended program. Fourteen schools have M.Div. programs that require only three years, which satisfies the ATS accrediting regulation. In 1986-87 all except four of these schools required a fourth year of study before ordination, however, and the four remaining schools have just added a fourth year of study before ordination. Seven or eight other schools are discussing the advisability of shortening the M.Div. program to three years and instituting an optional M.A. program during the fourth year.

The length of time needed for an adequate theological program is of course related to the preparation students bring to the seminary. A recent decline in the number of students who attended college seminaries, as well as the addition of lay students, has meant that many come with a less developed knowledge of their faith and a weaker liberal arts education, especially in philosophy. These students may have educational needs that would best be served by a longer program. In light of the diverse backgrounds of students, new ways of meeting special needs are being implemented. One means of preparing for the study of theology that has been introduced is a pretheology year. Twelve theologates have some form of such a program available to students, either a structured program, a set of courses in philosophy; or a college program on the same premises, where students can take the courses they need. It is common during this year for the students to be engaged almost totally in the study of philosophy. Unanswered questions about pretheology programs concern their relative quality, degree of success, appropriate length, and location, that is, whether they are better attached to a college as a fifth year or to the theologate as a pre-year.

Issues for the future: An ongoing dilemma faced by schools is how to incorporate all the contents of the ideal curriculum into the years of theology. Several approaches to the problem have been tried, such as extending the program with a pastoral or internship year, using summers for Clinical Pastoral Education (CPE) and field education, or increasing the number of credits and courses required of seminarians. From limited student feedback regarding each of these fairly new approaches, both positive and negative responses were reported by faculty. Inserting a pastoral year has been helpful for some students, who return to school with renewed interest and understanding of how and what to study in the light of ministerial demands. In other cases, the break in the academic program has proved detrimental to serious study. Of even greater concern is the significant number of students who fail to return after a pastoral year. Although this last pattern is viewed as negative by some, others feel that it is better for the ordination candidate to make the decision to leave before being ordained, or for the lay student to leave before investing further time and commitment in study that would not be directly applied. It can be expected that schools will continue to review the length and structure of academic programs.

Some seminaries have considered adding a fifth year, usually in the form of an internship program, but few have implemented the extension, in part because bishops are reluctant to wait another year for priests who are badly needed, and in part because some faculty believe that practical experience can just as well be gained after ordination. It is widely held that when students finish theology they still have much to learn about ministry, and that the only real solution is to incorporate continuing education and formation into the model for priestly formation not as a choice but as a requirement. The role of theologates in providing this education is addressed below.

5. OTHER PROGRAMS

Present reality: Twenty years ago almost every theologate offered one basic M.Div. program for seminarians. Since then a veritable explosion in types of degree programs and students has occurred at all but a few theologates. Although not every school offers every type of new program, several possibilities are now available at most schools. Among them are pretheology courses or programs at twelve schools, with at least four of these oriented specifically to the needs of older men. Six schools offer the possibility of a retroactive M.Div. for those priests who finished theology before the degree was conferred. Programs for permanent deacons are listed among the offerings of four seminaries. Many degree programs are also available: thirty-eight schools offer the M.A., nine the M.T.S., four the M.R.E., four others the Th.M., and two the S.T.M.; three have an S.T.L., S.T.B., or D.Min. program. One school currently offers the S.T.D., two the Ph.D., and three others a joint Ph.D. In addition, sixteen schools offer a formal continuing education or sabbatical program, and several provide various types of certification for religious educators and volunteer parish ministers.

It is obvious that the variety and diversity of programs could well strain the resources of theologates. It is also true that the number of seminarians has declined so sharply in recent years that, without these new programs and students, up to half of the present schools would not be able to survive. In 1966-67 the only students enrolled in just over one hundred theologates were 8,325 seminarians. By 1986-87 the number of seminarians had dropped to 3,859, but 2,459 (38.9 percent) other full-time students were enrolled in the fifty-four theologates. Because of the reduced number of institutions, the average number of seminarians in theologates has not changed drastically— declining from about eighty to about seventy—but these students are not evenly distributed among the theologates. A few schools have large numbers of seminarians, whereas some fifteen schools have such a small number that they are barely able to continue their programs. The latter schools must attract a diverse student body if they are to remain open.

Issues for the future: Questions about the future of theologates relate directly to the missions of the schools. The kinds of students who will be welcome to study in theologates in the years ahead will determine much about the nature of theological education, the number of schools that can be sustained, and the variety of programs that will be available. Many decisions about the schools hinge on the basic issue of mission.

Another consideration for the future relates to the need for continuing education for priests and lay ministers. Many academic deans and faculty members observed that everything priests need to know in order to minister effectively cannot be taught during the four years of theology. They propose that, just as updating is required of many other professionals, continuing education should become mandatory for priests and lay ministers. Theologates are in a position to provide the programs, but though the rhetoric to support such a plan is strong, most believe that bishops are not committed to it.

C. Pastoral Formation and Field Education

OVERVIEW STATEMENTS

Since Vatican II, greater emphasis on pastoral concerns has led to development of pastoral field education programs at every school, and faculty are becoming more aware of the need to incorporate the pastoral dimension in other courses.

The stated qualifications for directors of field education are varied, but the consensus is that persons with a background in pastoral theology and with organizational skills would be ideal. At present few directors have those credentials.

A major goal of directors of field education is to establish a coherent developmental approach to pastoral training that takes into account the backgrounds of students and the needs of the Church.

Theological reflection is the hallmark of the best field education programs; different ways of practicing it are being developed, and some models are satisfactory while others still need improvement.

Training for pastoral leadership is being emphasized more as parishes change and parishioners become more actively involved in parish life. These changes require skills in pastoral leadership, such as understanding group processes and conflict resolution. In all but a few cases, directors of field education indicate that courses teaching these skills have yet to be developed.

1. DEVELOPMENT OF FIELD EDUCATION

Present reality: Since Vatican II, greater emphasis on pastoral concerns has led to significant development of pastoral field experience in theologates. As more attention is given to practical training for ministry, those responsible for field education programs are attempting a variety of approaches. With the reestablishment of field education in the curriculum, the appropriate qualifications for directors are being examined and even the naming of the position and of the field experiences is undergoing change. At a few theologates "supervised ministry" is replacing "field education." Concurrently the structure and content of programs are being examined, and the effectiveness of the experiences more carefully evaluated. These changes signal a redirection of focus, time, and energy that affects the whole configuration of theological education.

Until about fifteen years ago, what is called field education in the theologate program today was a time set aside for practical experience, often occupying the final year of study before ordination. Essentially a deacon internship, it involved Christian education and some pastoral work associated with the office of deacon. In recent years pastoral field education has gained new emphasis and support in the curriculum, and now it is becoming an integral part of ministerial preparation. Because of its prominence in the third edition of the *PPF*, the need for pastoral preparation is being highlighted more and more by the educators who are preparing students and by the parishioners who will be receiving their services.

The goals of pastoral training as set forth in the *PPF* are numerous and comprehensive. One of its principal goals is "to teach seminarians the habit of theological reflection about the priestly mission. In the context of field education, theological reflection refers to that process by which they attempt to perceive how theology and the tradition of the Church shed light on various pastoral situations they have experienced, how God's saving power and presence are operative in these experiences, and what this means for their own life in Christ" (p. 55). Other reasons for introducing ministerial experience during theology, as indicated in the *PPF* and generally acknowledged by directors and students, are to nourish the call to priesthood or other ministerial service; to serve as a realistic test of what working in the Church will require; to teach students how to work within the structure of the Church; and to develop in them a sensitivity to people, their needs and aspirations, their circumstances of life, and their attitudes toward God and humankind.

Some schools are making serious efforts to synthesize theoretical and applied theology, but the synthesis is difficult to achieve. Although the integration of field education with academic and spiritual preparation is considered highly desirable, and several seminaries have worked diligently to create an adequate model, it is generally acknowledged that extensive work still needs to be done on this aspect of theological education. Developing leadership skills and other competencies needed in ministry settings, along with instilling the habit of theological reflection, cannot be adequately accomplished in such a short time. Nevertheless, the process can be begun and students can engage in theological reflection during the remainder of their education and in their future ministry. Since in most cases supervision in the pastoral setting is minimal, even if faculties agree on the importance of field education, the implementation of programs can be difficult.

Even more problematic are the school situations in which field education is given only minimal recognition, or is actually resisted because it is not "real theology." These institutions accord a lower status to the director of field education and are unwilling to give academic credit for field placement. The comment of one faculty member summarizes the concern of those who support field education: "Does this not indicate that academic formation is still conceived apart from ministry? Does a 'ministerial dimension' truly exist in 'academic courses,' or are faculty still teaching just the way they were taught in graduate school because they don't know how to integrate? It happened in the thirteenth century that theology was divorced from spirituality and ministry, and the results still affect teaching styles and promote an anti-intellectual clergy."

As suggested, the place of field education is a significant area of contention for some faculties. The structural model of the Church underlying the curriculum strongly influences the way ministry is perceived and, consequently, the way faculty believe education for ministry should be conducted.

Issues for the future: Among the challenges that directors of field education identify for the future are these: (1) bringing about full acceptance of pastoral training and field education by faculties in theologates; (2) clarifying the meaning of theological reflection and the role the faculty might play in assisting with this process; (3) employing trained supervisors in field settings for more adequate evaluation; (4) broadening participation of parishioners in the field education process; (5) incorporating changes in programs as parish structures and needs change, especially in light of the diminishing number of clergy and increasing involvement of professional lay ministers; (6) facilitating the transition from theologate to parish ministry, which a few schools already see as their responsibility; and (7) arranging for supervision at least through the early years of ministry as a means of ensuring continuity and growth.

Many of the changes that directors of field education hope to implement are intended to effect movement toward a collaborative model of ministry. In order to develop an effective model, more support and supervision will have to come from field placement sites. If a collaborative model of ministry is not clarified or refined, and the number of priests continues to decline, the negative consequences will be detrimental to parish life. A similar observation was made by more than half of those who work with students in supervised ministry settings.

2. ROLE AND COMPETENCE OF DIRECTORS OF FIELD EDUCATION

Present reality: Of the forty-nine schools being considered,[1] forty-six identify the position of Director of Field Education. At two of these schools co-directors are listed, and so forty-eight individuals are included in these statistics. As recommended in the *PPF*, faculty status is accorded to all except two directors. Traditionally the position of leadership in this area has been titled Director of Field Education, still the term most commonly used in Catholic theologates and therefore in this document. Recently some schools have shifted to other titles, such as Director of Supervised Ministry or Director of Pastoral Formation. The *vocational status* of the forty-eight directors is represented by sixteen women religious, sixteen diocesan priests, eleven men religious, three laywomen, one Protestant minister, and one layman. The *credentials* of forty-three were identified, and they are as follows:

Degree	Number	
Ph.D.	10	
S.T.D.	2	41.9%
D.Min.	6	
M.Div.	8|	
Masters (M.A. et al.)	15	
M.Th.	1	58.1%
B.A.	1	

---

[1] The American College of Louvain does not have a field education program; thus the number of theologates being considered is forty-nine instead of fifty.

A relatively small proportion of directors of field education hold doctoral degrees (41.9 percent) when compared with the entire body of faculties, among which 67.4 percent hold doctorates.

The *academic rank* assigned to directors of field education as a group is lower than that of the faculty in general, which may reflect their sometimes limited educational backgrounds or the relatively short duration of their appointments. Only eighteen (37.5 percent) are listed with rank in the catalogs of their respective schools:

Rank	Number
Professor	0
Associate Professor	5
Assistant Professor	8
Instructor	4
Lecturer	1

Although the *PPF* is clear about the status of directors of field education ("the field education program should be entrusted to a director who has full faculty status" [p. 58, #208]), not all schools follow this prescription. Acceptance of directors of field education as full-fledged faculty is progressing rapidly, but about 60 percent of the directors who were interviewed still feel that their credibility is questioned as is the validity of the pastoral field component. Indeed, lack of acceptance in some instances extends to the entire pastoral studies area, a condition that its faculty believe is due in large part to the lack of knowledge and understanding of their discipline by faculty in "traditional" theological areas. At twelve schools faculty rank is given but not to directors of field education, and at seventeen schools rank is not listed for anyone. About half of the administrators who were interviewed would concur with one dean who said, "Directors should have faculty status and comparable credentials. If not, then they and the programs will be marginalized by the academic faculty." Some attribute the negative attitudes of other faculty not to theological differences per se, but rather to differences in theological method.

The *PPF* is straightforward in prescribing the areas of preparation requisite for directors of field education: "first, in theology, so that field education may be a truly theological discipline; second, in supervisory techniques" (p. 58, #208). Nonetheless, considerable disagreement about what should be the role and professional preparation of directors still exists. In some settings they have credentials equal to those of other faculty, and the corresponding status; in others they have faculty status, but not the same credentials as most other faculty. A third alternative is that they have professional administrative status only, in spite of having credentials equivalent to those of faculty. The varying degrees of credibility and success that are evident in field education programs frequently reflect the varying backgrounds of directors and the rank and status accorded to them.

Issues for the future: The educational background that should be required of those responsible for field education has not yet been agreed on; but as the purpose of field education is clarified, more attention will be given to the credentials needed for this position. Most faculty and deans believe that directors should have substantial theological training, especially in light of the significance of theological reflection. Some current directors have considerable skills in the areas of supervision and program management, but minimal preparation in theology. In the future it is expected that it will be even more difficult to recruit directors who have both the theological preparation and the other competencies needed to implement programs successfully. The qualities and skills required for the position are diverse, and few individuals with all of these credentials are available.

3. STRUCTURE, CONTENT, AND EFFECTIVENESS OF FIELD EXPERIENCE

Present reality: The requirements for field education are variably structured; some are spread out over three or four years, most are concentrated in one year, and a few are completed in an intense summer experience. At seven or eight schools, a coherent developmental model of field education is in place. According to such a model, the involvement and responsibility of students increases during the four years of theology, and the student progresses from observation to participation to leadership in the ministry situation. One of the best examples of such a model is "The Teaching Parish," the program of the St. Paul School of Divinity, where each student's pastoral experience is based in one parish and student responsibility increases each year. Another fine example of a developmental program, the one at Mundelein Seminary, has students working in many different settings, but the level of responsibility is also incremental. The positive and negative features of these two models are easily identified. Although the first provides continuity, follow-through, and intense relationships, it does not offer as much variety or flexibility. The selection of parishes and the training of on-site supervisors are crucial to the success of this model. The second model gives students more breadth and diversity, but it also engages them less intensely, making it easier for them simply to wait out a difficult situation rather than confronting and solving problems. On the whole, most models lack a developmental approach and consist largely of one experience followed by another. While any of these experiences may be beneficial, the potential for growth is diminished with experiences that are scattered and less coherent.

At about ten schools where students are somewhat older and more experienced than the average seminarian, attention is given to building on the backgrounds and skills that students have acquired before theology rather than to multiplying experiences during theology that they have already had. Religious order candidates often fit into this category, since they have engaged in several years of ministry and are experienced in theological reflection. Lay students come with backgrounds as diverse as those of seminarians, and may be equally experienced. For field education to function well, therefore, discriminating diagnostic tools need honing so that students can be assigned to appropriate ministerial settings.

The number of semester hours in field education required by theologates ranges from four to twenty-four. Thirty-seven theologates specify the number of credit hours, two require field education but do not specify the number of hours, six require a deacon internship or pastoral year, three require a number of units or clock hours, and The American College of Louvain does not require fieldwork as part of its academic program. The statistics for the schools that specify semester-hour requirements (or the equivalent in quarter hours) are as follows:

M. Div. Requirements	*Seminarian Requirements*
< 7 hours = 8 schools	< 7 hours = 7 schools
7-9 hrs. = 5 "	7-9 hrs. =4 "
10-12 hrs. = 13 "	10-12 hrs. = 13 "
13-15 hrs. = 3 "	13-15 hrs. = 4 "

16-18 hrs. = 5"	16-18 hrs. = 6 "
> 18 hrs. = 3 "	> 18 hrs. = 3 "
Mean = 11.5 hrs.	Mean = 11.8 hrs.
Median = 12 hrs.	Median = 12 hrs.
Mode = 12 hrs.	Mode = 12 hrs.
Range = 4-24 hrs.	Range = 4-24 hrs.

PPF Models = 7 hrs.

The *locus* of pastoral field education for diocesan and religious seminarians, as well as for lay students, is most often either the parish or organizations and activities associated with parish life. In a few instances parish leaders are well prepared to supervise students who are doing their pastoral training, and take seriously their participation in the educational process. The concept of "the teaching parish," mentioned earlier, is the basis for several successful field education programs. One former long-term rector made the following comment: "Parish congregations are crying for this type of preparation for clergy. They are also *proud* to do their part in supporting it—again, part of the participatory approach to the Church. The ecclesiology of the local church does make a difference." For at least half of the directors, a primary goal is to work more closely with those who supervise students on location so that supervisors can arrive at greater clarity about the nature of their task, especially how to evaluate students properly.

One problem, often noted by those from rural areas or places less densely populated by Catholics, is that field placement sites tend to be in parishes where there are several priests, whereas actual ministry is likely to be carried out in a parish by only one priest. As one director queried: "How does the student, lay or clerical, learn to work in situations where there is only one priest and one or more professional lay minister? It is ever more likely that even first assignments for young priests will be as a pastor by himself. We have a long way to go before we understand shared responsibility, collaboration, and team work with lay people. We have an obligation to teach both lay and clerical students how to work together."

Some exceptions to placements in parishes are those in prison ministry or in ministry with special groups not associated with parishes, such as persons with AIDS. A few theologates require Clinical Pastoral Education (CPE) and most schools highly recommend it, but generally in addition to other field experiences. Other variations include one school that bases its entire field education program on the CPE model, and another that requires a year or more of mission experience appropriate to the charism of the religious order.

The desired outcomes of pastoral training are diverse. Most directors reported that their primary aim is to help students develop a habit of theological reflection on ministry that will last lifetime. Many directors also believe that the pastoral field experience enables students to integrate the spiritual, personal, and academic aspects of formation, and that it broadens their image of the Church. When asked whether field experience accomplishes what is intended, the vast majority of theologate personnel agreed that its development is progressing steadily and its goals are being more clearly delineated, but the same majority acknowledged that the best models for conducting field education have not yet been adopted in their own schools.

Issues for the future: As those responsible for pastoral education look to the future, four goals predominate. The first goal is to implement a more coherent program that is developmental and progressive, one in which experiences build on one another and increase in level of participation and responsibility. A second, related goal seeks to take into account the diverse backgrounds of students and thus calls for an individual approach to field experiences. Assessment of students' skills and their plans for future ministry is necessary for the successful implementation of this goal. Internships for those who are deacons and will be ordained as priests differ considerably from internships for those who will work as professional lay ministers. Making available a variety of field placements that meet specific needs of students is a constant challenge for directors.

The third goal is to develop a core of trained supervisors. The men and women who function as supervisors work in a variety of ministries, and have different levels of preparation and experience. Most directors of field education provide at least some specific in-service training for supervisors, so that expectations are clear and evaluations of students more fruitful. A major problem is to retain a group of individuals who understand the process of pastoral formation and are willing to give their time to the task of preparing future ministers. A fourth, related and comprehensive goal is to help students adapt to the changing needs of the people they are serving, both in parishes and in other settings. To achieve this goal, students must learn to be responsive to diverse groups, including a growing number of Hispanics and Asians, elderly, and college-educated professionals.

The goals of pastoral training as set forth in the *PPF* are numerous and inclusive. The relative importance of this area of formation is indicated by the fact that, although only seven hours are recommended for field education in the *PPF*, the average number required by theologates is nearly twelve. In the past decade pastoral field education, now sometimes called supervised ministry, has evolved and developed to the point of meeting many of the needs of students in preparation for competent entry into public ministry.

Part V

Future Goals and Directions of Theologates in Relation to the Needs of The Roman Catholic Church in the United States

A. Church and Society:
Theologate Response to Special Concerns

OVERVIEW STATEMENTS

As the Catholic population changes, so must preparation of those who will minister to it. Theologates tend to focus on preparing students to minister to the traditional, average white nuclear family, rather than to those who are elderly, ethnically diverse, and from nontraditional families.

Horizons must be expanded to include a wide range of persons who do not conform to our stereotypical notion of who is Catholic.

> Among ethnic groups, those of special importance are Hispanics, Blacks, and Asians.

> An increasing number of elderly persons, including those who are grieving and dying, require special ministry.

> A higher proportion of college-educated Catholics, many of whom are single and feeling neglected by the Church, need attention and special ministry.

Certain issues are of particular concern and call for more attention and greater knowledge:

Issues of peace and social justice

The universal Church and its mission

Ecumenism in its multiple dimensions

INTRODUCTION

As our analysis of all aspects of the formation program reveals, theologates tend to concentrate on preparing candidates for priesthood and for other professional ministry who will serve the general population, the mainstream of society. Much of formation—personal and spiritual, academic, and pastoral—is designed for middle-class white students who will serve in middle-class white parishes. However, our interviews indicate that faculty and administrators are concerned about issues transcending middle-class boundaries, and about specific populations that they believe deserve more attention. These issues and populations are discussed here.

1. SPECIAL ISSUES

Present reality: Peace and social justice issues, the mission of the universal Church, and ecumenism are among topics that many theologate faculty and administrators believe deserve more emphasis during formation. They are troubled by lack of awareness on the part of seminarians and other ministerial students about these topics, which are often put in second place because of an already crowded curriculum but also because of lack of commitment to them by some Church leaders. The thinking often expressed was that different ecclesial officials give contradictory signals about the stance that should be taken on these issues, and in an effort to be compliant theologates may ignore the issues altogether. One rector described this as a "survival" mentality: "We can survive only if we have students, and taking a forceful position, say on economic justice, can alienate some powerful people, so we stay with a low-keyed approach to topics like this." Yet many faculty and administrators underlined the urgency of addressing more specifically issues of peace and social justice, the mission of the universal Church, and ecumenism.

Peace and Social Justice. For the past ten years or more, the American people in general have shown little interest in peace and social justice issues. Faculty report that students reflect this cultural indifference about matters that were vital to the previous generation. Strong conviction about the imperative to learn about peace and social justice concerns is limited to a select minority of students, and only infrequently is it encouraged or promoted by theologate faculty. A few respondents who feel impassioned about the necessity of incorporating these concerns in the curriculum believe that the present tendency may be a consequence of "privatized," nonministerial spirituality, which in turn reflects the individualism so characteristic of our culture. A countercultural response may need to be articulated in formation programs to offset this tendency. As one moral theologian commented: "The nature of the Church is at issue. I believe it constitutive of its nature to speak out on peace and justice. If we don't educate the next generation of Church leaders to be conscious of significant moral questions, how do we expect to keep alive the Church's teachings in our congregations? Religion is not a private affair; it must affect behavior in the marketplace."

The U.S. bishops' pastoral letters on war and peace and on the economy have fulfilled an important function by placing these issues at center stage. Particularly faculty who teach moral theology have incorporated the documents in their courses. They report, however, that the content of the letters is not eagerly embraced by a sizable number of seminarians. According to one faculty member, "The positions of the bishops on war and peace and on the economy have greater potential to create a split between the hierarchy and the laity than any other issue. These negative attitudes are reflected by seminarians who are coming from a society where the bishops' authority to make such statements is questioned. If we succeed, as I think we must, in convincing our students of the significance of these documents, the result may be a widening gap between 'the leaders and teachers' and many people in the pews." In light of the pressure of time and the other tensions identified above, it is not surprising that determining the appropriate place of these topics in the curriculum has become a dilemma for theologate faculties.

The Universal Church and Its Mission. Two of the most significant documents of the Second Vatican Council dealt with the Church:

Dogmatic Constitution on the Church (*Lumen Gentium*) and *Pastoral Constitution on the Church in the Modern World* (*Gaudium et Spes*). One of the central teachings of these documents, which serve as cornerstones in ecclesiology courses, is the universal nature of the Church: It is for all peoples of all cultures. Yet faculty report that the concept of the Church as universal is elusive for students. It is a challenge to students to expand their image of the Church beyond the American experience, or even the local parish. The importance of being able to envision the Church as a multicultural and diverse body grows as its membership, in the United States alone, mirrors this reality more and more. Most students have been only minimally exposed to a broader sense of the Church; in fact, since with few exceptions faculty themselves lack the background that would prompt them to raise awareness of this dimension of the Church, rather limited attention is given to it. Recently the Association of Theological Schools has highlighted the notion of the globalization of theological education by making it a priority for the 1990s. This action has the potential to foster consciousness of the universal nature of the Church, and globalization is therefore an especially fitting theme for Roman Catholics.

Ecumenism. Another important document of the Second Vatican Council was the *Decree on Ecumenism* (*Unitatis Redintegratio*). During the years immediately following the council, the Church was involved in unprecedented ecumenical activity. According to faculty members who were teaching at that time, theologates then were deeply committed to ecumenical dialogue. Today ecumenism is still an espoused value at most theologates, and some efforts are made to provide an ecumenical perspective in courses and to participate in ecumenical projects. For example, almost every theologate is part of a cooperative arrangement or consortium with schools from other denominations. In a recent study of cooperative ventures in theological education, nearly all respondents gave personal testimony that ecumenical cooperation had had a significant impact on their development and thought. However, it was also reported that "ecumenism is on the decline, though there is substantial disagreement over how to detect or interpret evidence demonstrating that decline."[1] We

---

[1] J. W. Fraser et al., *Cooperative Ventures in Theological Education*, 56. This book reports on the experience of cooperation in theological education over the past twenty years. The important role of ecumenism in the developing stages of cooperative ventures is identified.

observed during our site visits that very little concrete effort is now made to teach special courses on ecumenism, and that students take minimal advantage of opportunities to cross-register at a school of a different denomination. This reluctance is related in part to the limited understanding students have of their own tradition, and in part to the fact that they are not tested in any significant way on their knowledge of ecumenism or their experience with it. Nor are they strongly encouraged to make ecumenical activities a priority.

Issues for the future: Because of preoccupation with other matters, theologates will probably not change meaningfully in their approach to these issues, though most faculty believe that all three—peace and social justice, awareness of the universal Church, and ecumenism— deserve more attention. It is likely that a few faculty members will keep these issues at the forefront of theological education, and other forces will also have a positive influence. About social justice, one faculty member said: "If the purpose of the theologate is to form Church ministers, it can't be changeless in a changing society. We need to alter our curriculum to incorporate more fully some of the pressing concerns that are at the heart of the Church's social teaching."

The necessity of understanding the concept of the universality of the Church, which is emphasized in chapter 2 ("The People of God") of the *Dogmatic Constitution on the Church*, will become even more urgent as the focus of the Church continues to shift to the Third World. Inculturation will create tensions that will affect the Church of the West, and Americans will not escape the changes brought about by demographic shifts in Church membership.

The attitude of Church leadership will be a key factor in determining the evolution of ecumenism in theologates. The tone will be set by the local Church and by the ordinary responsible for the theologate. Given all the other demands on formation programs, the probability of ecumenism attaining the prominence it had two decades ago is unlikely. Yet the phenomenon of the worldwide spread of Islam raises a new challenge that may dwarf previous challenges. The almost total lack of knowledge about Islam and its influence throughout the world may have serious consequences for the Church, and at least initial discussions about the need to rectify this lacuna should be undertaken.

2. SPECIFIC POPULATIONS

Many theologate leaders believe that formation programs fail to take adequately into account the needs of certain significant and growing groups in the Church, for example, the Hispanic population and the elderly. With the exception of a few theologates that focus on Hispanic ministry, one or two that have intercultural programs, and some religious communities that offer extracurricular training for ministry to special populations, almost all theologate education envisions ministry to middle-class whites, who would have been more characteristic of Church membership in the 1950s. Yet the reality is that the Church today no longer fits the stereotype of that earlier decade. Now more members are Hispanic and Asian, more are elderly and poor, more are college-educated, and more are alienated from Church and society. These changes suggest that the Church in the United States must greatly expand its horizons if it is to thrive in the next century, and the expansion must begin with formation programs.

Hispanic Ministry. When the U.S. bishops adopted the "National Pastoral Plan for Hispanic Ministry"[2] in November 1987, a critical step forward was taken in acknowledging the strength of the Hispanic people and their significance for the Church. The impact of this document, which focuses on the pastoral needs of the Hispanic Catholic, is only beginning to be felt. But as seminarians and other students prepare for ministry, the model of the Church that it proposes should have an enormous influence. The proposed model is described in the document as "communitarian, evangelizing, and missionary, incarnate in the reality of the Hispanic people and open to the diversity of cultures, a promoter and example of justice . . . that develops leadership through integral education . . . that is leaven for the kingdom of God in society. "[3] The emphases articulated in this statement would affect nearly every aspect of formation, especially courses in systematic and pastoral theology and field experience.

Our interviews showed that, in at least half of the theologates, a strong desire to respond to the needs of the growing number of

---

[2]*National Pastoral Plan for Hispanic Ministry* (Washington, D.C.: United States Catholic Conference, 1988).

[3]*National Pastoral Plan,* 7.

Hispanic Catholics in the United States was matched by uncertainty about what should be done to encourage vocations in the Hispanic community and how future ministers should be educated to serve this vital group of people. What programs and services are now in place? Four theologates reported that their programs are geared entirely to crosscultural bilingual ministry, or that they have a distinct Hispanic intercultural ministry program.[4] Another eighteen offer specific courses on Hispanic theological and cultural perspectives, and on ministering to the Hispanic community. Some of these courses are conducted in Spanish and others in English; most of the twenty-two schools also offer Spanish-language courses or make them available elsewhere. Field experience with Hispanic parishes is a possibility at twenty-six theologates. Other more limited programs and services are listed by most of the remaining theologates, for example, workshops and lectures about Hispanics, occasional liturgies in Spanish, and consciousness raising about different ethnic, cultural, and racial backgrounds. In the next decade, faculty and administrators anticipate further development of programs related to Hispanics.

Ministry to other groups. Preparing students for ministry to a much smaller but growing group of Asian Catholics, and a small but stable group of Black Catholics, is yet another dimension of theological education. While the level of awareness and concern for both groups is high, extremely limited programming directed to their needs is evident in theologates. No programs are geared entirely to Black students or to students who will minister to Blacks, but seven schools offer specific courses[5] and seventeen offer opportunities for field placement in a Black parish, mostly in large urban centers. About two-thirds of the theologates offer no formation that relates to Black Catholics. Programs and services geared to Asian Catholics

---

[4]The four are Seminary of St. Vincent de Paul in Boynton Beach, Florida; Oblate School of Theology in conjunction with Assumption Seminary in San Antonio, Texas; St. Thomas Seminary in Denver, Colorado; and Centro de Studios de los Dominicos del Caribe (CEDOC) in Bayamon, Puerto Rico. Each of these theologates has a unique approach to theological education and a unique student body.

[5]The three theologates that provide more activities related to Blacks than do any other schools are St. Mary's in Baltimore, Maryland; Notre Dame Seminary in New Orleans, Louisiana; and Mundelein Seminary in Mundelein, Illinois. Some of the theologates associated with universities also have access to the cultural opportunities and resources of those institutions.

are even more limited, in part because their immigration is so recent. Only one theologate, Notre Dame Seminary in New Orleans, has more than an occasional lecture or some pastoral services available to Asian students.

During interviews, especially with faculty, respondents mentioned other groups that they realize are present in greater numbers in the Church and require special ministry. For example, it is well documented that the number of elderly will continue to soar, the divorced Catholic population is increasing, and persons with AIDS and their families have acute needs. At the same time, a very different group— that of college-educated Catholics—is growing at an unprecedented rate. Although Catholics constitute only 25 percent of the general population, 40 percent of the college population is Catholic.

Should changes be made in formation programs with the hope of improving Church ministry to these groups? Most faculty believe that post-theology programs will be needed to meet the special needs of certain segments of the population. The curriculum is already crowded, and new material cannot be incorporated without dropping other requirements. A different solution proposed by some faculty is not necessarily to provide special classes or programs to teach students to minister to these groups, but rather to stress basic virtues and values—compassion, care for the poor, the dignity of all persons. As one faculty member observed: "How quickly we have forgotten our history. The Church in the United States has always served many different kinds of people—every nationality, every socioeconomic group, people of all ages and backgrounds. Our basic problem is that we have become too narrow in our understanding of who the Church really is. We need to expand our horizons and be willing to learn some new approaches."

Issues for the future: Ministry to any of these groups challenges the imagination, and demands time and resources that are now otherwise distributed. Consciousness of what it will mean to serve the changing Catholic population is increasing. One difficult problem is finding faculty and staff with the backgrounds and talents to prepare others for ministry to these various groups. For example, it is nearly impossible to find faculty who have the competence to teach in the area of Hispanic studies, let alone people who are themselves Hispanic or have worked with Hispanic parishes or communities. Whereas ministering to groups like the elderly blends more readily into general parish work, ministering to whole communities and parishes whose ethnic composition differs from that of the minister demands special preparation. The appropriate way to fulfill the rightful expectations of such groups in the future has yet to be determined.

More thought must be given to the method and language of theology if the Church hopes to remain in touch with the diverse groups it is attempting to serve today. The media and media language are being used by fundamentalist sects who, despite their recent setbacks, have made tremendous inroads on the American religious scene. If students experience new methods of teaching, they will be more likely to adopt new methods in their own teaching, which takes on so many forms in ministry. For the most part, courses are taught now in much the same way as they were in the past, though the material is different. The question is whether the material is adapted to "ministerial" education. The lecture method is used most commonly, with students tending to be passive recipients. This method proves to be ineffective in ministry settings. To what extent can a more experienced-based approach be introduced so that in future ministry students will be able to draw on the lives of the people to whom they are ministering?

Assessing the potential impact on theological education of trying to meet the needs of special groups brings to mind the overriding responsibility of every school to plan programs that are directed to the particular needs of its own region. No theologate can serve every group effectively, nor should it try, but in each special area at least a few schools should provide some resources.

B. The Futures of Roman Catholic Theologates: Challenges and Opportunities

OVERVIEW STATEMENTS

As concern about stewardship of resources becomes more acute, the number of theologates and where they will be located may change.

The mission of theologates will continue to be affected by changes in the Church, especially the phenomenon of more lay people becoming professional ministers; who will take responsibility for the education of lay ministers must be decided.

Adequate staffing will become even more crucial as theologates respond to the needs of a changing student population and changing requirements in preparation for ministry.

Parishes in the future will be characterized by more interaction and inclusiveness, and so it will be even more essential to teach skills that prepare ministers to work collaboratively; faculty and administrators will be making adjustments in the design and content of programs accordingly.

A longitudinal study of ministerial effectiveness will provide required information about what the best environment for theological education of seminarians and other students is.

Maintaining high standards in the selection of students will in the long run enhance vocational recruitment and lead to more effective ministers serving the Church.

Strategic and directional planning, both short- and long-term, will characterize the management of successful theologates in the future.

INTRODUCTION

During the course of the research on theologates conducted over the past four years, I found indications of many accomplishments and positive developments, as well as many signs of hope for the future. Important among the reasons for optimism are excellent personnel, well-conceived programs, and keen awareness of the needs of the Church in the United States. I have tried to give full expression to these positive findings. I have also focused attention on questions and concerns, and in this concluding chapter I will summarize some of the major issues that surfaced during my interviews with theologate faculty, administrators, and students.

1. REFLECTIONS ON THE FUTURE

At the conclusion of each interview, respondents were asked to reflect on some areas that have significant implications for the future: What factors will ensure success for theologates? What Church leadership issues will have an impact on theologates? What problems and concerns will theologates face? And what creative visions do theologate leaders have for the future of their institutions?

In answer to the first question, six factors were most often mentioned as critical to the success of theologates:

a. Enrolling a sufficient number of qualified students was given the highest priority. To achieve this goal, recruiting practices will have to be more effective and selection criteria more satisfactorily defined.

b. Securing an adequate number of faculty who can teach in academic programs and serve as role models, and of administrators who can provide vision and stability, is another critical factor. Since faculty and administrators are often assigned to and removed from theologate positions by bishops and religious superiors, there may be an absence of long-term commitment to institutions by individuals.

c. Improving the image of theologates, especially among priests who look back on their seminary days without satisfaction or pride, is a significant factor, because the morale of priests affects their willingness to recruit qualified candidates. Information shared between those working in theologates and those involved in other ministries would be helpful.

d. Establishing criteria to determine the effectiveness of the preparation undergone by ordination candidates and other students is essential.

e. Preventing a dual-track priesthood that would divide men who are preparing for diocesan priesthood from those who are preparing for religious order priesthood is imperative. The growing discrepancy between the values and visions of these two groups is becoming more noticeable, as are the differences between the institutions in which they are being educated. This potential division could be destructive to the mission of the Church.

f. Intensifying fund-raising efforts to ensure financial stability is also important. Expenditures that have been deferred can then be implemented, for example, for maintenance and improvement of facilities and salary increases. More efficient use of facilities will in turn add to needed revenues.

Respondents then commented on Church leadership issues—changes in patterns of responsibility and relationship—that they believe will have an impact on theologates. These were (1) establishing more clearly the identity of priests in their changing ministerial roles, and thus helping to raise morale among priests; (2)providing better education for collaborative ministry, parish leadership, and pastoral communication; (3)developing better working relationships with lay people, and enabling them to assume leadership roles as the number of priests drops; (4)learning to manage change and its impact, especially when coping with decline rather than growth; and (5) resolving questions of governance for theologates.

Problems and concerns for the future were identified as these: (1)deciding to enroll unqualified candidates because of declining numbers, and especially accepting a large number of older candidates without considering the impact they will have on the Church; (2) failing to respond to the changing position of lay people, especially women, in the Church;(3)making unclear distinctions between priestly ministry and other types of professional ministry; (4)being oblivious to the changing population of the Church, for example, with respect to ethnic composition, age levels, and ministry needs; (5) designating separate training for new or growing minority groups that would lead to several classes of clergy, an approach that would be risky, ill-advised, and problematic for our culture; and (6) tolerating an increasing dichotomy between a hierarchical and a collaborative model of Church.

When asked about a creative vision, respondents expressed less agreement about what the features of ideal theologates should be in the future. Though not all would subscribe to every feature listed here, those most often mentioned were (1) having more interaction and exchange with other theologates, including their students, faculty, and administrators; (2) incorporating more women religious and lay people in theologates as students, faculty, administrators, and board members; (3) giving more attention at some theologates to special areas of ministry, for example, to Hispanics, the elderly, or better-educated Catholics; (4) having stronger regional theologates or, alternatively, having national theologates with different program emphases; (5) taking more responsibility for lay ministry training, thus enabling more theologates to remain open in various parts of the country so that future ministers can be educated in their own geographical regions; and (6) affiliating with other Catholic institutions of higher education where feasible, so that limited theological resources can be most judiciously used.

Some theologate leaders stated that they simply lack the vision to make the choices that are required. These leaders feel stymied by inadequate resources and by the unwelcome intervention of Church officials who seem unaware of many of the dynamics that are affecting theologates, such as changing Church membership and competition for qualified candidates and personnel.

2. SUMMARY OF ISSUES

When all the data derived from the research—interviews, surveys, and statistics—are considered, certain issues recur again and again. The future of the Church in the United States will be significantly affected by the way these issues are resolved. The six that I believe merit special consideration are a) divergent models of preparation for priesthood; b) future staffing; c) vocations and screening of candidates; d) the impact of the changing context for ministry, especially in parishes, on priestly formation; e) the impact of changing Church membership on priestly formation; and f) the necessity of planning for the future.

a. Church leaders must decide which model or models are suitable and acceptable for preparing men for priesthood. Representatives of the various schools of thought spoke strongly and clearly about the particular contexts and structures they prefer for programs of priestly formation. They have well-articulated reasons for adhering to one or another model. Different models can be distinguished, for example, on the basis of who is enrolled or the geographical area from which students come. Some theologates enroll only seminarians in M.Div. programs, while others enroll a combination of students—lay, religious, and clerical—in several different programs. The single-purpose theologate is preferred by some ordinaries and the more diverse model by others; but if all ordinaries chose theologates that restricted admission to seminarians, at least half of the schools would be forced to close for lack of enrollment. A collapse of this magnitude would have serious negative repercussions for the Church, especially in those areas of the country that would be left without theological resources.

Related to the issue of formation models is the geographical spread of the constituencies served by theologates, regional or national. As competition for students increases, theologates that were previously used by a few nearby dioceses or a limited number of religious communities are extending their recruitment much more widely. A few of them, for reasons sometimes related to the ideology rather than the quality of the theologate, are very successful in their recruitment efforts. The result is an irregular distribution of seminarians, and a depletion of theologates where the newly recruited students previously enrolled. When theologates can no longer count on seminarians from dioceses that traditionally supplied them, planning becomes difficult and the overall effect is deleterious.

This recent phenomenon of more widespread recruitment is not a reflection on those centers that have a long history of serving a national constituency, such as the Catholic University of America in Washington, D.C.; St. Mary's in Baltimore; St. Meinrad's in St. Meinrad, Indiana; and the Pontifical College Josephinum in Columbus, Ohio. For many years these theologates have served the Church on a national level, and their programs are designed to meet the needs of students from all over the country. Other theologates that enroll students on a national basis have a specialized purpose; among these are the Catholic Theological Union in Chicago and the Washington Theological Union in Silver Spring, Maryland, which were founded to serve many religious orders, as well as Pope John XXIII National Seminary in Weston, Massachusetts, which was founded to educate older men for priesthood. Religious orders such as the Jesuits, Dominicans, and Oblates, which previously had regional theologates that are now closed, also serve a national constituency. The variety provided by the broad spectrum of theologates is enriching for the whole Church. These theologates have a different rationale for national recruitment than do the theologates that have only recently enlarged the scope of their recruitment efforts.

As missions are reviewed and programs adjusted, the following questions should be asked: Are decisions being made about mission based on principles or because of pressure? Are actions being taken out of conviction or convenience? Associated with these questions is the problem of where responsibility should fall for the education of lay people who will be involved in Church ministry. If several models continue to be employed, how can support for these different models be conveyed by Church leaders?

b. A second major issue concerns the staffing of theologates. Three topics under this heading deserve attention: administrative leadership, availability of faculty; and preparation of personnel for nonteaching positions, especially in the areas of personal and spiritual formation and pastoral field education. First, regarding administration, the role of rectors/presidents has shifted considerably over the years from a largely internal to a significantly external one. Concurrently the role of academic dean has continued to expand, so that many internal functions related to the progress of individual students now fall to the dean, as does the leadership of the faculty and academic program planning. The positions of rector/president and academic dean have in common an exceedingly high rate of turnover; in the past three years, half of the rector/president positions and more than half of the deanships have changed hands. The question is, What kind of preparation and support are needed to enhance the desirability of serving at length in these key leadership posts?

Availability of adequately prepared faculty is a second personnel concern. At the present time, theologates are enjoying a kind of windfall in being able to draw from the faculties of the many schools that have been closed over the past twenty years. The fact that this supply will not be available again raises the following questions: What kind of planning is being done to guarantee an adequate number of well-prepared faculty for the future? How can the exodus of premier Catholic theologians from theologates to other Catholic graduate schools and secular universities be prevented? What changes in sabbatical policies, teaching loads, and salaries and benefits will be needed in order to provide faculty with the time and money to pursue more scholarship?

The third personnel concern is the lack of sufficient preparation received by those who will assume responsibility for personal and spiritual formation and for pastoral field education. In this case an obvious question arises: To what extent is it recognized that these increasingly specialized positions require more than a person of good will with some pastoral experience?

A final, overriding personnel issue involves the morale of all who work in theologates. It is my observation that many individuals are strongly dedicated and committed to this very specialized work in the Church. It is also clear that few experience the concrete and consistent support of Church leaders. Priest faculty and administrators, in particular, miss the encouragement and understanding of their fellow priests who work in parishes and other ministries. Memories of past personal experiences in seminaries are not always positive and, according to current priest staff, the changed nature of theologates is not apparent to many priests in other ministries today. More planned interaction and information sharing between priests in seminaries and those outside would be fruitful both for morale and for future vocations.

c. A third major issue concerns vocations to the priesthood and the selection of candidates. A major problem not only for theologates, but for the Church generally, is the small number of vocations to the priesthood. Most theologate leaders anticipate a decline in the total number of seminarians in the next five years, few of them believe that intensified vocational recruitment will increase the numbers significantly, and fewer still believe it their responsibility to do the recruiting. Given this profile, several theologates are likely to close or merge in the next five years, not by virtue of careful planning but rather out of necessity or by default.

These factors have enormous consequences for the future. On one level, the pressure on schools to accept marginal candidates and then to retain them with little regard for their aptitude is a serious and frequently expressed concern. Some schools have strictly adhered-to standards, but they report that students rejected by them can readily find another theologate at which to enroll. As the number of strong candidates continues to dwindle, should there be a reevaluation of minimal standards for acceptance? At issue are questions about the backgrounds of students: Should they be admitted if they have been dismissed from other theologates? If they are converts, how long should they have been members of the Church before acceptance?

What degree of self-understanding, especially about sexuality, should students attain before admission, and how can this important area be measured? Vocation directors and others need training if they are to make accurate assessments of applicants.

Transcending the level of institutional problems is concern about factors negatively affecting vocations to the priesthood. During my research, many speculated about the causes for the decline in numbers of priesthood candidates. They cited such nebulous but important factors as the nature of American culture and society, which strongly emphasizes materialism and individualism and tends to undervalue commitment and service. Another factor is the excessively negative press coverage of the Church on issues ranging from the pastoral letter on homosexuality to sexual misconduct among clergy. The lack of vocations is also attributed to the role and treatment of women in the Church and to the evolving role of lay ministry. Lack of clarity about the role of priests, coupled with extremely high expectations in parishes, adds to the problem. But, according to a survey published in the *The Future of Catholic Leadership,*[1] the major reason for the lag in the number of vocations is the requirement of celibacy. The survey finds that 70 percent of men who were campus ministry leaders would not consider priesthood because they would not be allowed to marry, and 62 percent of a random sample of all male college students gave the same answer (p. 124). The great majority of those we interviewed confirmed that the survey findings correspond with their perceptions. It is perhaps no wonder, then, that young men are hesitant to embark on a vocation that places them at the heart of multiple controversies.

d. A fourth issue involves preparing men for a priestly ministry that is different from the experience of most faculty currently teaching in theologates. Virtually every person interviewed believes that priestly ministry already is, or in the near future will be, quite different from what it has been even in the recent past. The anticipated change is mainly attributed to the smaller number of priests, which has necessitated increased involvement by lay people in professional ministry. Seminarians identify the need for role clarification as one of the two or three major preoccupations with which they face

---

[1]Dean R. Hoge, *The Future of Catholic Leadership,* 119-129.

their future priesthood. The Church in the United States seems to be hesitating between accepting the fact that more and more professional ministers who are not ordained will be working in parishes, and hoping against hope that a sudden surge in vocations will make that acceptance unnecessary. During this moment of hesitation, changes in staffing are occurring at a breathtaking pace in parish structures and other Church institutions. Seminarians are aware that ministry in collaboration with others who are not ordained is inevitable, but for the most part they feel unprepared to cope with the new context. Thus the inevitable questions provoked by this issue are, How must programs for priestly formation change in light of the impending new reality? What adjustments in personal and spiritual formation may be required? in theological curriculum? in teaching methods? and especially in pastoral field education?

e. A fifth issue is closely related to the context of ministry, but deals more specifically with Church membership, that is, those to whom ministry will be directed. We are keenly aware of changes in the demography of Church membership. By the year 2000, it is projected that perhaps half of all Catholics in the United States will be of Hispanic background, a sizable proportion will be Asian, and cutting across ethnic boundaries will be an enormous number of elderly, as well as a better-educated but smaller number of young people. Growing numbers of persons alienated from Church and society will also demand attention. Priests in the future will have to address the needs of these groups as a matter of course. It will not be possible to label such work as "specialized ministry" or to relegate preparation for it to a post-theology program. It was often said by those interviewed that schools focus on preparing students for ministry to the middle range of the Catholic population, which in the near future will be greatly diminished. The profile of the "average Catholic" has changed. Is it not mandatory that the curricula of theologates be adjusted to meet these needs? Is not an updated understanding of American culture and societal structures the precondition for an appropriate response?

f. The final issue is one that in a sense embraces all the foregoing issues. It concerns the need for planning. As the interviews indicated, few comprehensive institutional planning efforts are in place. A consequence is that changes are happening without reference to their contexts or implications. It is nonetheless possible to design a desirable future scenario for theologates, and then to work systematically toward the goals implicit in that scenario and thus the enhancement of the future Church. In order to conceive a reasonable plan, key leaders must be given time to think about and imagine the future. Leisure must be made available to listen to the Spirit, to explore and channel creativity.

Planning is needed on the national no less than the institutional level. Hesitation about planning on a national level is expressed because of fear of imposed uniformity. Another concern is the issue of competition; would planning for the "system" negatively affect certain institutions? One result of these perhaps legitimate fears is that very little comprehensive national planning is in fact done. Unexplored questions remain: Should a whole new model of preparation for priesthood be considered? Who is even to consider such a possibility, for example, for the Hispanic candidate? How can a pool of qualified personnel be guaranteed in the future? Should methods of teaching be adjusted to meet the needs of a changing student population? How can ministerial effectiveness be measured so that theologates can make adjustments in programs with shortfalls? The list could be expanded indefinitely, but suffice it to say that with comprehensive and systematic planning a creative vision will emerge in the future.

My final comment returns to the theme of hope. In the course of the past four years of doing this research, I have been deeply impressed by the quality of persons performing the special task of preparing candidates for priesthood and other professional Church ministry. Their dedication, skill, and goodness persuade me that "all things are possible" for a Spirit-filled future. We may all be surprised by the direction in which the Spirit leads, but let us pray that there will be openness to the Spirit so that we may continue to give expression to the "reason for the hope" that we have in our hearts.

Appendix A

THEOLOGATES WHERE INTERVIEWS WERE CONDUCTED

Franciscan School of Theology
Jesuit School of Theology
Dominican School of Theology
Saint Patrick's Seminary
Saint Thomas Seminary
Dominican House of Studies
Oblate College
School of Religious Studies, The Catholic University of America
DeSales Hall School of Theology
Seminary of Saint Vincent de Paul
Catholic Theological Union
Saint Mary of the Lake Seminary
Saint Meinrad School of Theology
Mount St. Mary's Seminary
St. Mary's Seminary and University
Washington Theological Union
Pope John XXIII National Seminary
Saint John's Seminary
Weston School of Theology
School of Theology of St. John's University
St. Paul Seminary
Seminary of the Immaculate Conception
Pontifical College Josephinum
Oblate School of Theology

Appendix B

SUMMARY OF MAJOR POINTS

1. The length of terms of vocation directors is expected to increase by an average of nearly two years, a positive change in terms of experience and expertise.

2. Vocation directors are willing to continue in some form of vocation work after their terms as directors. Consideration should be given to ways of utilizing their experience.

3. Few vocation directors have had extensive preparation for vocation work, and most (165; 72.1 percent) would welcome some form of educational experience, especially an internship.

4. In the screening of candidates, interviewing and testing are the two most widely used means of selection. More training in both areas could make the process more effective.

5. Vocation directors indicate a willingness to consider candidates who may be regarded as high-risk by either ordinaries or seminaries, for example, those who have been rejected by another diocese or religious community, nonpracticing homosexuals, and recent converts. Seminaries with restricted resources or programs may not be able to accommodate high-risk candidates.

6. Among the characteristics in candidates that vocation directors rank highest are sound psychological makeup, leadership potential, and desire for priesthood. The lowest ranked are orthodoxy and willingness to be celibate. These values may conflict with what is expected by ordinaries and seminaries.

7. The principal concern about the selection of candidates relates to their psychological and personal characteristics.

8. Ordinaries/religious superiors generally make the final decision about which seminary a student will attend. Yet only 77 of them (33.6 percent) interview candidates.

9. Diocesan directors prefer freestanding (42.3 percent) and university-affiliated seminaries (36.5 percent), primarily because of their spiritual formation programs and secondarily because of their academic programs. Religious order directors prefer the union model (51.1 percent) and, to a lesser degree, the university-affiliated model (28.3 percent) primarily because of the diversity of the settings and the academic programs.

10. Seminaries could best assist vocation directors by helping with the selection of candidates and with maintaining open communication about the school and the students.

Appendix C

STRUCTURAL MODELS OF THEOLOGATES

I. FREE-STANDING SEMINARIES/SCHOOLS OF THEOLOGY

This type of school "provides the entire program of spiritual, intellectual, and pastoral formation/education" (PPF, p. 7). Within this broad category fall 30 schools, which can be further sub-divided on the basis of their mission as follows:

- A. For Diocesan Priesthood Candidates

  - Saint John's Seminary, CA (CM)*
  - Saint Patrick's Seminary, CA (SS)
  - Mount Saint Mary's Seminary, MD (Diocesan)
  - Saint John's Seminary, MA (Diocesan)
  - Kenrick Seminary, MO (CM)

- B. Diocesan and Religious Priesthood Candidates

  - Saint Meinrad School of Theology, IN (OSB)
  - Pope John XXIII National Seminary, MA (Diocesan)
  - Pontifical College of Josephinum, OH (Diocesan)
  - Sacred Heart School of Theology, WI (SCJ)

- C. Diocesan Candidates with Separate Programs for Others

  - Saint Mary of the Lake Seminary, IL (Diocesan)
  - Saint Mary's Seminary and University, MD (SS)
  - Saint Joseph's Seminary, NY (Diocesan)
  - Saint Charles Borromeo Seminary, PA (Diocesan)

- D. Diocesan Candidates and Lay Students

  - Holy Apostles Seminary, CT (MSsA, changing to involve dioceses)

*Indicates the group conducting the school.

- Seminary of Saint Vincent De Paul, FL (Several dioceses)
- Saint John's Provincial Seminary, MI (Several dioceses, changing to one)
- SS. Cyril and Methodius Seminary, MI (Diocesan)
- Immaculate Conception, NJ (Diocesan)**
- Christ the King Seminary, NY (OFM)
- Seminary of the Immaculate Conception, NY (Dioceses)
- Mount Saint Mary's of the West, OH (Diocesan)
- Saint Mary Seminary, OH (Diocesan)
- Saint Francis Seminary, WI (Diocesan)

- E.   Religious Candidates and Other Students

   - Maryknoll School of Theology, NY (MM)
   - St. Anthony-on-the-Hudson, NY (OFM Conv.)

- F.   Diocesan, Religious, and Lay Students

   - Saint Thomas Seminary, CO (CM)
   - Notre Dame Seminary, LA (Diocesan)
   - Mount Angel Seminary, OR (OSB)
   - Saint Vincent Seminary, PA (OSB)
   - Mary Immaculate Seminary, PA (CM)

II. SUPPLEMENTAL MODEL - UNIVERSITY-RELATED

This model is described in the PPF (p. 7), as one "which provides one or more parts of the program from its own resources while other parts (such as the academic) are provided by another institution (such as a university)." This category covers all houses of formation which do not have academic programs. Since this study is intended to examine all institutions which provide the academic programs for priesthood candidates, the houses of formation are not included unless the students are enrolled in a university that would not otherwise be considered a theologate. For purposes of this study, these are listed under university-related programs. The houses of formation are not listed here, so as to avoid counting the students twice, once in their residence and once in the academic institution.

**   Although Immaculate Conception, NJ, is located on the campus of Seton Hall University, it considers itself a free-standing seminary. Mt. St. Mary's Seminary, Emmitburg, MD, is located on a college campus, but its programs make it freestanding.

- The Catholic University of America, DC (Diocesan)
  (A large group of diocesan priesthood students come from
  Theological College, operated by the Sulpicians, but also some
  from other houses of formation.)
- St. John's University, MN (OSB)
  (Priesthood students from St. Cloud Diocesan Seminary and
  from St. John's Abbey.)
- Moreau Seminary, IN (CSC)
  (Students attend University of Notre Dame)
- St. Paul Seminary, MN (Diocesan)
  Seminary is part of School of Divinity, St. Thomas College)
- Aquinas Institute, MO (OP)
  (Students take some courses at St. Louis University)
- Saint Mary's Seminary, TX (Diocesan)
  (Students attend St. Thomas University)
- Mater Dei Institute, WA (SJ)
  (Students attend Gonzaga University)
- Centro de Estudios Dominicos (CEDOC), PR (OP)
  (Affiliated with Bayamon University)
- The American College at Louvain, BEL (Diocesan)
  (Students attend Catholic University of Louvain)
- The North American College, Rome (Diocesan)
  (Students attend several universities)

III. COLLABORATIVE SCHOOLS

This model is described as one which "recognizes the sharing of
resources in a different way for the formation and education of
priests." Three expressions of the collaborative model are identified.

A. Union Model

- Catholic Theological Union, IL
- Washington Theological Union, MD

B. Federation Model

- Franciscan School of Theology, CA (OFM)
- Jesuit School of Theology at Berkeley, CA (SJ)

- Dominican School of Theology, CA (OP)
- Weston School of Theology, MA (SJ)
- Oblate School of Theology, TX (OMI)

C.   Mixed Model

- Dominican House of Studies, DC (OP)
- Oblate College, DC (OMI)
- DeSales School of Theology, DC (OSFS)

IV. OTHER

- St. Gregory the Theologian Seminary, MA
  (Eparchy of Newton) Melkite Greek Catholic Seminary
- Byzantine Catholic Seminary of Saints Cyril and Methodius,
  PA (Byzantine Archdiocese)

Monastery Training

- Monastery of the Holy Spirit, GA (OCSO)
- St. Joseph's School of Theology and Institute of Monastic
  Studies, MA (OCSO)

Categories are based on descriptions from the Program of Priestly Formation.

Bibliography

Bleichner, Howard, Daniel Buechlein, and Robert Leavitt. *The Preparation of a Diocesan Priest,* 1987.

CARA Seminary Directory 1987: U.S. Catholic Institutions for the Training of Candidates for the Priesthood, ed. Adrian Fuerst. Washington, D.C.: Center for Applied Research in the Apostolate.

Consulting the American Catholic Laity: A Decade of Dialogue, ed. Moira Mathieson. Washington, D.C.: United States Catholic Conference, 1986.

Documents of Vatican II, ed. Austin P. Flannery. Grand Rapids, Mich.: Eerdmans, 1984.

Fact Book on Theological Education, 1986-87, ed. William L. Baumgaertner. Vandalia, Ohio: Association of Theological Schools in the United States and Canada.

Fraser, James W., Monica E. Friar, Barbara A. Radtke, Thomas J. Savage, and Katarina Schuth. *Cooperative Ventures in Theological Education.* Lanham, Md.: University Press of America, 1988.

The Good Steward: A Guide to Theological School Trusteeship. Washington, D.C.: Association of Governing Boards of Universities and Colleges, 1983.

Hemrick, Eugene F., and Dean R. Hoge. *Seminarians in Theology: A National Profile.* Washington, D.C.: United States

Catholic Conference, 1986.

_____ *Seminary Life and Visions of the Priesthood: A National Survey of Seminarians.* Washington, D.C.: National Catholic Educational Association Department of Seminaries, 1987.

Hoge, Dean R. *The Future of Catholic Leadership: Responses to the Priest Shortage.* Kansas City, Mo.: Sheed and Ward, 1987.

Larsen, Ellis L., and James M. Shopshire. *A Profile of Contemporary Seminarians* [*Theological Education* 24 (Spring 1988)].

National Pastoral Plan for Hispanic Ministry. Washington, D.C.: United States Catholic Conference, 1988.

Planning for the Future: Catholic Theology Schools/Formation Houses 1975-1983. Washington, D.C.: Center for Applied Research in the Apostolate, 1980.

Potvin, Raymond H. *Seminarians of the Eighties: A National Survey.* Washington, D.C.: National Catholic Educational Association, 1985.

The Program of Priestly Formation, 3rd ed. Washington, D.C.: United States Catholic Conference, 1982.

Rosinski, Bernard J. *An Academic Profile of Catholic Seminaries: Preliminary Survey.* Washington, D.C.: National Catholic Educational Association, 1987.

A Shepherd's Care: Reflections on the Changing Role of Pastor. Washington, D.C.: United States Catholic Conference, 1987.

Index

Index